Q<small>IN</small>uest <small>OF</small> <small>THE</small> O<small>RDINARY</small>

In Quest of the Ordinary

Lines of Skepticism and Romanticism

STANLEY CAVELL

UNIVERSITY OF CHICAGO PRESS
Chicago and London

The University of Chicago Press, Chicago 60637
The University of Chicago Press, Ltd., London
© 1988 by The University of Chicago
All rights reserved. Published 1988
Paperback edition 1994
Printed in the United States of America

97 96 95 94   5 4 3 2

LIBRARY OF CONGRESS
CATALOGING-IN-PUBLICATION DATA

Cavell, Stanley, 1926–
    In quest of the ordinary : lines of skepticism and
romanticism /
    Stanley Cavell.
        p.   cm.
    Bibliography: p.
    Includes index.
    ISBN 0-226-09818-4 (paper)
    1. American literature—19th century—History and
criticism—Theory, etc.   2. Philosophy in literature.
3. Philosophy, American—19th century.   4. Romanticism.
5. Skepticism.   6. English literature—History and criticism—Theory, etc.   I. Title.
PS217.P45C38   1988
810'.9'003—dc19   88-22651
                                                CIP

♾ The paper used in this publication meets the minimum
requirements of the American National Standard for
Information Sciences—Permanence of Paper for Printed
Library Materials, ANSI Z39.48-1984.

To Eugene Smith

Contents

Contents

At Stanford
THE TANNER LECTURE (1986)

At Vienna
CELEBRATORY LECTURE (1986)

Preface and Acknowledgments

IN THE FIRST OF THE LECTURES collected here, I note a perplexity that began making its presence felt to me some ten years ago. As I was trying to follow the last part, part 4, of my book *The Claim of Reason* to a moment of conclusion, my progress kept being deflected by outbreaks of romantic texts—a quatrain from Blake, Wordsworth's Boy of Winander, Coleridge's Ode on Dejection, *Frankenstein*, a division in Emerson's "Transcendentalism," a passage from *Walden*. After completing the manuscript I would from time to time ask myself for some account of this interference. What is philosophy for me, or what has it begun showing itself to be, that it should call for, and call for these, romantic orientations or transgressions? Each time the question arose I put it aside in favor of other pressing matters about which my ignorance felt less vast or less galling. Two years after the publication in 1979 of *The Claim of Reason*, Professor Michael Fischer of the English Department at the University of New Mexico invited me to participate in a series of lectures and class discussions that he and his colleague Morris Eaves were organizing on the topic of Romanticism and Contemporary Criticism. He overcame my plea of ignorance by saying that what was wanted from me, among the invited speakers, was a discussion of how I viewed the appearance of romantic texts in my own writing, in *The Senses of Walden* and especially in part 4 of *The Claim of Reason*. Caught off guard, and on the basis that no one was in a better position to learn about these appearances to me than I was, I accepted. The Beckman lectures, given under the title of the present

ix

volume, incorporate and expand the material I developed for the New Mexico series.

One who is as bent as I seem to be on intellectual adventures that require conducting my continuing education in public must count on friendly and productive occasions. No one could be luckier than I have been in this regard. The texts to follow bear specific marks of the interventions in discussions at Albuquerque, apart from those of Fischer and of Eaves, of Gus Blaisdell, Russell Goodman, and Ira Jaffe; and at Berkeley of Paul Alpers—whose introduction of me in his capacity as Chair of the Department of English, my hosts for the occasion, set so excellent a tone of consideration—and of his colleagues Janet Adelman, Joel Fineman, Stephen Greenblatt, Steven Knapp, William Nestrick, Norman Rabkin, and Henry Nash Smith. It is also a pleasure to note here that some months before getting together my thoughts for Albuquerque, an invitation from the University of Utah gave me a chance to broach some raw versions of things in response to which Virgil Aldrich, Brooke Hopkins, and Barry Weller were precise and encouraging.

I knew that I did not want my set of Beckman lectures to be published alone; too much seemed left without clear and useful ways of going on. For example, the material on *The Winter's Tale*, while it continues the problematic of skepticism and tragedy on which *The Claim of Reason* ends, rasies new problems so massively or crudely as to steal attention from the interplay of skepticism and romanticism that led to them. Two problems in particular: (1) Because *The Winter's Tale* represents skepticism as the question whether I can know that my children are mine, the question of a father and distinctly not that of a mother, the implication now seems to me irresistible that the issue of skepticism in this text—and therewith where not in any romantic text? and where not in philosophy?—is inflected by question of gender. (2) The problematic of telling as counting in this "tale" begins as an unfolding of the themes in *The Claim of Reason* associated with a Wittgensteinian criterion as a form of counting and recounting in contrast with an Austinian criterion as a mode of telling and identifying, hence themes associated with different aspects or levels of the claim to know. But the unfolding moves so far and so fast as to further unnerve my grasp of the motivations of and to skepticism. Certain paths are, however, indicated, here and elsewhere. It is in the introduction to my recent collection *Disowning Knowledge: In Six Plays of Shakespeare* that I have reached a certain development in the engendering of skepticism, finding it worked on a historical scale in the tasks of *Antony and Cleopatra;* and the themes of counting and recounting are brought in what follows here to a further place in "Being Odd, Getting Even," where at the same time Poe's appearance in the Beckman lectures comes to seem

less arbitrary. Philosophical and literary issues of, let us say, encounter-
ing, meet in Emerson's question, in the second paragraph of "Experience": "How many individuals can we count in society?"—meet, I
mean, if we listen to Emerson's question, as I urge in "Being Odd,
Getting Even," as a re-asking, or recounting of Descartes's question,
"Am I alone in the world?"; listen to the edge Descartes's question gives
to the Pascalian question of cosmic isolation: Am I *so much as* alone?
Without providing an answer to this question of skepticism you do not
know whether the world has become a plenum, that is, a statistical
crowd, or else a void of others. The concluding lectures to follow here,
on the uncanny and on the fantastic, further specify this issue.

My classes at Harvard have been the critical continuing occasions
for conducting my education in each of these developments. Of the
members of these classes who have pressed me on matters directly related to romanticism's skepticism, I mention, from recent years, Chris-
topher Benfey, Daniel Brudney, James Conant, Juliet Floyd, Marian
Keane, Joshua Leiderman, Peter de Marneffe, Richard Moran, Susan
Neiman, Marya Schechtman, Saadya Sternberg, Charles Warren, and
Liliane Weissberg; and while the classes are less recent, conversations
and writing about these topics continue with Norton Batkin and with
Timothy Gould. On the occasion of the Tanner lectures (there was a
second, on cinema, to appear in a more appropriate setting)—where
Julius Moravcsik and his colleagues in Stanford's Department of Phi-
losophy were most welcoming and the Stanford Humanities Center
provided so congenial a place to work—Ted Cohen, Arnold Davidson,
Karen Hanson, and William Rothman were invited to Stanford by The
Tanner Lectures on Human Values in order to join me in what proved
to be rich discussions with students of the material I presented publicly.

As I pack off the present material, a general misgiving is focused
for me in my having just read *The Literary Absolute: The Theory of Literature in German Romanticism* (Albany, 1988), a translation of *L'absolu
littéraire* by Philippe Lacoue-Labarthe and Jean-Luc Nancy, published
in 1978. There I find features of my Beckman lectures preceded, gen-
erously and practically, in certain opening themes and strategies, from
the other side of the philosophical mind—the German by way of
France, opposed to the English by way of America—specifically, the
theme of a romantic call for the unity of philosophy and poetry precipitated by the aftermath of Kant's revolution in philosophy, traced
strategically with respect to a limited collection of romantic texts (ones
associated with the six issues of the *Athenaeum* published by Friedrich
and August Schlegel from 1798 to 1800—years marking the first and
the second editions of the *Lyrical Ballads*). An understandable reaction
of mine was to ponder once more the costs, linked to certain privileges,

of my American belatedness, a reaction I recount at some length in the preface to a book pairing two long lectures of mine, on Wittgenstein and on Emerson, written in 1987, the year after the last piece of the present volume was in place—*This New Yet Unapproachable America*, to be published in the same season as the present volume. My reaction to the reaction of belatedness has been to wonder whether and how it would have helped me to have read *The Literary Absolute* earlier. When?

My preface about American belatedness is recurrently about what it means to be ready to read certain texts, and to fear reading them (too late? too soon?). In taking on the implied question posed to me by part 4 of *The Claim of Reason*—concerning the place where philosophy is to be encountered by me as attested by the outcropping of romantic texts—I locate the pertinent dimension in Kant's intellectual aftermath to be the legacy of the thing in itself; whereas Lacoue-Labarthe and Nancy locate the romantic problematic as engaged by Kant's "weakening of the subject" (*The Literary Absolute*, p. 30), something like the polar twin of the line I took. It would have been, it seems to me, of exactly no philosophical use for me to have sought to weigh the relative merits of these starting places apart from establishing to my own satisfaction that, among other matters, Emerson's writing bears up under the pressure of the call for philosophy, that he constitutes a fair realization of the bonding of philosophy and poetry that both Coleridge and Friedrich Schlegel had called for. Satisfaction will depend on supposing, for example, that the idea of relying in Emerson's word *self-reliance* knows its relation to the idea of binding or bonding in the word *religion*, so that the self's (perpetual, step-wise, circle-wise) construction of the self, say in "Self-Reliance," has to pass through an idea of the self's alliance with and rallying of itself, its self-authorizations, as on a path, or succession, in the aftermath of religion's dominance. This by no means implies that Emerson persists in seeking a resubstantializing of the self, the hope for which Hume and Kant, let us say, had shattered. It would make more sense of Emerson to say that he sought the desubstantializing of God. It is, I think, mostly because of the fatefulness of Emerson's work that I decided to place the material of the preface to be published with *This New Yet Unapproachable America* at the start of that volume rather than of the present one, which it equally fits. The study in that later work given to Emerson's "Experience" is the most sustained reading I have given of a single Emerson essay, hence most single-mindedly to date sets out the philosophical stakes I find in play in his writing. Then again, that reading would not exist but for the set of experiments to follow here, with their confirmation of the work of *The Senses of Walden*.

Of the opening lecture, "The Philosopher in American Life," not hitherto published, the middle third, along with its title, is from an address delivered on the occasion of the sesquicentennial celebration at Wesleyan University in the fall of 1981. The remanining lectures and postscripts have appeared in various contexts. James Conant had suggestions about matters of substance and of format that I have gratefully accepted in making the cuts and new transitions that collecting these pieces entailed. It was, for example, his suggestion, in which format implies substance, that I not only list in the bilbiography those texts I quote from, in the editions used, thus obviating the need for individual note references, but that I add titles I may only refer or allude to without quoting, thus registering the fact that juxtaposing a text to the text of another can be as significant a response to that text as juxtaposing it to a text I produce myself, more commonly called an act of reading.

Chapter 2 is reprinted from *Raritan*, Fall 1983, pp. 34–61, with the permission of the publisher.

Chapter 3 and postscript B to chapter 5 are reprinted from *Romanticism and Contemporary Criticism*, edited by Morris Eaves and Michael Fischer. Copyright 1986 by Cornell University. Used by permission of the publisher, Cornell University Press.

Chapter 4 was first published in *Disowning Knowledge: In Six Plays of Shakespeare*, copyright Cambridge University Press 1987. Reprinted with the permission of Cambridge University Press.

Chapter 5 and its postscript A are reprinted from *Reconstructing Individualism: Autonomy, Individuality, and the Self in Western Thought*, edited by Thomas C. Heller, Morton Sosna, and David E. Wellbery, with the permission of the publishers, Stanford University Press. Copyright 1986 by the Board of Trustees of the Leland Stanford Junior University.

Postscript C to chapter 5 was originally published as "Reply to Robert Mankin on *The Claim of Reason*," in *Salmagundi*, Summer 1985, pp. 90–96.

Chapter 6 is reprinted with permission of the University of Utah Press from the *Tanner Lectures on Human Values*, vol. 8, Salt Lake City/Cambridge (U.K.): University of Utah Press/Cambridge University Press, copyright 1988.

Chapter 7, "The Fantastic of Philosophy," was first published in the *American Poetry Review* 15, no. 3 (May–June 1986): pp. 45–47.

At Berkeley:

THE MRS. WILLIAM BECKMAN LECTURES (1983)

1

The Philosopher in American Life
(Toward Thoreau and Emerson)

WHEN IN ACCEPTING THE INVITATION to deliver a set of
Beckman Lectures I asked what expectations are placed on such
occasions, and I was assured by my hosts that they would be interested
in whatever I wanted to talk about, I wasn't certain whether I was being
answered or humored. It is true that since the time I was an undergraduate at Berkeley in the forties, and an assistant professor here (and
movie-goer) in the fifties and early sixties, there have been at this university more members of its faculty from whom I have learned more
about more things—from the art of music to Shakespeare and from
skepticism to transcendentalism—than have been together at any other
place. So I have the uncanny feeling that I could say anything here and
be understood completely. But I will try not to press my luck.

I will not even explore the urgency of the wish to be understood
completely, for example trace the source of the wish in my intermittent
sense that no utterance of mine could be acceptable simultaneously to
all those by whom I desire understanding, say by the primarily philosophical and by the primarily literary. Some may accuse me of trying to
reconcile my father and my mother. But if these terms (I mean philosophy and literature) name halves of my own mind, it is perhaps all the
more immediately urgent for me to see that they keep in touch.

What I have done for these lectures, wishing to take the occasion
of old memories and aspirations to form some measure of my progress,
is to propose as their primary business the reading of a set of texts that
represent the oldest and the newest of my interests, placing them in a

3

loosely woven net of concepts. The point of the loose weave is to register that I am as interested in the weaving together of these texts as I
am in their individual textures, and that I wish to leave open, or keep
open usefully, how it is one gets from one to another of them.

One set of these connections forms perhaps the most pervasive,
yet all but inexplicit, thought in these lectures: that the sense of the
ordinary that my work derives from the practice of the later Wittgenstein and from J. L. Austin, in their attention to the language of ordinary or everyday life, is underwritten by Emerson and Thoreau in their
devotion to the thing they call the common, the familiar, the near, the
low. The connection means that I see both developments—ordinary
language philosophy and American transcendentalism—as responses to
skepticism, to that anxiety about our human capacities as knowers that
can be taken to open modern philosophy in Descartes, interpreted by
that philosophy as our human subjection to doubt. My route to the
connection lay at once in my tracing both the ordinary language philosophers as well as the American transcendentalists to the Kantian insight
that Reason dictates what we mean by a world, as well as in my feeling
that the ordinariness in question speaks of an intimacy with existence,
and of an intimacy lost, that matches skepticism's despair of the world.
These routes from, say, Emerson to Wittgenstein are anticipated in a
thought I have put many ways over the years, never effectively
enough—the thought that ordinary language philosophy is not a defense of what may present itself as certain fundamental, cherished beliefs we hold about the world and the creatures in it, but, among other
things, a contesting of that presentation, for, as it were, the prize of the
ordinary. So that epistemologists who think to refute skepticism by
undertaking a defense of ordinary beliefs, perhaps suggesting that there
is a sense in which they are certain, or sufficiently probable for human
purposes, have already given in to skepticism, they are living it.

But this thought of mine virtually says of itself that it must be
ineffective, as well as abusive. For think of it this way. What it comes to
is the claim that such an expression as "The world exists and I and
others in it" does not express a belief about the world; or in other words
it comes to the claim that belief is not the name of my relation to the
existence of the world and I and others in it; and that to insist otherwise
is at variance with our ordinary word "belief." But if that is so, one who
has arrived at the surmise that perhaps the world and I and others do
not exist, or anyway that we cannot know with certainty that they do,
must simply feel, So much the worse for our ordinary words, and for
whatever you imagine that other relation to the world might have been.

After enough repetitions and variations of this pattern of incon-
sequence or irresolution—or put otherwise, after some five hundred

pages of a belated doctoral dissertation on the subject—I concluded that the argument between the skeptic and the antiskeptic had no satisfactory conclusion, or that I would search for none. This left me at a place I called Nowhere, or more specifically it left me disappointed. I mean that as I began to think and to write my way out of my nowhere, what I found I was writing about was disappointment, the life-consuming disappointments in Shakespearean tragedy, but also the philosophy-consuming disappointments with knowledge as expressed in Wittgenstein's *Philosophical Investigations*. It was in following out these paths, with some reason to believe that their crossings were definitive for my philosophical direction, that I came to the idea that philosophy's task was not so much to defeat the skeptical argument as to preserve it, as though the philosophical profit of the argument would be to show not how it might end but why it must begin and why it must have no end, at least none within philosophy, or what we think of as philosophy.

Here my thought was that skepticism is a place, perhaps the central secular place, in which the human wish to deny the condition of human existence is expressed; and so long as the denial is essential to what we think of as the human, skepticism cannot, or must not, be denied. This makes skepticism an argument internal to the individual, or separate, human creature, as it were an argument of the self with itself (over its finitude). That this is expressed as a kind of argument of language with itself (over its essence) is how it came to look to me as I worked out the thought that Wittgenstein's *Investigations* is not written—as it had in my experience uniformly been taken—as a refutation of skepticism (as if the problem of skepticism were expressed by a thesis) but as a response to what I have come to call the truth of skepticism (as if the problem of skepticism is expressed by its threat, or temptation, by our sense of groundlessness). The way I work this out in relation to the *Investigations* starts from the thought that we share criteria by means of which we regulate our application of concepts, means by which, in conjunction with what Wittgenstein calls grammar, we set up the shifting conditions for conversation; in particular from the thought that the explanatory power of Wittgenstein's idea depends on recognizing that criteria, for all their necessity, are open to our repudiation, or dissatisfaction (hence they lead to, as well as lead from, skepticism); that our capacity for disappointment by them is essential to the way we possess language, in perhaps the way that Descartes found our capacity for error to be essential to our possession of the freedom of the will. (If we could not repudiate them they would not be *ours*, in the way we discover them to be; they would not be our responsibility.) The record of this work is given in the first and especially in the fourth and last part of *The Claim of Reason,* the middle two parts of which consist essentially of the dissertation that some twenty years earlier had led to my nowhere.

The lead I wish to follow in these lectures is something that kept pressing for attention in the fourth part of that book, the outcropping of moments and lines of romanticism. While I tried at each of these outbreaks to give expression to this pressure (for future reference, so to speak) I felt it was threatening the end of my story, if for no other reason than that I did not know enough, or how, to accept it. But my ignorance has become a luxury I can no longer afford to excuse, because the pressures to make a beginning, consecutive to the book, at uncovering the connection with romanticism have become irresistible. A signal of these pressures is my having marked my sense of the underwriting of ordinary language philosophy in the work of Emerson and Thoreau by speaking of an intimacy with existence, or intimacy lost—a signal recognizing the claim that the transcendentalism established in their pages is what became of romanticism in America.

Accordingly, given my interest in putting Wittgenstein's and Austin's preoccupation with the ordinary and the everyday together with Emerson's and Thoreau's emphasis on the common, the near, and the low, it is understandable that I would eventually want to understand more about Wordsworth's notorious dedication of his poetic powers, in the preface to the *Lyrical Ballads,* to "[making] the incidents of common life interesting," and his choosing for that purpose "low and rustic life" together with the language of such men as lead that life, which he calls "a far more philosophical language than that which is frequently substituted for it by Poets." My concern with Coleridge more or less follows, but it has special features which will come forward when I read him in a certain detail in succeeding lectures. What I mean by romantic is meant to find its evidence—beyond the writing of Emerson and Thoreau—in the texts of Wordsworth and Coleridge that I explicitly consider. If what I say about romanticism is false to these texts, then for my purposes here it is false of romanticism, period. If what I say is true but confined to just the texts I consider, I shall be surprised but not abashed; I know very well that there is in any case work ahead of me. I have chosen to talk about war-horses not only because I want my evidence, if narrow, to be as widely shared as possible, but also because I am not concerned here with subtleties of definition or with history. What I say about romantic exemplifications can only be useful if it is obvious—as obvious as the other examples philosophers use. (Here I am siding with philosophers for whom the obvious is the subject of philosophy, as for example, Wittgenstein, and partially, Heidegger.)

But look for a moment, before coming back to America, at the magnitude of the claim in wishing to make the incidents of common life interesting. Beyond the word "common" take the words "make" and "interesting." Wordsworth's modest statement first of all carries on its face its competition with other conceptions of poetry, since the verb "to make" is forever being cited as what the word poetry declares itself to take on. Presumably this is meant to call attention to the fact that poems are made, invented, that they are created, hence by creators; this would be confirmed in such a remark as Auden's, that "poetry makes nothing happen." What the words "make interesting" say is that poetry is to make something happen—in a certain way—to the one to whom it speaks; something inside, if you like. That what is to happen to that one is that he or she become interested in something, aligns the goal with what I have taken as the explicit presiding ambition of *Walden,* and with the enterprises of such philosophers as Wittgenstein and Austin. They perceive us as uninterested, in a condition of boredom, which they regard as, among other things, a sign of intellectual suicide. (So metaphysics would be seen as one more of the false or fantastic excitements that boredom craves. So *may* be the activities appealed to in refuting or replacing metaphysics, for example, appeals to logic or to play.) This is what Wittgenstein has against metaphysics, not just that it produces meaningless propositions—that, even in the sense in which it is true, would be only a derivative of its trouble. His diagnosis of it is rather that it is empty, empty of interest, as though philosophy were there motivated by a will to emptiness. When Austin says of philosophical examples that they are "jejune" (*Sense and Sensibilia,* p. 3), he is using a common room word to name, with all due differences of sensibility, the Nietzschean void. What worse term of criticism does he have? (As if J. P. Morgan were to say of a business's collateral that it is jejune.)

I realize that connections of the kind I am proposing here are not exactly native to professional philosophy, that reading texts of Wordsworth and Coleridge, for example, as though they are responding to the same problems philosophers have, even responding in something like the same way (a way that cannot be dissociated from thinking), is not how you would expect a philosopher from our English-speaking tradition and profession of philosophy to proceed. The interest for me in mentioning this is that my connections and procedures here are not exactly foreign to that profession either, that they represent, to my mind, rather a quarrel with it, which hence acknowledges a kinship with it. But then I had better get on soon with the main burden of this first or introductory lecture, to say something about a way I see the differences of my connections and procedures from those of that profession, which will mean saying something about philosophy as a profession, something that for me will mean saying something about why Emerson and Thoreau are not regarded as belonging to it.

Another word or two before that, by way of indicating my path from *The Claim of Reason* to the lead of romanticism.

That book is heavily indebted to an idea I call acknowledgment, which forms a key to the way I see both the problematic of skepticism and that of tragedy. This idea has been criticized on the ground, roughly, that in offering an alternative to the human goal of knowing, either it gives up the claim of philosophy to reason or else it is subject to the same doubts that knowing itself is. Perhaps this takes my idea as offering something like a mode of feeling to replace knowing, and it may be that moves of this sort have been made in theology and in moral philosophy when proofs of God's existence were repudiated and the rational ground of moral judgment became incredible. These results can seem the wish of a sentimental romanticism; if they were ones I had been moved to, I would surely feel that I owed a better understanding of feeling or sentiment than any I have had from such philosophies. Or perhaps the criticism of acknowledgment takes my idea as offering an alternative to knowing in a different direction, say as embodied in Santayana's title *Skepticism and Animal Faith*. But Santayana's notions of skepticism and of faith refer to a realm of things (namely, essence) which he defines as fixed beyond knowledge, an impulse just about perfectly hostile to the way I think. However the word "animal" is supposed to modify the word "faith" in Santayana's title, it puts faith out of the reach of our ordinary word. I put the suggestion, when it came up for me in my dissertation, as the concluding question of its pages on skepticism, declaring my nowhere: "How is that faith achieved [the supposed faith that the things of our world exist], how expressed, how deepened, how threatened, how lost?" (*The Claim of Reason*, p. 243).

But I do not propose the idea of acknowledging as an alternative to knowing but rather as an interpretation of it, as I take the word "acknowledge," containing "knowledge," itself to suggest (or perhaps it suggests that knowing is an interpretation of acknowledging). In an essay on the tragedy of *King Lear* I say, "For the point of forgoing knowledge is, of course, to know" ("The Avoidance of Love," p. 325), as if what stands in the way of further knowledge is knowledge itself, as it stands, as it conceives of itself; something not unfamiliar in the history of knowledge as expressed in the history of science. Otherwise the concept of acknowledgment would not have its role in the progress of tragedy.

But it is not in this direction that my concept of acknowledgment has mainly caused suspicion, not in the claim that tragedy is the working out of skepticism; but in the reverse direction, as I might put it, that skepticism is the playing out of a tragedy, that accordingly our ordinary lives partake of tragedy in partaking of skepticism (Chekhov calls these lives comedies, no doubt as a concession to our constricted circumstances). This means than an irreducible region of our unhappiness is natural to us but at the same time unnatural. So that the skepticism is as live in us as, let me say, the child.

Thoreau calls this everyday condition quiet desperation; Emerson says silent melancholy; Coleridge and Wordsworth are apt to say despondency or dejection; Heidegger speaks of it as our bedimmed averageness; Wittgenstein as our bewitchment; Austin both as a drunken profundity (which he knew more about than he cared to let on) and as a lack of seriousness. To find what degrees of freedom we have in this condition, to show that it is at once needless yet somehow, because of that, all but necessary, inescapable, to subject its presentation of necessity to diagnosis, in order to find truer necessities, is the romantic quest I am happy to join. In writing about Samuel Beckett's *Endgame* I express this perception of the everyday as of "the extraordinary of the ordinary," a perception of the weirdness, or surrealism, of what we call, accept, adapt to, as the usual, the real; a vision captured in the opening pages of *Walden* when its writer speaks of his townsmen as appearing to be absorbed in fantastic rituals of penance, a perception of arbitrariness in what they call necessities. In this *Walden* links with those works of our culture specifically devoted to an attack on false necessities, say to Plato's vision of us as staring at a wall in a cave, or Luther's idea of us as captives, or Rousseau's or Thoreau's sense of us as chained, or the perception of our self-subjugation in the case histories of Marx and Freud.

It is this history of devotion to the discovery of false necessity that brought me to the ambiguity of the title I give to these lectures, *In Quest of the Ordinary;* to the sense that the ordinary is subject at once to autopsy and to augury, facing at once its end and its anticipation. The everyday is ordinary because, after all, it is our habit, or habitat; but since that very inhabitation is from time to time perceptible to us—we who have constructed it—as extraordinary, we conceive that some place elsewhere, or this place otherwise constructed, must be what is ordinary to us, must be what romantics—of course including both E. T. and Nicholas Nickelby's alter ego Smike—call "home."

PROBABLY THE MOST FAMOUS TEXT adducible on the topic of the professionalizing of philosophy is Thoreau's, in the early paragraphs of *Walden:* "There are nowadays professors of philosophy, but not philosophers" (chap. 1, paragraph 19 [hereafter cited as 1.19]). In my hearing this sentiment is invoked always as a crack at academics, and of course in part it surely is that. But to suppose that is all, or primarily, the target of the sentiment is to underrate Thoreau's complexity, let alone the extent of his hopes and his disappointments; and certainly it is to overrate the attention he is giving to what we call professors of philosophy. The thing he is saying about "nowadays"—its loss of philosophy—is not something that a particular group of people, call them professors of philosophy, either have caused or could reverse. It will help even the balance if we quote the much less famous sentence following the one just quoted: "Yet it [i.e., philosophy] is admirable to profess because it was once admirable to live." But since Thoreau will say later on in this first chapter that by philosophy he means an economy of living (1.72), and since "an economy of living" is a perfectly accurate brief description of *Walden* as a whole, it should follow that *Walden* is meant to establish his claim as a philosopher. Then why does he say there are nowadays no philosophers?

I think of a number of reasons. First, the very openness of his avowal to the aspiration of philosophy makes him, literally, a professor of philosophy, one who acknowledges it, and if that is something other than a philosopher then he is not a philosopher. Second, if being admirable is essential to the living of philosophy then again he is not a philosopher because his life neither is found admirable (he rather depicts its effects on others as one of being questionable) nor ought to be found so (it ought, if it attracts you, to be lived). Third, when this writer uses a word like "nowadays" we should be alert to the ways in which time is one of his favorite playthings: he will, in the third chapter, identify himself with "the oldest Egyptian or Hindoo philosopher [when they] raised the veil from the statue of the divinity," saying that "no time has elapsed"—"it was I in him that was then so bold and it is he in me that now reviews the vision"; and in the second chapter he describes a spot he has sat down in as one he has lived in ("What is a house but a *sedes*, a seat?—better if a country seat. I discovered many a site for a house. . . . There I might live, I said; and there I did live, for an hour, a summer and a winter life."). Accordingly he might mean "nowadays" to cover the entire period of philosophy since Plato, or the pre-Socratics, that is, since what we call the establishment of philosophy; or he might well mean precisely that *now*, since he is writing his book, he is professing and not living philosophy, and that this is admirable (only) because that former life, which his writing depicts, was admirable. However, fourth, since I also take him to claim that his writing is *part* of his living, an instance of the life of philosophy, I take him to be saying, or implying, that the reader could not understand his claim to be a philosopher until he or she understands what it is to be his

10

reader, what he asks of understanding. "Nowadays" inscribes the fact that the reader comes to his words after the writer has left them, hence—this is a central claim of my book on *Walden*—he makes good on his identification of his book as a testament; a promise, as Luther puts it, in view of the testator's death; so that the life depicted in Thoreau's book is declared over by the time you come to its page. There is, accordingly, no philosopher there nowadays, unless you are one, that is, unless you accept the promise as yours, which would mean to identify yourself as one who "reviews its vision."

At one point in writing *The Senses of Walden,* I found myself asking: "Why has America never expressed itself philosophically? Or has it . . . ?" (p. 33)—a form of question that implies that if we have expressed ourselves philosophically we may not recognize that we have, as if we continued to lack the authority to take authority over our minds. And the context of the question implied that I was taking the question of American philosophical expression to be tied up with the question whether Thoreau (and Emerson) are to be recognized as philosophers. It isn't as if I did not know in 1970 that America was pretty well assuming the leadership of what is called Anglo-American analytical philosophy, which is half of what the Western world calls philosophy. Nor is it that I felt this half to be foreign to the American genius, as if it were still trading on importations from the Vienna and the Berlin of the 1930s. Logical positivism found genuine intellectual comradeship with, for example, strains in American pragmatism. It was and is just as much a question for me whether pragmatism, often cited as the American contribution to world philosophy, was expressive of American thought—in the way I felt that thought could be or had been expressed. Is this a reasonable question?

Something I had in mind can be seen by recalling Max Weber's celebrated address, "Science as a Vocation," delivered in 1918, about half way between this lecture and the year Thoreau finished *Walden.* The term science here would include philosophy as a separate discipline. Weber begins by "practically and essentially" identifying the question as to the material conditions of science as a vocation with the question: "What are the prospects of a graduate student who is resolved to dedicate himself professionally to science in university life?" In America at any rate, practically speaking this identification still holds, that the conditions for devoting oneself to philosophy are essentially the prospects of holding a position in the philosophy department of a University. Yet we should find an uneasiness in granting this that Weber could scarcely have known. He had a pair of assurances that I take us to lack. He was assured simultaneously that in his culture authoritative philosophy could be achieved by professors of philosophy (it can be taken as the mission of Kant and Hegel to have demonstrated this, somewhat to our confusion); and he was assured that this achievement was a part of the common literary inheritance that had, for example, produced and profited from him. Whereas American intellectuals can be said to hold nothing in common, nothing, that is, of high culture. (Perhaps it follows from this that no American philosophy *could*, of itself, give expression to America.)

I can imagine a number of responses to what may appear as my wish for the participation of philosophy and literature in one another, some ruder than others. One response would be that it is exactly the nature of professional philosophy—whether of Anglo-American analysis or of Continental systematizing—to give up, even to escape, the pleasures and the seductions of literature. And isn't this faithful to philosophy's origins in Plato, who ruled poetry out of his philosophical republic? But this is hardly an answer until we know why he ruled it out; and we cannot, I think, know why until we know what it means for philosophy to be in *competition* with poetry, as for the same prize. Besides, something Plato ruled *in* to his philosophy is what we might call the obligation of therapy, and professional philosophy does not on the whole follow Plato slavishly in this. Philosophy was seen, like poetry, to possess the power to change people, to free the soul from bondage. In the past couple of millennia other contestants have presented themselves, in addition to philosophy and poetry, on the field of therapy; religion has, and, most recently, psychotherapy (though here we need a separate term to cover the direct assault on the mind by practitioners from Mesmer to Freud). Certainly there are good grounds for rejoicing that philosophy has escaped the business of therapy; I dare say they are roughly the same grounds for rejoicing that philosophy has become professional. It is my impression that those professionals who take Wittgenstein with limited seriousness as a philosopher do not take at all seriously his likening of philosophical procedures with therapies. Certainly I do not wish to see philosophy, as a profession, get back into the business of therapy, anyway not as philosophy stands, and not into what we are likely to think of as therapy; but I confess that the idea is more painfully ludicrous than I wish it were, because I am of the view that philosophy is, or ought to be, haunted by the success of its escape from this obligation. I might express my outlook by saying that if you conceive philosophy and poetry and therapy in ways that prevent you from so much as seeing their competition with one another then you have given up something I take as part of the philosophical adventure, I mean a part of its intellectual adventure.

That nothing of high culture is common to us means that for us no text is sacred, no work of this ambition is to be preserved at all costs. But then this is a conclusion, or rather a premise, Emerson and Thoreau want us to arrive at, that as Emerson puts it, "around every circle another can be drawn," that "all that we reckoned settled shakes and rattles; and literature, cities, climates, religions, leave their foundations and dance before our eyes" ("Circles"). All this has its ecstacies of expectation and equality, which is so far to the good. But think what it means about our everyday intellectual life. If Emerson and Thoreau are the founding thinkers of American culture, but the knowledge of them, though possessed by shifting bands of individuals, is not possessed in common by that culture, then what way have we of coming to terms on the issues that matter most to us, as say the fundamental issues of philosophy and of art can matter to us?

So extraordinary a cultural amnesia must have many sources. As food for thought I cite three sentences from Bruce Kuklick's recent book entitled *The Rise of American Philosophy: Cambridge, Massachusetts, 1860–1930*. It presents the story of American philosophy proper as beginning with the conflict engendered by Transcendentalism's attack on Unitarianism, the Christianity of the Boston gentry. Kuklick describes the situation this way: "When Transcendentalism attacked the foundation of accepted faith, Unitarian laymen looked to philosophy [specifically to the philosophers at Harvard] to buttress the established religion. The laity were not disappointed. . . . Adept and knowledgeable in argument, the Harvard thinkers consistently outmaneuvered the Transcendentalists philosophically. Although Emerson and his well-known circle won over a band of converts, the philosophical bases of Unitarianism remained unshaken" (p. 10). Kuklick, I gather, takes this as rather a grand day for American philosophy; but without disputing this as the beginning of American philosophy as a discipline, nor directly contesting a positive evaluation of it, consider how extraordinary a beginning it is, extraordinary even that it should be plausible as such a beginning. The period in question is the middle of the nineteenth century, a time at which Marx could announce (in the introduction of his proposed book on Hegel's *Philosophy of Right*) that "the criticism of religion is in the main complete." While thinkers like Nietzsche and Heidegger will come to show how far from complete that criticism was, Marx's remark calls to mind the centuries in which European philosophy was establishing its modern basis by quarreling with religion, posing a threat to religion whether it appeared to attack it (say as in Hume) or to defend it (say as in Kant), because the price religion pays for philosophy's defense is a further dependence on philosophy's terms;

and the philosophical is as jealous of its autonomy (call this Reason) as the religious is (call this Faith).

Even if one accordingly interpreted the Harvard philosophers' defenses of an established religion in the middle of the nineteenth century not as the beginning of the story of the American discipline of philosophy but as a sign that this discipline had not yet begun independently, the moral to draw may be only that American intellectual development is not in phase with European developments, something we perhaps already knew. But the other half of the story Kuklick tells is that the philosophical defense was precisely taken against Emerson and Transcendentalism, and here the defense seems to have been much more lasting. There has been no serious move, as far as I know, within the ensuing discipline of American philosophy, to take up Emerson philosophically. The moral to draw here may of course be the one Kuklick draws, that Emerson and Thoreau are to be comprehended as philosophical amateurs, toward whom, it would be implied, there is no professional obligation. But suppose the better moral is that Emerson and Thoreau are as much threats, or say embarrassments, to what we have learned to call philosophy as they are to what we call religion, as though philosophy had, and has, an interest on its own behalf in looking upon them as amateurs, an interest, I think I may say, in repressing them. This would imply that they propose, and embody, a mode of thinking, a mode of conceptual accuracy, as thorough as anything imagined within established philosophy, but invisible to that philosophy because based on an idea of rigor foreign to its establishment.

Before giving a name to this foreign rigor I have at least to indicate some way to avoid, or postpone, a standing and decisive consideration that professional philosophers will have for refusing to hear out an articulation of the intuition that Emerson and Thoreau warrant the name of philosophy—the consideration that no matter what one may mean by, say, conceptual accuracy, a work like *Walden* has nothing in it to call *arguments*. And while someone may rest undisturbed at the prospect of philosophy forgoing its therapeutic dimension, no one should rest easy at the idea of philosophy abandoning the business of argument. But suppose that what is meant by argumentation in philosophy is one way of accepting full responsibility for one's own discourse. Then the hearing I require depends upon the thought that there is another way, another philosophical way (for poetry will have its way, and therapy will have its way) of accepting that responsibility.

This other philosophical way I am going to call reading; others may call it philosophical interpretation. This associates Emerson and Thoreau with the Continental tradition of philosophizing and at once dissociates them from it. It associates them according to the thought,

14

as I express it at the opening of *The Claim of Reason*, that philosophy may be inherited either as a set of problems to be solved (as Anglo-American analysts do) or else as a set of texts to be read (as Europe does—except of course where it has accepted, or reaccepted, analysis). You can sense how different imperatives for training, different standards for criticism and conversation, different genres of composition, different personas of authorship, will arise from this difference in modes of inheritance.

This sense is enforced by seeing how the devotion to reading at the same time dissociates Emerson and Thoreau from the Continental tradition. To say how, I must first describe what I have sometimes called the two myths of philosophizing, or myths of the role of reading in philosophical writing.

In the one myth the philosopher proceeds from having read everything, in the other from having read nothing. Perhaps this duality is prefigured in the division between Plato's writing and Socrates' talking, but it is purely enough illustrated in this century by contrasting Heidegger's work, which assumes the march of the great names in the whole history of Western philosophy, with that of Wittgenstein, who may get around to mentioning half-a-dozen names, but then only to identify a remark which he happens to have come across and which seems to get its philosophical importance only from the fact that he finds himself thinking about it. Common to the two myths is an idea that philosophy begins only when there are no further texts to read, when the truth you seek has already been missed, as if it lies behind you. In the myth of totality, philosophy has still not found itself—until at least it has found you; in the myth of emptiness, philosophy has lost itself in its first utterances.

Now I can put my idea about a difference between the Transcendentalists and the Continentals, within the affinity between them, this way: While Emerson and Thoreau proceed with the tasks of philosophy—for example with the task of endless responsibility for one's own discourse—by something they portray as reading, and not as argumentation, they are nevertheless not interested in what we are likely to call philosophical texts more than in others, and indeed nothing is more constant in their philosophical mission than to warn the student against much book reading altogether. It is no wonder if they are an embarrassment to a university curriculum.

Then what, or how, do they recommend reading? I will begin an answer to this by spending the rest of this lecture reading a few further sentences from *Walden* on the subject, and then from Emerson's "Self-Reliance."

Having praised the written beyond the spoken word and finding that the "heroic books . . . will always be in a language dead to degen-erate times," the writer of *Walden* interprets "the noblest written words" by a startling identification: "*There* are the stars, and they who can may read them" (3.4). This is an interpretation of nature as a text, of course, but it is one of Thoreau's clearest interpretations of what reading itself is. It interprets reading (dangerously invoking, to revise, the idea of the astrological) as a process of *being read*, as finding your fate in your capacity for interpretation of yourself. "Will you be a reader, a student merely, or a seer? Read your fate, see what is before you, and walk on into futurity" (4.1). What is before you is precisely not, if you catch Thoreau's tune, something in the future; what is before you, if you are, for example, reading, is a text. He asks his reader to see it, to become a seer with it. Only then can you walk beyond where you are. In the course of *Walden* he depicts himself reading in two or three spe-cific books, and each time he is interrupted. One time, at the beginning of "Brute Neighbors," the interruption is openly allegorized as the per-sonification of the Poet inviting the personification of the Hermit to leave off his meditation on some sentences of Confucius and to come fishing. The Hermit stalls for a moment, but then accedes to this other pleasure and need. Since Thoreau typically uses openness to conceal something, one may take this personified exchange as being with him-self, hence to betoken that his own wish to write (to fish with the poet in him) interrupts his wish to read, which would according to his way of thinking mean that his writing is continuously a matter of interrupt-ing writing, genuine writing being a matter of breaking in upon some-thing, call this meditation, or silence, or call it language, or the present. (If "the present" here may be figured as metaphysical "presence," and this, further, as narcissistic "self"-presence, then writing in this allegory occurs as the expression or creation of desire, something beyond, some-thing wanted, lacking, "breaking in." Then writing figures the reception of language, of others, as such. Then when Thoreau insists on writing alone, writing only, as opposed to speaking ["a labor of my hands only" as in his opening paragraph—here, not a labor of my mouth; but this will come forth against the dedication of his mouth to God's words], he is withdrawing his investment in others, taking his voice back to itself, enacting a "return" to the presocial [it would take an "advance" to the postsocial]; and then his writing figures as it were the states before writing, before its contrast with voicing, before its breaking in [Thoreau will call this "running amok against him"]. This suggests the level at which what Thoreau calls "disobedience," refusing to listen, makes his neighbors anxious: as if, if society persists in the error of its ways, there is no assurance that society will in the future be able to break into metaphysical solitude, that is, that it will be *wanted*, and *consented* to.) [1]

Another interruption of reading, in "Sounds," goes this way. The writer describes himself as "look[ing] up from my book" upon hearing a train pass, and it takes a moment to realize that what he calls "my book" is the one he is now writing. And when he looks up at the train here is what happens. "This carload of torn sails is more legible and interesting now than if they should be wrought into paper and printed books. Who can write so graphically the history of the storms they have weathered as these rents have done?" (4.12). What happened when he looked up from his book is that he went on reading (and writing). He went on seeing what was before him, he found the train legible, hence he walked on into futurity, for example into his book. So his reading and writing were not interrupted after all. That reading is a way, or a goal, of seeing, is something attested—as I found in *The Claim of Reason*—by the history of the word *reading* in a word for advising, which in turn contains a word for seeing. Now here in his book *Walden*, what its writer was reading then is now before *us*, and not only in a narrative

---

1. In the introduction to *The Senses of Walden* in 1972, in response to an earlier query whether I had been reading Derrida and Lévi-Strauss, and as a way of explaining, not without a certain worry even then, why I thought my ignorance of other work would not compromise the specific effort of mine, I said, "My remarks about writing as such are not meant as generalities concerning all of literature but as specific acknowledgements of the intention of the writer in this book, in particular two phases of this intention: to rest his achievement of the condition of writing as such specifically upon his achievement of a genuine Scripture; and to alarm his culture by refusing it his voice, i.e., by withholding his consent. . . ." This response has, I believe, been taken by some readers of *The Senses of Walden* to mean that my book is without theoretical ambition. What the response meant was that no theory I was aware of had the power to account for *Walden*'s practice and the theory of writing that is part of that practice; and that it itself, on the understanding I had reached of it, contained a theory of itself, hence of any text—to the extent that another text's relation to it, call this its difference, is specifically measured. It is, I trust, somewhat understandable why, in 1987, revising the present chapter, I have added this footnote and the parenthetical observation to which it attaches. I do not wish to seem unteachable, or unresponsive to the demand to relate what I do to the practice and theory of deconstruction. But those who wish me well, and I hope some others, will appreciate that 1972 (and the years preceding, during which the work that goes into *The Senses of Walden* was in preparation), is as yet an immeasurable distance in American time. Naturally I am aware of the possibility that intellectual events of the past two decades may have preempted the fields I find myself in; but it is my fortune, good or bad, to imagine otherwise. I was early enough so that it was quickly too late for me for a different start. If this were a race, I would bet on the hare every time. But if it is not, if there is not just one course, and if indeed we are not on the ground but at sea, the turtle may make sense.

of it as, say, a newspaper might have it, but in an account of it (an account is Thoreau's habitual economic term for what his writing is), which means a calculation of its value. He has wrought (written, and, since they already contained writing, he has translated) the torn sails into a book of printed pages, and in this transaction it is still by the rents of these sheets, evidence of what has happened to them, by the distress that caused them and the distress and the satisfaction they will cause, that they still write the history of the storms they have weathered. The transaction of sails into pages reduces their interest, he says; so apparently writing is for him a capital expenditure. And in his translation, those "rents" also go to make good his claims as an economist, or accountant, and become the payments he gives in return for his weathering of his history.

These two sentences of Thoreau's about the legible train prompt me to add up what he means by reading along the following lines. Reading is a variation of writing, where they meet in meditation and achieve accounts of their opportunities; and writing is a variation of reading, since to write is to cast words together that you did not make, so as to give or take readings. Since these accounts are of what Thoreau calls economy, which is his philosophical life, it follows that his economics, resulting from the interplay of writing and reading, is what he claims as philosophy. An implication of this line of interpretation is that while philosophizing is a product of reading, the reading in question is not especially of books, especially not of what we think of as books of philosophy. The reading is of whatever is before you. Where this happens to be a verbal matter what you read are words and sentences, at most pages. Whole books are not read, any more than they are written, at a sitting; not exactly or simply because they are too long but because they would dictate the length of a session of reading, whereas meditation is either to be broken off or to bring itself to an end. (The theme here is of the ending of philosophy as one of philosophy's unshaken tasks.) Books of philosophy would especially not be read, I imagine for two reasons: (1) Philosophical books are forever postponing their conclusions (this is roughly the criticism made of Hegel by Kierkegaard). Being outwardly systematic, everything is made to depend on how it works out; that is, it is a narrative—a narrative of concepts, it so happens—hence based on suspense. In this respect books of philosophy are of no more philosophical use than novels are. A book of philosophy suitable to what Thoreau envisions as "students" would be written with next to no forward motion, one that culminates in each sentence. This sounds like a prescription for a new music, say a new discourse, and hence like a negation of poetry as well as of narrative, since it implicitly denies, in a work of literary originality, the role of the line; the sentence

18

is everything. Naturally I hope it also sounds like a description of *Walden*. (2) Americans are not, anyway not yet, what might be called professors of philosophy, obliged to read any and every text that gives itself out as philosophy and to find a place for it in our thoughts. We are possessed of no standing discourse within which to fit anything and everything philosophers have said. We are either philosophers or nothing; we have nothing to profess. Either we are able to rethink a thought that comes our way, to own and assess it as it occurs, or we must let it pass, it is not ours.

The discourse Thoreau invents for this assessment, his economics, proceeds, in the absence of a philosophical vocabulary, by taking us, as suggested, over the fantastically elaborated network of terms of assessment—terms of economy—our language naturally possesses, assessing words as they are employed, which often and critically comes to turning the face of a word to a value of it we would ordinarily not notice as economic—for example, faces of the words *account, settle, redemption, living, interest, terms.* Whether you accept Thoreau as a philosopher depends on whether you accept his invention of a discourse, along with his other beginnings, as a beginning of a philosophical discourse. The implication of this invention may seem the biggest of the brags in this book of brags. The writer is claiming to be writing the *first* book of philosophy. —But *is* this really so exceptional a brag? It is a claim of authority, that he has a right to his words; in his terms, that they are earned, a labor of his hands only. But he does not say that he is the *only* such writer or earner. He emphatically does not think he comes to his work earlier than the "oldest" (Egyptian or Hindoo) philosophers we heard him invoking; merely coevally with them: there is no philosophy present until the philosopher is *being* read (at least, necessarily by himself, by herself.) Nor does he claim that he is unique *nowadays;* he emphatically denies this. The uncomfortable implication is rather that philosophical authority is nontransferable, that each claim to speak for philosophy has to earn the authority for itself, say account for it.

I spoke earlier of philosophy as a bequeathing; now I am speaking of it as an inheriting. Anxious not to be misunderstood in emphasizing the nationality of philosophy, the demand a philosophy places upon its nation, forcing it to put its philosophy on trial, to repress it, so that it can return (in chapter 8 of *Walden:* "It is true, I might have . . . run 'amok' against society; but I preferred that society should run 'amok' against me, it being the desperate party"), I do not wish to leave the impression that Thoreau is shunning the influence of foreign philosophy. His invocation of the oldest Egyptian and Hindoo philosophers should itself secure that fact, along with its implication that America must inherit philosophy not—or not alone, not primarily?—from Europe, but also from where Europe inherited it, from wherever Plato inherited it (which only philosophy will know). Here is just another version of *Walden*'s mythical brag to philosophy, specifically announcing, in all modesty, that to inherit philosophy you have already to be in the way of philosophy.

Walden, as said, opens with its writer declaring that when he wrote his pages he earned his living "by the labor of [his] hands only," and whatever debt or guilt he is there disclaiming, he goes on to work out a chain of economic terms to figure his debt to philosophy. *The Senses of Walden* more or less says of itself that it may be derived from two axioms: that the house being built in *Walden* is *Walden* (which also means America, the spiritual construction, or discovery, or constitution, of, Thoreau tells us, Walled-In, which may image imprisonment, but which is what Paradise says); and that accordingly every act of its writer is an allegory, or staging, of its writing. So that when in the chapter falling first he says, "It is difficult to begin without borrowing," and reports that on the day he went down to the woods he borrowed an axe, adding that "I returned it sharper than I received it," he is to be understood as describing his literary-philosophical borrowing, which entails his competing with it. Such confession is reinforced by claims like, "Nothing was given me of which I have not rendered some account," which suggests (not that it follows) that his account is of nothing other than what was given him. Perhaps most unmistakably, or summarily, there is the scene in which he, "takes down" a shanty for which he had bargained and which he bought for boards for his envisioned house, where the picture of dismantling, and removal to a new site, and the figuration of buying as believing and of bargaining as coming to terms, all figure in his account of his account.

To say that Emerson and Thoreau "found" philosophy for America is to say, among other things, that, in teaching the nation that it is, and how it is, to be born into thought, they demonstrate how thinking (from Europe, from the past, from where it finds philosophy) is to be brought to these shores, which in Thoreau's book means turned to account.

I have emphasized that the writing and the reading or seeing that Thoreau exemplifies are not about something *else,* something past or future, to be called his living; they are themselves either exemplifications, modes, of philosophical life or they are philosophically worthless. To say that the central narrative of *Walden* is the building of home is to say that the book is about what you might call edification. Edification might also be a reasonable term for what we were calling therapy. It is, under this description, exactly the thing that good professionals, like Hegel, are at pains to deny to philosophy. I do not assert that Thoreau

20

would mean by edification what Hegel means by it. The issue is alive in works like *Being and Time* and in *Philosophical Investigations,* where one feels that some spiritual claim (call it) is leveled at the reader and that this claim cannot, or must not, be interpreted as some specifically moral claim. It may be the case that in a given age the edification to which philosophy may aspire can only happen when philosophy is professional, or in touch with the professional. Ours is perhaps such an age. Edification of any kind may be taken as what Max Weber deplores in the university classroom; he describes the wish he deplores, making science into something it cannot be, as a wish for a substitute redemption. (I see on late night television that a professor of philosophy and theology, arguing against a secular humanist, so he called him, appeals to science to prove that the universe is caused, hence has a source in some intelligence. I take it Weber would not approve. Neither did the secular humanist. Such also is our age.)

And Thoreau's case is worse, from a professional point of view, than has so far come out, for he will accept no substitute for redemption. One of his most innocuous, hence most suspicious, sentences goes this way: "You only need sit still long enough in some attractive spot in the woods that all its inhabitants may exhibit themselves to you by turns" (12.11). All of *Walden* is condensed in these few drops. Grant for now that this attitude of sitting allegorizes the reading and writing we have noted. I will also just assert that, among many other things, "by turns" means by verses and by conversions. (You may imagine that it also means "by tropes." But this would only be the case where Thoreau's figures [stressed by his numbers in his "account"] are taken as figurations of, or refigurings, recountings of, figuration, according to which "by turns" would have to mean "by turning around the idea of trope itself.") Then what he is saying is that he—that is, his book—has a power of stillness, say silence, that is sufficiently attractive to be looked to as redemptive. This should be put together with *Walden*'s interpretation of being seated that we cited earlier, the one that identifies a house as a seat, hence being seated anywhere as a way and a time you might be living, spending your life, in a word, taking up residence. The context of that remark (the opening paragraphs of chapter 2) is one in which Thoreau goes to extravagant lengths—that is, his usual lengths—to show that this being seated or residence is part, as the word says, of possessing the landscape that radiated from him, and the farms and the trees and, in short, everything within the dozen miles on every side of where, sitting, he is living; the country is taking its origin in him. Why the equation of the postures of writing and reading and those of owning should be noted in this way is something we will have occasion to speculate about.

21

I would like to take the claim of Thoreau's sentence that concerns (and shows) the writer sitting still long enough (in attraction) as fulfilling one of what I had meant by the tasks or predicates of philosophy—here the task of inviting questions by its silence, or of confronting by not speaking the first word. (Socrates is overtaken in the public street; Wittgenstein's *Investigations* opens with a quotation, the words of someone else; so does Heidegger's *Being and Time;* the writer of *Walden* begins, after a brief paragraph introducing himself, by saying that he is answering some very particular inquiries made by his townsmen concerning his mode of life.) But the use of a seductive or attractive silence to elicit another's revelation of themselves suggests procedures and powers which, even if they are well thought of as teaching, universities have no credentials for.

In turning to Emerson for his testimony about reading, I note that the story of his and Thoreau's cultural neglect needs complication. Emerson's story has to include an account of the tremendous fame attaching to him in his lifetime, which persisted for some decades after his death and which, after further decades in which he seemed unreadable, there have been recurrent efforts to revive, themselves invariably producing counter-efforts to destroy it again. How one understands these twists of his reputation generally seems tied up with what one takes his writing to be, as if the writing and the reputation formed one case for us, and the case is always undecided, as if we do not yet know what this man is and what he wants.

A way of considering what it is about his writing that produces this wavering toward it, this not knowing how it is to be taken, is to consider that Emerson makes the question of how to take it (how seriously, I would like to say, *he* takes it, the question of authenticating its own seriousness), a guiding question he asks for himself, of himself.

I have more than once cited the following passage from "Self-Reliance" as one in which he is dramatizing his mission as a writer, presenting the credentials of his vocation: "I shun father and mother and wife and brother when my genius calls me. I would write on the lintels of the doorpost, *Whim*. I hope it is better than whim at last, but we cannot spend the day in explanation." I will not recall again the biblical contexts which show Emerson there to be specifying the call to write as following the new promise of redemption, and specifying the act of writing as marking his old dwelling as with a mezuzah, or with blood, as on passover. The question is pushed at us, How seriously does he mean these specifications? Is there any philosophical point to them beyond the literary, whatever that may be?

I go on here to note that the entire essay "Self-Reliance," for all its fame as preaching individualism (which is not wrong certainly, but certainly not clear), is a study of writing, as if one's wish to write simply *Whim* already took upon oneself the full-blown burden of writing. The writer writes *Whim* in the place others place the word of God, as if to mock the commoner habit of taking God's name in the place of Whim. As if there is no greater standing authority for using the word *Whim*—or any other word, however small—than for using the word *God;* no justification for language apart from language.

That "Self-Reliance" is a study of (philosophical) writing (hence of reading and of thinking) is insistently established in the essay by Emerson's draw upon the reach of the words "expression" and "character" and "communication," using them throughout to call attention at once to the externals of writing and to the internals of the one doing the writing, backing it, fronting it, hence to assert that both writing and writer are to be read, which is about to say, both are texts, perhaps testing, contesting, one another. (It is from that essay that I will go on to take my quotations from Emerson here, unless I specify otherwise.) He says, for example, that "A character is like an acrostic or Alexandrian stanza—read it forward, backward, or across, it still spells the same thing." And after warning near the beginning "we but half express ourselves" and claiming in the middle that while we "may err in the expression" of our intuitions we know that they are so (they are *so, this* way) and are "not to be disputed," he speaks near the end of the wise man as "[making] men sensible [of something] by the expression of his countenance." What the wise man is making us sensible of, says Emerson in this instance, is that the soul stays home, that even when he is called from his house he is still, whatever others say, at home. But since being called, for a wise man, is evidently being called by his genius, and since for Emerson that is to write, Emerson is submitting his writing to the condition of acquiring whatever authority and conviction is due to it by looking at its countenance, or surface.

Our philosophical habits will prompt us to interpret the surface of writing as its manner, its style, its rhetoric, an ornament of what is said rather than its substance, but Emerson's implied claim is that this is as much a philosophical prejudice as the other conformities his essay decries, that, so to speak, words are no more ornaments of thought than tears are ornaments of sadness or joy. Of course, they may be seen so, and they may in a given case amount to no more; but this just means that expressions are the last things to take at face value.

What countenance will count as the writing of the wise? Emerson finds in the communication of those who "conform to usages," who, that is, are without self-reliance, that "every word they say chagrins us and we do not know where to begin to set them right." If every one of our words is implicated in the conformity to usage, then evidently no word assures a safe beginning; whether a given word will do must accordingly depend upon how it allows itself to be said, the countenance in which it puts its utterer, whether it can be uttered so as not to chagrin us, which is to say sadden us, but rather, to use a favorite Emersonian phrase, to raise and cheer us. As if these were the fixed alternatives for the practice of philosophy.

Here we come upon the most familiar of all the complaints leveled at Emerson, the complaint that more than any other has clouded his reputation among intellectuals in this century: that he is recklessly affirmative, that he lacked the sense of tragedy.

Whatever this means, and however often it has ineffectually been denied, a prior question is bound to rise to the lips of a philosopher, simply the question what difference it makes, what philosophical difference, whether the countenance of speech saddens or cheers us, which are psychological matters of the *effects* of words; whereas what matters philosophically is whether what is said is true. But then it is up to us at least to get the psychology straight. Emerson says in a companion essay ("Circles") "The simplest words,—we do not know what they mean except when we love and aspire." Whatever states these words are meant to name, this remark says not that the states are the effects of words but rather on the contrary that they are their causes, or rather conditions of understanding words. While it may not be unprecedented for a philosopher to tell us that the words we use every day are imprecise or prompt illusions, it is not usual, even not normal of philosophy, to say that the way to their meaning lies through a change of heart.

Whatever this itself means will presumably depend on how accurately it describes Emerson's own practice of writing and thinking, that is, on his particular countenancing of words. Let us look finally at two further sentences exemplifying his practice of describing his practice. When he says, "Who has more obedience than I masters me" this is to be taken in connection with his speaking of writing as something to which one is called, something to which one is harkening, showing obedience. Then to "master" him is not exactly to overcome him, as if he were an unruly impulse or an insubordinate slave, but to have command of him as of a difficult text or of language. And however difficult the text may be that concerns the subject of being called, I find it no harder to command, and more serviceable, than any number of texts that less affirmative aestheticians have produced concerning the subject of intention.

Both the idea of grasping the intention of a text and the idea of sharing or hearing what has called it, are interpretations of reading, of following a text. But the idea of being intended can close out what the idea of being called and of obedience, of listening, brings into investigation: namely, how it is that one writes better than one knows (as well as worse) and that one may be understood better by someone other than oneself (as well as understood worse). These are things worth looking into. Emerson is looking into it when he remarks: "Character teaches above our wills. Men imagine that they communicate their virtue or vice only by overt action, and do not see that virtue or vice emit a breath every moment." I find this a frightening notation of an anxiety in writing; an acknowledgement that one must give over control of one's appropriations, as if to learn what they are.

To write knowing that your words emit a breath of virtue or vice every moment, that they communicate the means by which you are expressing your desires, know them or not, is to leave your character unguarded. To leave what I say unguarded has been a point of honor with me, even though I know that some risks are not worth taking. If one could not write better than one is, and understand a writer better than he or she may understand themselves, if we were not capable of better obedience than we have shown, obedience to something better, then the case of writing would be more pitiable than it is, because then it could propose no measures for putting itself aside, no relief for writer or reader. It follows that I am at any time subject to indictment by what I set down, or else it goes for nothing.

I have not wished to disguise a certain pathos in my sense of struggle for the writing of philosophy, in the position and the place I find myself in, I mean for example as a Professor of Philosophy in America, and elsewhere. At the same time I have not wished to make the struggle unduly personal, because the struggles it joins are nothing if not common—those between philosophy and poetry, between writer and reader, between writer or reader and language, between language and itself, between the American edifice of fantasy and the European edifice of philosophy, between the hope and the despair of writing and reading redemptively.

But how about the very pathos in posing these issues as struggles? Isn't that to romanticize what are merely intellectual problems? Is philosophy as such—nowadays? still?—to be cloaked as a romantic undertaking? I suppose my finding Emerson and Thoreau to underwrite Wittgenstein and Austin suggests a certain romantic taint in what I regard as some of the most advanced thought of our time; and Heidegger's relation to romantic literature, especially of course to Hölderlin, suggests that it is a taint he takes on willingly. It may be that the claim upon the reader I have pointed to in Heidegger's and Wittgenstein's work, the claim I said is not to be captured exactly as moral, may be thought of as a romantic demand for, or promise of, redemption, say self-recovery. But in all philosophical seriousness, a recovery from what? Philosophy cannot say sin. Let us speak of a recovery from skepticism. This means, as said, from a drive to the inhuman. Then why does this present itself as a recovery of the self? Why, more particularly, as the recovery of the (of my) (ordinary) (human) voice? What is romantic about the recovery of, the quest for, the ordinary or everyday? What business is it of philosophy's?

2
Emerson, Coleridge, Kant
(Terms as Conditions)

IN THIS SECOND LECTURE I follow out certain intuitions of the
first—that philosophy's essential business has become the response to skepticism, as if philosophy's business has essentially become
the question of its own existence; that the recovery of the (my) ordinary
(voice) from skepticism, since it is itself a task dictated by skepticism,
requires the contesting of skepticism's picturing of the task; that in philosophy the task is associated with the overcoming, or say critique, of
metaphysics, and in literature with the domestication of the fantastic
and the transcendentalizing of the domestic, call these movements the
internalization, or subjectivizing, or democratizing, of philosophy; and
that this communication between philosophy and literature, or the refusal of communication, is something that causes romanticism, causes
at any rate my present experiments with romantic texts, experiments
caused by the discovery of these texts among the effects of *The Claim of
Reason*.

Working within an aspiration of philosophy that feeds, and is fed
by, a desire to inherit Emerson and Thoreau as thinkers, I take it for
granted that their thinking is unknown to the culture whose thinking
they worked to found (I mean culturally unpossessed, unassumable
among those who care for books, however possessed by shifting bands
of individuals), in a way it would not be thinkable for Kant and Schiller
and Goethe to be unknown to the culture of Germany, or Descartes
and Rousseau to France, or Locke and Hume and John Stuart Mill to
England. While I have been variously questioned about what this

means, and what it betokens, I am not yet prepared to describe the mechanisms that have made it possible and necessary. But since I rather imply that the repression of Emerson and Thoreau as thinkers is linked with their authority as founders, I should at least note the preparation of their repression by their self-repressions.

Founders generally sacrifice something (call this Isaac, or call this Dido), and teach us to sacrifice or repress something. And they may themselves be victimized by what they originate. I take such matters to be in play in the way Emerson and Thoreau write in and from obscurity, as if to obscure themselves is the way to gain the kind of standing they require of their fellow citizens. As if to demonstrate their self-repression, hence their powers to undo this repression, were to educate us in self-liberation, and first of all to teach us that self-liberation is what we require of ourselves. That this is within our (American) grasp means that to achieve it we have above all to desire it sufficiently. This achievement of desire is equally an intellectual and a spiritual, or say passionate, exercise. In "Thinking of Emerson" (added to the reprinting of *The Senses of Walden*), I characterize the thinking that Emerson preaches and practices in terms of abandonment, abandonment of something, by something, and to something. Those who stay with the entering gentilities of Emerson's prose will naturally take his reputed optimism as a sign of his superficiality and accommodation; it is an understandable stance, because to follow his affirmations to their exits of desire is to be exposed to the intransigent demands they place upon his reader, his society. (As an exercise in these demands, in obscurities amounting to self-repression, in the incessant implication that the language does not exist in which to stake claims quite philosophically, or say nationally, you may assign yourself a meditation on the opening question of Emerson's great essay "Experience": "Where do we find ourselves?" Hint [as they used to say after posing a tricky problem in American high school math textbooks]: Take the question as one staked for American thinkers by the thinking and practice of Columbus [say by the fact that native Americans are called Indians], as if the very direction to America, the brute place of it, and that we call it discovered, say found, threaten the assured edifice of metaphysics. And then take Emerson's question where we find ourselves as asking how we are founding ourselves, since there is no *one* voyage to America. As if Emerson's self-repression is to enact the wish to found a tradition of thinking without founders, without foundation; as if we are perhaps to ratify ourselves with Foundling Fathers.)

Heidegger's idea that thinking is something to which we stand to be attracted is exactly not an idea he expects to attract his fellow citizens, but at best is to single out rare, further, thinkers. A thinker is one drawn, you may say seduced, by the authority of thinking, that is, drawn to the origin of thinking (say in Parmenides) that philosophy has obscured, or repressed in establishing itself, or say founding itself. But in the way I conceive of Emerson and of Thoreau it is as if they play Parmenides to their own Plato, Dido to their own Aeneas, Hölderlin to their own Heidegger. (I am not here speaking of comparative quality but of comparative structure, although without my conviction in the soundness of the Americans' quality, I do not know that I would be interested in their structure.) Even in the absence of an understanding of how it is that the repressed performs its own repression, one may surmise that a thinker would wish to acquire the authority of thinking in this way in order to teach the authority whose acquisition consists in its relinquishment. I think of this as philosophical authority. If something like this is an intelligible and practical background to bring to Emerson and Thoreau, the advantage, to it and to them, is that it can be investigated with as it were, one's own hands, and in open air; as if the origins of philosophy were hardly different in age from the origins of movies. Someone my age will have had a teacher whose teacher could have heard Emerson. So that the philosophical waltz of obviousness and obscurity is—most obviously, if *therefore* most obscurely—of one's own calling.

It is habitually said, I suppose correctly, that what we think of as romanticism is a function of (whatever else) how we conceive the philosophical settlement proposed in the achievement of Kant. Since what we think about any view of the relation of the mental and the material, so to speak, is bound to be some such function (that is, since Kant's achievement is part of how we think) this is not a very specific claim. In this essay I specify what I understand a certain force of the Kantian function to be. That I confine myself to working this out only relative to a reading of one essay of Emerson's—"Fate," from *The Conduct of Life*—and a few passages from Coleridge's autobiograhical prose will naturally require various justifications, not to say excuses. The fact that these texts do not undertake to quote and refute particular passages from Kant's writing would not for me be enough to show that, on a reasonable view of argument, they are not in argument with his philosophy. This too depends on what you understand Kant to have accomplished (what you think the name *Kant,* means) and on what you understand to be the cause of the kind of writing in which romantics have expressed themselves. That it is not what we may expect of philosophical prose would hardly take such writers by surprise, as if they wrote as they did inadvertently, or in ignorance of the sound of philosophy. Consider that they were attacking philosophy in the name of redeeming it. Should professional philosophers, now or ever, care about that? It is true that philosophy habitually presents itself as redeeming itself, hence struggling for its name, famously in the modern period, since Bacon, Locke, and Descartes. But can philosophy be redeemed *this way,* this romantic way? To consider further what that way is, is a motive for taking up the texts in question here.

To prepare for them I had better set out some version of what can be said to be Kant's accomplishment. Or let Kant say it for us, in two summary paragraphs from his *Prolegomena to Any Future Metaphysics* (section 32).

> Since the oldest days of philosophy inquirers into pure reason have conceived, besides the things of sense, or appearances (phenomena), which make up the sensible world, certain creations of the understanding, called noumena, which should constitute an intelligible world. And as appearances and illusion were by those men identified (a thing which we may well excuse in an undeveloped epoch), actuality was only conceded to the creations of thought.
>
> And we indeed, rightly considering objects of sense as mere appearances, confess thereby that they are based upon a thing in itself, though we know not this thing in its internal consitution, but only know its appearances, viz., the way in which our senses are affected by this unknown something. The understanding therefore, by assuming appearances, grants the existence of things in themselves also, and so far we may say, that the representation of such things as form the basis of phenomena, consequently of mere creations of the understanding, is not only admissible, but unavoidable.

You can take these paragraphs as constituting the whole argument of the *Critique of Pure Reason,* in four or five lines: (1) Experience is constituted by appearances. (2) Appearances are of something else, which accordingly cannot itself appear. (3) All and only functions of experience can be known; these are our categories of the understanding. (4) It follows that the something else—that of which appearances are appearances, whose existence we must grant—cannot be known. In discovering this limitation of reason, reason proves its power to itself, over itself. (5) Moreover, since it is unavoidable for our reason to be drawn to think about this unknowable ground of appearance, reason reveals itself to itself in this necessity also.

Then why do we need the rest of the eight-hundred-plus pages of the *Critique of Pure Reason*? They can be said to be divided between those that set up or fill in the pictures or structures necessary to get this argument compellingly clear (clear, you might say, of the trucks that are invited to drive through it), and those pages that set out the implications of the argument for human nature, hence for our moral and aesthetic and scientific and religious aspirations. I am prepared to call all of these pages pages of philosophy. What I claim is that if you are not at some stage gripped by a little argument very like the one I just drew out, your interest in those eight-hundred-plus pages will be, let me say, literary. The question would still remain whether you are seriously interested in that argument—interested more than, let me say, academically—if you are *not* interested in those eight hundred pages. A good answer, I think, and sufficient for my purposes, is yes and no. I am going to focus here on the yes side.

What would the argument, supposing it is convincing, accomplish? Kant had described his philosophical settlement as limiting knowledge in order to make room for faith. This is a somewhat one-sided way of describing his effort concerning knowledge, since what he meant by "limiting" it was something that also secured it, against the threat of skepticism and powers of dogmatism. It can accordingly be seen as one in the ancient and mighty line of the philosophical efforts to strike a bargain between the respective claims upon human nature of knowledge or science and of morality and religion. Kant's seems to be the most stable philosophical settlement in the modern period; subsequent settlements have not displaced it, or rather they have only displaced it. I take this stability, for the purposes of the story I have to tell, as a function of the balance Kant gives to the claims of knowledge of the world to be what you may call subjective and objective, or say to the claims of knowledge to be dependent on or independent of the specific endowments—sensual and intellectual—of the human being. The texts I am using as examples of romanticism I understand as monitoring the stability of this settlement—both our satisfaction in the justice of it and our dissatisfaction with this justice.

The dissatisfaction with such a settlement as Kant's is relatively easy to state. To settle with skepticism (and dogmatism, or fanaticism, but I won't try to keep including that in the balance), to assure us that we do know the existence of the world, or rather, that what we understand as knowledge is *of* the world, the price Kant asks us to pay is to cede any claim to know the thing in itself, to grant that human knowledge is not of things as they are in themselves (things as things, Heidegger will come to say). You don't—do you?—have to be a romantic to feel sometimes about that settlement: Thanks for nothing.

The companion satisfaction with the settlement is harder to state. It is expressed in Kant's portrait of the human being as living in two worlds, in one of them determined, in the other free, one of which is necessary to the satisfaction of human Understanding, the other to the satisfaction of human Reason. One romantic use for this idea of two worlds lies in its accounting for the human being's dissatisfaction with, as it were, itself. It appreciates the ambivalence in Kant's central idea of limitation, that we simultaneously crave its comfort and crave escape from its comfort, that we want unappeasably to be lawfully wedded to the world and at the same time illicitly intimate with it, as if the one stance produced the wish for the other, as if the best proof of human existence were its power to yearn, as if for its better, or other, existence. Another romantic use for this idea of our two worlds is its offer of a formulation of our ambivalence toward Kant's ambivalent settlement, or a further insight into whatever that settlement was a settlement of—an insight that the human being now lives in *neither* world, that we are, as it is said, between worlds.

Emerson and Thoreau joke about this from time to time. "Our moods do not believe in each other," Emerson says in "Circles"; "I am God in nature; I am a weed by the wall." And Thoreau identifies his readers as, for example, those "who are said to *live* in New England." That Wittgenstein and Heidegger can be understood to share this romantic perception of human doubleness I dare say helps account for my finding its problematic unavoidable—Wittgenstein perceiving our craving to *escape* our commonness with others, even when we recognize the commonness of the craving; Heidegger perceiving our pull to *remain* absorbed in the common, perhaps in the very way we push to escape it.

About our worldlessness or homelessness, the deadness to us of worlds we still see but, as it were, do not recollect (as if we cannot quite place the world)—about this Wordsworth and Coleridge do not joke (though they can be funny), as though they hadn't quite the American confidence that world-changing change would come, or that they could help it happen. When Wordsworth dedicated his poetry, in his preface to *Lyrical Ballads,* to arousing men in a particular way from a "torpor," the way he sought was "to make the incidents of common life interesting," as if he saw us as having withdrawn our interest, or investment, from whatever worlds we have in common, say this one or the next. This seems to me a reasonable description at once of skepticism and of melancholia, as if the human race had suffered some calamity and were now entering, at best, a period of convalescence. The most familiar interpretation of this calamity has seen it as the aftermath of the French Revolution; Nietzsche will say the death of God. However this calamitous break with the past is envisioned, its cure will require a revolution of the spirit, or, as Emerson puts it at the close of "The American Scholar," the conversion of the world. Wittgenstein accounted for his appearance by saying that history has a kink in it. I am not interested here in comparing romantic writers in terms of whether they saw redemptive possibilities in politics, or in religion, or in poetry. My subject is rather how such an idea may pressure philosophy to think about its own redemption.

Since those who are said to live in New England, or for that matter in England, are after all alive, a vision such as that expressed in *The Ancient Mariner* has recourse to the idea of the living dead, or rather of death-in-life, for example, of re-animated bodies. Here the relation to Kant's worlds is, as I read it, all but explicit, as is the idea that the place we inhabit, in which we are neither free nor natural, is itself a world, as it were a Third World of the spirit, so that our consciousness is not double, but triple.

Of course all such notions of worlds, and being between them and dead to them and living in them, seeing them but not knowing them, as if no longer knowing them, as it were not remembering them, haunted by them, are at most a sheaf of pictures. How seriously one takes them is a matter of how impressed one is by the precision and comprehension of their expression. To test this is a purpose of the texts under discussion here.

EMERSON'S FLUCTUATING REPUTATION IS A gaudy expression of the tendency of romantic writing to go dead for one periodically, perhaps permanently, as if in obedience to its perception both of our capacity to reabsorb our investment in the world, and of our capacity, or nerve, to ask, and sometimes to get, a melodramatic exaggeration of one's life in response to its investment. I have had occasion to say how long it took me to forgive Emerson, so to speak, for his nerve, and to follow my sense of his precision and depth. The essay "Fate" is especially useful here because of its pretty explicit association with Kantian perplexities. "The bulk of mankind believe in two Gods," it declares, having established the two Gods, or poles of the essay, as Freedom and Fate (or say determinism, or nature). It would be Emerson's reputation as much as his sound that makes it hard for one to credit him with the philosophical stamina to take on Kant and his worlds, and I pause before that essay in part to make that reputation one more feature of the problem Emerson presents to one who acknowledges him as a thinker.

Of all the moments in the history of what I am calling the repression of Emerson in American philosophy, none seems to me more decisive, apart from the professionalization of philosophy itself, than Santayana's marking of him as a pillar of the Genteel Tradition. (This moment of the professionalization of philosophy is gone into at somewhat greater length in my essay entitled "Politics as Opposed to What?"). It is hard for me, coming from the Harvard Philosophy Department to lecture at Berkeley on subjects in romanticism and skepticism, to put aside a discussion of Santayana's fantastically influential essay named, and naming, "The Genteel Tradition in American Philosophy," delivered at Berkeley a little over seventy years ago, written by a man who was living in Boston during the last ten years of Emerson's life, and who at Harvard had been the most glamorous teacher of one who would be my glamorous teacher of *Walden* when I was an undergraduate at Berkeley halfway back those seventy-odd years. Particularly hard since Santayana remains, I believe, the figure most likely to occur to an American intellectual who hears that someone is proposing, or remembering, some confrontation of philosophy and poetry by one another. For some, Santayana will represent the last serious writer in America in whose work such a confrontation was undertaken, for others a warning that such an undertaking is doomed to posturing: if infectious for a while, in the end ineffectual. I hope that both representations are wrong, but I will not argue against them now. What interests me here is that when, in "The Genteel Tradition," Santayana describes Emerson as "a cheery, childlike soul, impervious to the evidence of evil" he does not show (there or anywhere else I know that he mentions Emerson) any better understanding of Emerson's so-called optimism than, say, his contemporary H. L. Mencken shows of Nietzsche's so-called pessimism—he merely retails, beautifully of course, but essentially without refinement, the most wholesale view there is of him.

In recent years this charge of cheeriness has been under attack, by, among others, Stephen Whicher and Harold Bloom, and a more sophisticated picture has emerged according to which Emerson's early optimism is tempered by a mature or more realistic acceptance of life's limits and ravages, signaled most perfectly in "Fate," the opening essay of *The Conduct of Life,* published two decades after his first volume of essays. But in what is the new maturity in "Fate" supposed to reside? It strikes me that people who talk about Emerson on the whole quote him (if they do—Santayana, so far as I know, harps on him without quoting one line of his prose) as they would quote a writer of incessant public celebrations, as though he wears all he means that way. Whereas an essay such as "Fate" sems to me excruciatingly difficult to come to terms with, presenting writing that is as indirect and devious as, say, Thoreau's is, but more treacherous because of its care to maintain a more genteel surface.

I guess the new maturity is supposed to be announced in sentences like the following:

The book of Nature is the book of Fate. . . . Nature is what you may do. There is much you may not. We have two things,—the circumstance, and the life. Once we thought positive power was all. Now we learn that

negative power, or circumstance, is half. Nature is the tyrannous circumstance, the thick skull, the sheathed snake, the ponderous, rock-like jaw;
necessitated activity; violent direction; the conditions of a tool, like the
locomotive, strong enough on its track, but which can do nothing but
mischief off of it. . . .

Is the change in this marked by "Once we thought . . . Now we learn"?
But why take this as sheer autobiography? It would be more like Emerson to be speaking of the human race, or human maturation, generally. As for himself personally, he says somewhere, I seem to remember,
that he was born old.

In any case, if this is the sort of thing that is supposed to show a
new maturity, our new respect for it is bound in turn to fade. In 1930
the historian James Truslow Adams published in the *Atlantic Monthly* a
piece called "Emerson Reread" (Stephen Whicher cites it as perhaps
one of the two most intelligent anti-Emerson statements), in which
Adams finds Emerson, who had been for him, as he was for so many
others, an inspiration when he was a youth, no longer able to sustain
the man of fifty. Adams has the grace to ask whether this is his or Emerson's fault; but not for long; he knows the answer. Emerson fails because he does not know about evil—about war, disease, misfortunes of
every kind. As far as I can tell these evils are the very sort of circumstances Emerson is summarizing when he says, halfway through "Fate,"
drawing a breath for a new response, "No picture of life can have any
veracity that does not admit the odious facts." He had listed some facts
earlier in the essay in a well-remembered pair of sentences: "The way of
Providence is a little rude. The habit of snake and spider, the snap of
the tiger and other leapers and bloody jumpers, the crackle of the bones
of his prey in the coil of the anaconda,—these are in the system, and
our habits are like theirs." But these are lists of matters no less obvious
than "the heart-ache and the thousand natural shocks / That flesh is heir
to. . . ." What could it mean to suppose that Emerson, in his early writing, had not known of their existence? That he mostly does not mention
them, early or late, is surely more plausibly to be attributed to his finding them too obvious to mention than too obscure to have noticed.

But I think I know by now what the man of fifty finds distasteful
that made the boy of sixteen or seventeen ecstatic. It is an idea that
Emerson and any Romantic would be lost without, that the world
could be—or could have been—so remade, or I in it, that I could *want*
it, as it would be, or I in it. In time the idea is apt to become maddening
if kept green (certainly it makes one's grown-up acquaintances impatient), a continuous rebuke to the way we live, compared to which, or
in reaction to which, a settled despair of the world, or cynicism, is luxu-

rious. This dual perspective, of hope and of despair, proves to be internal to the argument of the essay on Fate, which I might summarize as the overcoming of Kant's two worlds by diagnosing them, or resolving them, as perspectives, as a function of what Emerson calls "polarity." It is as if Emerson's present essay is prophesying the fate of his reputation when it says, "In youth we clothe ourselves with rainbows and go as brave as the zodiac. In age we put out another perspiration—gout, fever, rheumatism, caprice, doubt, fretting and avarice."

Yet there is, I agree, a departure in the essay "Fate," a steady awareness that may present itself as a new maturity or realism. I find it contained in the statement, "In the history of the individual is always an account of his condition, and he knows himself to be party to his present estate"—as if we are conspirators either for or against ourselves. The departure, or advance, shows in comparing this with a remark from "Self-Reliance": "Society everywhere is in conspiracy against the manhood of every one of its members." Now, in "Fate," it emerges that we, in so to speak taking our place in the world, are joining the conspiracy, and we may join it to our harm or to our benefit. "If Fate follows and limits Power [elsewhere called will], Power attends and antagonizes Fate. . . . [Man is] a stupendous antagonism, a dragging together of the poles of the Universe."

Living this antagonism (as relentless as electricity), we polar beings are either victims or victors of Fate (a remark about Fate as much as about us, the sort of thing Wittgenstein calls a grammatical remark); the remark above all means that Fate is not a foreign bondage; human life is not invaded, either by chance or by necessities not of its own making. "The secret of the world is the tie between person and event. . . . He thinks his fate alien, because the copula is hidden." Freud and Marx say no less. (I think here of a remark from the *Investigations:* "It is in language that an expectation and its fulfillment make contact" [§445].)

Of course this is all, if you like, mythology, and as such cannot philosophically constitute what Emerson claims for it; namely "one key, one solution to the old knots of fate, freedom, and foreknowledge." But suppose I emphasize, on his behalf, that he is offering his solution *merely* as a key; and, as Pascal had put it, a key is not a hook—a key has just what Pascal calls the *aperitive* virtue, that is, it only opens, it does not further invite, or provide. Whether you find Emerson entitled to such a gloss will depend on who you think Emerson is, something I am trying to leave, or to get, open. It would be, to my mind, key enough if Emerson's thought here opens to us the thought, or opens us to the thought, that our past solutions to these mysteries, however philosophical in aspect, are themselves mythology, or as we might more readily say today, products of our intuitions, and hence can progress no further until we have assessed which of our intuitions are satisfied, and which thwarted, by the various dramas of concepts or figures like fate, and freedom, and foreknowledge, and will. Disagreements over such matters do not arise (as they do not arise in skepticism) from one of us knowing facts another does not know, but, so Emerson is saying, from how it is one aligns the facts, facts any of us must have at our disposal, with ideas of victimization, together with whatever its opposites are. (One of Emerson's favorite words for its opposite is Lordship.) Something you might call philosophy would consist in tracing out the source of our sense of our lives as alien to us, for only then is there the *problem* of Fate. This looks vaguely like the project to trace out the source of our sense of the world as independent of us, for only then is skepticism a problem.

Even someone willing to suspend disbelief this far might insist that Emerson's writing maintains itself solely at the level of what I was calling mythology. So I must hope to indicate the level at which I understand the onset of philosophy to take place.

One key to Emerson's "Fate" is the phrase "the mysteries of human condition." I take the hint from the awkwardness of the phrase. I assume, that is, that it is not an error for "the mysteries of *the* human condition," as if Emerson were calling attention to mysteries of something which itself has well-known attributes. One attribute of what is called *the* human condition may be said to be that man must earn his bread by the sweat of his brow, another that the spirit is willing but the flesh is weak, another that we are subject to Fate. Such are not Emerson's bread, but his grist. The hint the phrase "the mysteries of human condition" calls attention to is that there is nothing Emerson will call *the* human condition, that there is something mysterious about condition as such in human life, something which leads us back to the idea that "in the history of the individual is always an account of his condition," and that this has to do with his "[knowing] himself to be a party to his present estate." "Condition" is a key word of Emerson's "Fate," as it is of the *Critique of Pure Reason*, as both texts are centrally about limitation. In the *Critique:* "Concepts of objects in general thus underlie all empirical knowledge as its a priori conditions" (A93; B126). I am taking it that Emerson is turning the *Critique* upon itself and asking: What are the conditions in human thinking underlying the concept of condition, the sense that our existence is, so to speak, had on condition? (Descartes pivotally interpreted an intuition of conditionality, or limitation, or finitude, as the dependence of human nature on the fact and on the idea of God, from which followed a proof of God's existence. Nietzsche reinterpreted such an interpretation of dependence as an excuse for our passiveness, or self-punishment, our fear of autonomy, hence as a cover for our vengefulness, from which follows the killing of God.)

It is as if in Emerson's writing (not in his alone, but in his first in America) Kant's pride in what he called his Copernican Revolution for philosophy, understanding the behavior of the world by understanding the behavior of our concepts of the world, is to be radicalized, so that not just twelve categories of the understanding are to be deduced, but every word in the language—not as a matter of psychological fact, but as a matter of, say, psychological necessity. Where Kant speaks of rules or laws brought to knowledge of the world by Reason, a philosopher like Wittgenstein speaks of bringing to light our criteria, our agreements (sometimes they will seem conspiracies). Starting out in philosophical life a quarter of a century ago, I claimed in "The Availability of Wittgenstein's Later Philosophy" that what Wittgenstein means by grammar in his grammatical investigations—as revealed by our system of ordinary language—is an inheritor of what Kant means by Transcendental Logic; that more particularly when Wittgenstein says, "Our investigation . . . is directed not towards phenomena but, as one might say, towards the 'possibilities' of phenomena" ($90) he is to be understood as citing the concept of possibility as Kant does in saying, "The term 'transcendental' . . . signifies [only] such knowledge as concerns the a priori possibility of knowledge, or its a priori employment" (A56, B80–81). Here I am, still at it.

Whatever the conditions are in human thinking controlling the concept of condition they will be the conditions of "the old knots of fate, freedom, and foreknowledge," immediately because these words, like every other in the language, are knots of agreement (or conspiracy) which philosophy is to unravel; but more particularly because the idea of condition is internal to the idea of limitation, which is a principal expression of an intuition Emerson finds knotted in the concept of Fate. His first way of expressing Fate is to speak of "irresistible dictation"—we do with our lives what some power dominating our lives knows or reveals them to be, enacting old scripts. The problem has famously arisen with respect to God, and with God's or nature's laws. Emerson adds the new science of statistics to the sources of our sense of subjection to dictation, as if to read tables concerning tendencies of those like me in circumstances like mine—Emerson spoke of circumstances as "tyrannous"—were to read my future; as if the new science provides a new realization of the old idea that Fate is a book, a text, an idea Emerson repeatedly invokes. Then further expressions of the concept of condition are traced by the rest of the budget of ways Emerson hits off shades of our intuition of Fate, for example as predetermination,

38

providence, calculation, predisposition, fortune, laws of the world, necessity; and in the introductory poem to the essay he expresses it in notions of prevision, foresight, and omens.

Emerson's initial claim on the subject (and it may as well be his final) is this: "But if there be irresistible dictation, this dictation understands itself. If we must accept Fate, we are not less compelled to affirm liberty, the significance of the individual, the grandeur of duty, the power of character." This sounds like a nice little bale of genteel sentiments. Perhaps we can now begin to unpack it.

Dictation, like *condition*, has something to do with language— dictation with talking, especially with commanding or prescribing (which equally has to do with writing), condition with talking together, with the public, the objective. "Talking together" is what the word *condition*, or its derivation, says. Add to this that conditions are also terms, stipulations that define the nature and limits of an agreement, or the relations between parties, persons, or groups, and that the term *term* is another repetition in Emerson's essay. Then it sounds as though the irresistible dictation that constitutes Fate, that sets conditions on our knowledge and our conduct, is our language, every word we utter. Is this sound attributable to chance? I mean is the weaving of language here captured by (the conditions, or criteria of) our concept of chance?

"This dictation understands itself," Emerson says; but the essay sets this understanding as our task. And he says: "A man's fortunes are the fruit of his character." The genteel version of this familiarly runs, "Character is fate," and it familiarly proposes anything from a tragic to a rueful acquiescence in our frailties. But to speak of the fruit of one's character is to suggest that our character is under cultivation by us, and Emerson says of it, in line with a line of his from "Self-Reliance," that it constantly "emits" something, that it is "betrayed," betrays itself, to anyone who can "read [its] possibility." (In that earlier essay, which in chapter 1 I claimed is about communication, and specifically writing, he had said, unnervingly: "Character teaches above our wills. Men imagine that they communicate their virtue or vice only by overt actions, and do not see that virtue or vice emit a breath every moment.") He emphasizes that this reading is a trivial, daily matter: "The gross lines are legible to the dull." And now add that by "character," associated with ideas of being read, and with communicating itself, Emerson is again, as in "Self-Reliance," proposing us as texts; that what we are is written all over us, or branded; but here especially the other way around, that our language contains our character, that we brand the world, as for example with the concept of Fate; and then listen again to such an idea as that one's character is one's fate.

Now it says openly that language is our fate. It means hence that not exactly prediction, but diction, is what puts us in bonds, that with each word we utter we emit stipulations, agreements we do not know and do not want to know we have entered, agreements we were always in, that were in effect before our participation in them. Our relation to our language—to the fact that we are subject to expression and comprehension, victims of meaning—is accordingly a key to our sense of our distance from our lives, of our sense of the alien, of ourseles as alien to ourselves, thus alienated.

"Intellect annuls Fate. So far as a man thinks, he is free." This apparently genteel thought now turns out to mean that we have a say in what we mean, that our antagonism to fate, to which we are fated, and in which our freedom resides, is as a struggle with the language we emit, of our character with itself. By the way, "annul" here, I feel sure, alludes to the Hegelian term for upending antitheses (*aufheben*), or what Emerson calls our polarity, our aptness to think in opposites, say in pitting together Fate and Freedom. "Annul" also joins a circle of economic terms in Emerson's essay, for instance, *interest, fortunes, balances, belongings,* as well as *terms* and *conditions* themselves; and in its connection with legislation, in the idea of voiding a law, it relates to the theme of the essay that "We are lawgivers." The terms of our language are economic and political powers, and they are to be positioned in canceling the debts and convictions that are imposed upon us by ourselves; and first by antagonizing our conditions of polarity, of antagonism.

In putting aside Emerson's essay for a moment, I note that this last idea of us as lawgivers suggests that the essay is built on a kind of philosophical joke, a terrible one. Philosophy, as in Kant and as in Rousseau, has taken human freedom as our capacity to give law to ourselves, to be autonomous. Emerson's essay shows that fate is the exercise of this same capacity, so that fate is at once the promise and the refusal of freedom. Then on what does a decision between them depend? I think this is bound up with another question that must occur to Emerson's readers: Why, if what has been said here is getting at what Emerson is driving at, does he write that way? That he shows himself undermining or undoing a dictation would clearly enough show that his writing is meant to enact its subject, that it is a struggle against itself, hence of language with itself, for its freedom. Thus is writing thinking, or abandonment. Still the question remains why it is a genteel surface that he works at once to provide and to crack.

I TURN TO COLERIDGE, the figure from whom the American transcendentalists would have learned much of what they know about Kant, and about German philosophy generally, and by whom Emerson would have been preceded in his emphasis on polarity in human thinking.

I had opened the *Biographia Literaria* many times, increasingly in the past few years, recognizing in its mode of obsession at once with the existence of the external world and with German philosophy a forerunning of my own excitements in linking transcendentalism, both in Kant and later in Emerson and Thoreau, with ordinary language philosophy's confrontation of skepticism. But I had never been able to stay with it for longer than a chapter, and maybe half of the next, before closing the book with fear and frustration—both at the hopelessness in its ambitions for reconstituting the history of thought, by means, for example, of its elated obscurities as it translates Schelling on the task of something called uniting subject and object; and at its oscillation of astounding intelligence and generosity together with its dull and withholding treatment of Wordsworth's sense in claiming for poetry the language of the rustic and the low. I do not know that anything short of my growing sense of its pervasive bearings on the issues I have recently found myself involved with would have taken me all the way through it. The pain in it mounts, the more one feels the hatred in Coleridge's ambivalent address toward Wordsworth, praising his power and promise in terms reserved for the heroes of language, but cursing him, no doubt in the profoundly friendliest way, for not doing what it was given to him to do, for failing his power and breaking his promise.

I do not see how one can fail to sense projection in this; but of course the claim could still—could it not?—be true. Then, has it been considered that it may also be false, or worse, that whatever Coleridge had in mind in demanding of Wordsworth "the first genuine philosophic poem" (*Biographia,* chap. 22), it was something Wordsworth had already produced, and not just massively in *The Prelude* but fully in, for example, the Intimations Ode—that, so to speak, such achievements are all Coleridge could have *meant* in his prophecies? That it was critical for him to deny these achievements in this light, to project the achievements back into promises, is proven for me in the very incessance of his brilliance about them.

Since it was Coleridge who defined what many of us mean by literary criticism, he is, I assume, beyond praise in this regard. But what he actually says, in the *Biographia,* when at last he gets around to mentioning the intellectual drive of a work like the Intimations Ode, while it is as brilliant as his technical discussions of poems and of what poetry should be, is as dismissive and supercilious as anything he felt in the poisonous critics he so bravely and tirelessly defends his friends against. He dismisses thinking about what Wordsworth may have meant in invoking Plato's notion of Recollection, beyond saying that he cannot have meant it literally (then why insinuate that perhaps he did?), and he concludes that by describing the child as a philosopher Wordsworth can have meant nothing sensible whatever. It is this sudden—when Wordsworth flies his philosophical colors, then Coleridge's seemingly limitless capacity for sympathetic understanding toward other writers he thought genuine, is stripped away, his tolerance for mysticism and his contempt for reductive empiricisms forgotten, and he starts firing at will. I do not deny that Wordsworth is in trouble when he talks philosophy. But we are speaking of what one is to expect of Coleridge.

I propose one day—even alerted to the folly in being, or remaining, promising—to write something about this book based on the assumption that it is composed essentially without digression. May I remind you how perverse a claim that must seem, as if contesting with the perverseness of the book itself, which cannot be foreign to its permanence. Its fourth chapter opens with the remark, "I have wandered far from the object in view," when he has described no such object; the tenth chapter explicitly summarizes itself in its headnote as "A chapter of digressions and anecdotes, as an interlude preceding that on the nature and genesis of the imagination . . ." but the chapter it precedes—the eleventh—is not about imagination, but, as its headnote describes it, is "An affectionate exhortation to those who in early life feel themselves disposed to become authors," and that chapter opens with a sentence whose second clause is fully worthy to be considered the title of an essay of Montaigne's: "It was a favorite remark of Mr. Whitbread's, that no man does any thing from a single motive." The next chapter, twelve, describes itself as "A chapter of requests and premonitions concerning the perusal or omission of the chapter that follows," and what follows, chapter 13, which actually entitles itself "On the imagination," consists mostly of its absence; more specifically it consists largely of the printing of a letter the author says he received—a letter in prose self-evidently identical with the prose which we have all along been treated to—which he says persuaded him not to print the chapter, on the ground that it really belongs with that major work he has been (and will be forever) promising. The last sentence of that chapter refers the reader, for further amplification, to an essay said to be prefixed to a new edition of *The Ancient Mariner,* an essay which turns out also to be nonexistent. Thus ends the first volume of the *Biographia Literaria.*

To say that the book is composed without digression means accordingly that if it has some end, the approach to it is followed in as straightforward a path as the terrain permits. This suggests that the end is, or requires, continuous self-interruption. But then this will be a way of drawing the consequence of philosophy's self-description as a discourse bearing endless responsibility for itself. And this could be further interpreted as a matter of endless responsiveness to itself—which might look to be exactly irresponsible.

The end is indicated by the surface of the book's concern to preserve or redeem genuine poetry from its detractors and its impersonations, in a world that, as he demonstrates, cannot read; and to demonstrate that this preservation is bound up with the preservation or redemption of genuine philosophy, where the preservation of poetry and philosophy by one another presents itself as the necessity of recovering or replacing religion. This contesting of philosophy and poetry and religion (and I guess of politics) with one another, for one another, together with the disreputable sense that the fate of the contest is bound up in one's own writing, and moreover with the conviction that the autobiographical is a method of thought wherein such a contest can find a useful field, and in which the stakes appear sometimes as the loss or gain of our common human nature, sometimes as the loss or gain of nature itself, as if the world were no more than one's own—some such statement represents the general idea I have of what constitutes serious romanticism's self-appointed mission, the idea with which I seek its figures. Our current humanist appeals to the interdisciplinary would be traces of such contests.

From where is such an intellectual ambition to gain backing? Having repudiated the English and the French philosophical traditions because of their basis in the occurrence to the mind of ideas construed as representations and subject to laws, Coleridge turns for inspiration—and teaches us to turn—to German philosophy, both to the religious and mystical Germans who preceded Kant and to the idealists, preeminently Schelling, who thought to overcome Kant's limitations. And an essential preparation for the success of the ambition is the diagnosis of the fear and hatred of those who oppose such writing as he is undertaking and championing, as though an understanding of the hatred and the fear of poetry and of philosophy is internal to (grammatically related to) an understanding of what those aspirations are. No wonder Coleridge remarks, "Great indeed are the obstacles which an English metaphysician has to encounter" (*Biographia,* near the end of chap. 12). I take it as to Coleridge's philosophical credit that he finds the initial obstacle—perhaps therefore the greatest, the image of all the rest—to be the finding of a place to begin, undigressively. Such is a cost of refusing to identify the vocation to philosophy with the vocation to science, enviable, and glamorous as that may be.

The Kantian pressure upon the *Biographia* is conveniently measured in taking the book as the key to a Kantian reading of *The Ancient*

Mariner. For this purpose we can expose the issue by breaking in on a moment of the *Biographia* in which Coleridge is struggling with two of his main obsessions: his particular, engulfing sense of indebtedness to the work of others, and his tendency to deal in shady regions of learning.

The moment is occupied by a pair of sentences (from chap. 9, para. 6) in which he is expressing his gratitude, his debt, to the writings of mystics, the boon he has received from them in "[preventing my] mind from being imprisoned within the outline of any single dogmatic system. They contributed to keep alive the *heart* in the *head;* gave me an indistinct, yet stirring, and working presentiment, that all the products of the mere *reflective* faculty partook of DEATH." It is they, he goes on to say, who "during my wanderings through the wilderness of doubt . . . enabled me to skirt, without crossing, the sandy deserts of unbelief." Now since it is of objects, or what he calls "objects as objects," that Coleridge otherwise speaks of as "dead, fixed" in contrast to the will or to imagination, and since he speaks of "the writings of the illustrious sage of Königsberg" as having "[taken] possession of me as with a giant's hand," I interpret the death, of which the reflective faculty partakes, as of the world made in our image, or rather through our categories, by Kant's faculty of the Understanding, namely that very world which was meant to remove the skeptic's anxieties about the existence of objects outside us.

Here is extreme testimony that what both the world and the faculty of the world need redeeming from is felt to be at once skepticism and the answer to skepticism provided in the *Critique of Pure Reason.* And I think the feeling or intuition can be expressed by saying: since the categories of the understanding are ours, we can be understood as carrying the death of the world in us, in our very requirement of creating it, as if it does not yet exist.

Naturally it may be imagined that someone will profess not to understand how the world could die. But then there will also be those who will profess not to understand how the existence of the world may be doubted. A difference between these cases is that a philosopher might undertake to provide you with skeptical considerations that lead you to the possibility he or she has in mind, whereas a romantic will want you to see that his vision expresses the way you are living now. Both may fail in their demands. No one wants to be a skeptic; to be gripped by its threat is to wish to overcome it. And for each one who wants to be a romantic, there is someone else who wishes him to outgrow it.

Against a vision of the death of the world, the romantic calling for poetry, or quest for it, the urgency of it, would be sensible; and the sense that the redemption of philosophy is bound up with the redemption of poetry would be understandable: the calling of poetry is to give the world back, to bring it back, as to life. Hence romantics seem to involve themselves in what look to us to be superstitious, discredited mysteries of animism, sometimes in the form of what is called the pathetic fallacy.

Now this quest of poetry for the recovery of the world (which I am interpreting as the recovery of, or from, the thing in itself), this way of joining or paralleling the philosophical effort to recover from skepticism, will look to poetry very like the quest for poetry, as if the cause of poetry has become its own survival. For what is poetry without a world—I mean, what is a fuller expression of the romantics's sense of the death of the world than a sense of the death of the poetry of the world? But then again, how can the loss of poetry be mourned *in poetry*? (If it is gone, it is gone.) Which I take as the twin of the question: How can philosophy be ended *in philosophy*? (If it is here, it is here.) Yet ending philosophy is something a creative philosophy seems habitually to undertake.

I recognize that certain of these recent formulations concerning romanticism are under the influence at once of a decisive indebtedness to what I have so far read on these subjects by M. H. Abrams, Harold Bloom, Geoffrey Hartman, and Paul de Man; and at the same time of an uneasiness with those readings. For all their differences, they seem to share (in the writings in question) an assumption, as Bloom has expressed it in *Romanticism and Consciousness,* "that the central spiritual problem of Romanticism is the difficult relation between nature and consciousness." Of course I do not think this assumption is wrong, and its receipts have been rich; but I find that I do not know how to assess the price of so fundamental a stake in the concept of consciousness. By its price I mean two matters primarily; that the concept takes in train a philosophical machinery of self-consciousness, subjectivity, and imagination, of post-Kantianism in general, that for me runs out of control; and that it closes out a possible question as to whether what is thought of as fundamental to romanticism, especially to what any of its critics will feel as its sense of estrangement, is first of all the relation of consciousness and nature, or first of all, say, the relation of knowledge and the world; whether accordingly self-consciousness is the cause or the effect of skepticism, or whether they are simultaneous, or whether one or other of these possibilities leads from and to one or another version or notion of romanticism.

Provisionally taking skepticism as fundamental, or anyway more under my control, I will propose *The Ancient Mariner* as a study of the issue of Kant's two worlds, in the following way. I begin with the prose argument that prefaced its first printing in 1798, which was replaced, to be amplified, by the running marginal prose gloss in 1817, the year of the *Biographia*.

> How a Ship having passed the line was driven by Storms to the cold Country towards the South Pole; . . . and of the strange things that befell; and in what manner the Ancient Mariner came back to his own Country.

(We are bound, I guess, to hear this as inviting us to pass, and by warning us against passing, beyond and below the lines of poetry and prose. I am taking it as asking us to go beyond this way of taking it.) I note an implied image of a mental line to be crossed that is interpreted as a geographical or terrestrial border, in the following passage early in chapter 12 of the *Biographia*.

> A [philosophical] system, the first principle of which is to render the mind intuitive of the *spiritual* in man (i.e., of that which lies *on the other side* of our natural consciousness) must needs have a greater obscurity for those who have never disciplined and strengthened this ulterior consciousness. It must in truth be a land of darkness, a perfect *Anti-Goshen*, for men to whom the noblest treasures of their own being are reported only through the imperfect translation of lifeless and sightless *notions* [i.e., for us drifters]. . . . No wonder, then, that he remains incomprehensible to himself as well as to others. No wonder, that, in the fearful desert of his consciousness, he wearies himself out with empty words, to which no friendly echo answers.

Earlier in that paragraph Coleridge says of this "common consciousness" that it "will furnish proofs by its own direction, that it is connected with master-currents below the surface." I will relate this to the Mariner's returning "Slowly and smoothly / Moved onward from beneath" back toward the line, in particular moved onward by what the marginal gloss calls "The Polar Spirit."

Later in the *Biographia* chapter, as he is announcing his philosophical theses, Coleridge gives the geographical or civilian name of what the Mariner's glosses only call "the line," and places that feature of the earth at the center of thinking:

> For it must be remembered, that all these Theses refer solely to one of the two Polar Sciences, namely, to that which commences with, and rigidly confines itself within, the subjective, leaving the objective (as far as it is exclusively objective) to natural philosophy, which is its opposite pole. . . . The result of both the sciences, or their equatorial point, would be the principle of a total and undivided philosophy.

That Coleridge is part of a tradition obsessed with the polarity of human thought needs no confirmation from me. (See, for instance, Thomas McFarland, "Coleridge's Doctrine of Polarity and Its European Contexts.") In the passage just cited I understand the very impossibility of the idea of an "equatorial point," taken as an image or picture, to express his diagnosis of the Mariner's curse—that in being drawn toward one pole he is drawn away from the other, that is, that he is enchanted by a way of thinking, an isolated Polar Science, one in which, let me say, a diagram of the mind (as by a line below which knowledge cannot reach) is not an allegory but a representation, as of a matching substance. So the "Polar Spirit" with which the Mariner returns has yet to enter into the "two Polar Sciences" which in the vision of the *Biographia* will institute an undivided philosophy.

I end here with two remarks about this proposal for reading *The Ancient Mariner*.

1. By 1798 Coleridge knew something about Kant, but scholars agree that the giant's hand did not take hold of him until his return from Germany a few years later. Accordingly I am not saying that when he wrote his poem he meant it to exemplify Kant's *Critique of Pure Reason*, merely that it does so, and that there are passages in the *Biographia* where Coleridge is summarizing his hopes for philosophy in the form of post-Kantian idealism, primarily in Schelling, in which he virtually states as much. Conviction in this idea obviously depends on how strongly or naturally one envisions the first *Critique* as projecting a *line* below which, or a circle outside which, experience, hence knowledge, cannot, and must not presume to, penetrate. Here I must appeal to the experience of those who have tried to explain Kant's work, if just to themselves; I mean to that moment at which, quite inevitably, one pictures its architectonic by actually drawing a line or circle, closing off the region of the thing in itself. I realize that I imply, in this appeal, not merely that such a gesture is not accidental, but that so apparently trivial a sketch can control, or express, one's thinking for a long lifetime, like a Fate. Then one profit in thinking through the Mariner's journey by means of the poem is to assess that Fate, to suggest, for example, that if the Mariner's experience *is* to be imagined or conceived as of the region below the line, showing that its structure can be mapped, then it is not an a priori limitation of reason that prohibits its penetration by knowledge, but some other power, less genteel; call it repression.

This cautions me to be explicit that the region of the thing in itself, below the line, underlies both the inner and the outer horizons of knowledge (using Kant's distinction), toward the self or mind as much as toward the world or nature. Here is a way I can understand something of Freud's contempt and fear of the standing of philosophy. One reason Freud gives for shunning philosophy is that it identifies the mental with consciousness, but this seems no truer of Kant than it does of Plato. Something like the reverse would be a cause to fear Kant. If Freud's unconscious is what is not available to knowledge (under, let us say, normal circumstances) then Kant's Reason projects a whole realm of the self or mind which is even more strongly unavailable to knowledge; but, as part of reason, it is surely mental! What Freud must object to, however, is Kant's ground for excluding this realm from knowledge, namely that this realm cannot be *experienced,* hence that there is something in the self that *logically* cannot be brought to knowledge. If this is the wisdom of reason, Freud *must* try to outdistance it, which is to say, to change the shape of reason. Here is a sense in which he was preceded by romanticism.

2. I do not take this projected reading of *The Ancient Mariner* as in competition with the familiar reading of it as an allegory of the Fall. Rather on the contrary, I take it to provide an explanation of why it fits the Fall, that is, of what the Fall is itself an allegory of. Accordingly, I take the story in the poem to allegorize any spiritual transgression in which the first step is casual, as if, to borrow a phrase, always already taken, and the downward half of the journey—to the cold Country—is made "Driven by Storms," as if by natural, or conceivably logical, consequences. On this understanding the transgression fits what I understand the idea to come to of the craving to speak, in Wittgenstein's phrase, "outside language games." (It had better fit, since I take that idea as itself an interpretation of the Kantian *Critique.*) For that description ("outside language games") from the *Philosophical Investigations* (§47) itself is hardly more than an allegory, or myth. I use it in *The Claim of Reason* to record the pervasive thought of that book that a mark of the natural in natural language is its capacity to repudiate itself, to find arbitrary, or merely conventional, the lines laid down for its words by our agreement in criteria, our attunement with one another (which is to say, in my lingo, that the threat of skepticism is a natural or inevitable presentiment of the human mind), together with the discovery that what presents itself upon a skeptical repudiation of this attunement is another definite, as it were, frozen, structure—one to which I habitually say (I now realize afresh) that we are "forced" or "driven."

But if the Fall is also to be read as an interpretation of this condition, it is no wonder that it seems a romantic's birthright, not to say obligation, at some point to undertake an interpretation of the story of Eden. A dominant interpretation of it, as in Hegel, if I understand, is that the birth of knowledge is the origin of consciousness, hence self-consciousness, hence of guilt and shame, hence of human life as severed and estranged, from nature, from others, from itself. Hence the task of human life is of recovery, as of one's country, or health. I find myself winding up somewhat differently.

The explicit temptation of Eden is to knowledge, which above all means: to a denial that, as we stand, we know. There was hence from the beginning no Eden, no place in which names are immune to skepticism. I note that the story in the Bible as told does not equate the knowledge of nakedness with being ashamed, or self-consciousness (however consequential such things will be), but with fear. "I was afraid, because I was naked; and I hid myself," Adam says. And when God thereupon asks him, "Who told thee that thou wast naked?" the very fantasticality of that question of course drives us to ask what nakedness is and what it is to learn it of oneself. The feature of the situation I emphasize is that its sense of exposure upon the birth of knowledge pertains not only to one's vulnerability to knowledge, to being known, to the trauma of separation, but as well to the vulnerability of knowledge itself, to the realization that Eden is not the world, but that one had been living as within a circle or behind a line; because when God "drove out the man" the man was not surprised that there was an elsewhere.

3

Texts of Recovery
(Coleridge, Wordsworth, Heidegger . . .)

IN TAKING A FEW PASSAGES from Coleridge's *Biographia Liter-*
aria to declare that his *Ancient Mariner* can be understood as a
response to the *Critique of Pure Reason,* I wished to specify an example
of romanticism's internal relation to the philosophical settlement
worked out in Kant's Critical Philosophy. In particular, when Coleridge's "prose gloss" beside the poem speaks of the Mariner's ship drift-
ing across a line and of its being guided back toward the line, I took the
line in question to be (among other things, no doubt) the line implied
in the *Critique* "below" which or "beyond" which knowledge cannot
penetrate. On Kant's view, the effort to breach it creates, for example,
skepticism and fanaticism, efforts to experience what cannot humanly
be experienced. Coleridge's poem demonstrates that Kant's lined-off region *can* be experienced and that the region below the line has a definite, call it a frozen, structure. This way of interpretation (say as a
romantic craving for experience, as if doubting whether one now has
any experience to call one's own) is not incompatible with interpretations of the poem as of the Fall; indeed it provides an interpretation of
that interpretation.

So Kant's Critical Philosophy may itself be taken as philosophy's
an interpretation of the Fall. To declare as much is a way of understanding the extraordinarily interesting document Kant produced under the
title "Conjectural Beginning of Human History." There he speaks (of
the origin) of reason as (or in) a kind of "refusal," a power of opposition. You may take it as the ideology of Kant's "Conjectural Beginning"

to make out that this opposition is not to God's law but to nature's, that is, to the rule of instinct. (This, however, would seem to make what happened in Eden a Rise, not a Fall. Kant does not gloss over such an issue at this point. The question of the direction in which the human is conceived to appear, as from above or below, is touched on in *The Claim of Reason* in an observation concerning Kant's concept of the human not as the animal being who is rational but as the rational being who is animal [p. 399].)

I would like to emphasize here an analogous implication of my thought (as expressed, for example, in the early pages of chapter 1) that acknowledging is not an alternative to knowing but an interpretation of it. In incorporating, or inflecting, the concept of knowledge, the concept of acknowledgment is meant, in my use, to declare that what there is to be known philosophically remains unknown not through ignorance (for we cannot just not know what there is to be known philosophically, for example, that there is a world and I and others in it) but through a refusal of knowledge, a denial, or a repression of knowledge, say even a killing of it. The beginning of skepticism is the insinuation of absence, of a line, or limitation, hence the creation of want, or desire; the creation, as I have put it, of the interpretation of metaphysical finitude as intellectual lack. (So speaks serpentine infinity.)

In this connection it pleases me to cite something one may take merely as a curiosity, a passing remark from Austin's essay "Other Minds," which constitutes perhaps his major version of an ordinary language assault on skepticism. His assault involves, as one would expect of Austin, a tireless detailing of the errors, grammatical and semantical, in, among other things, the idea that there is a special class of empirical statements (unlike all the other classes of such statements) about which we can be certain, free of doubt; namely, so-called sense-statements, statements, that is, that confine themselves to the deliverances of our sensations, as opposed, say, to statements about material objects. In the passing remark I refer to, Austin momentarily turns aside from his work to observe: "It [viz., the view of an epistemologically favored class of sense-statements] is perhaps the original sin . . . by which the philosopher cast himself out from the garden of the world we live in" (p. 90).

While Austin would scarcely be interested in interpreting his little allegory of the garden very far (not, I take it, really believing in original sin, literally or allegorically) his unprecedented and unrepeated (so far as I recall) display of emotion toward the world here is a claim to his inheritance—even his—of English romanticism. I mean by this that, as I read it, this display of emotion toward the garden of the world is not, indeed is meant to declare that it is not, a claim to his inheritance of

English common sense, say in the form given it by G. E. Moore's "A Defense of Common Sense"; it is not a claim to be defending common beliefs or common knowledge about the world, as if the world we live in were Eden because it *could* not overthrow our certainties. Austin can grant that the world is more than we can ever bargain for. The idea is rather that for all our human liability to error, the world is Eden enough, all the Eden there can be, and what is more, all the world there is: risks and error are inherent in the human, part of what we conceive human life to be, part of our unsurveyable responsibilities in speech and in evil (in, as Descartes put it, our being provided with free will); and this condemnation to an unsurveyable freedom is not well described by saying that we can never, or can only in a certain class of cases, be certain. If the earth opens and swallows me up, this need not prove that my trust in it was misplaced. What better place for my trust could there be? (The world *was* my certainty. Now my certainty is dead.) Of course there is a spirit in which you may feel like saying, "Trust nothing!" But would it express that spirit to say, "Take no further step on the earth!"? So there is a question about whether we can live our skepticism, and if we cannot, what kind of threat skepticism poses. Which is to say that there ought to be a question whether philosophy is the best place, or the only place, to consider the matter (philosophy as it stands).

The chief fault I find with Austin's parable of the world as Eden lies in the clause "the philosopher cast himself out from the garden of the world we live in." Gender identity aside, Austin is taking it that it is clear how philosophy is special in this casting of itself out, as though one can tell by looking, so to speak, which of us is and which of us is not philosophizing; as though it is clear how to end philosophy (to bring philosophy peace, Wittgenstein has said [§133]), hence how to tell whose life is found and whose lost by philosophy.

I CONTINUE IN THIS LECTURE to be guided by the thought of romanticism as working out a crisis of knowledge, a crisis I have taken to be (interpretable as) a response at once to the threat of skepticism and to a disappointment with philosophy's answer to this threat, particularly as embodied in the achievement of Kant's philosophy—a disappointment most particularly with the way Kant balances the claims of knowledge of the world to be what you may call subjective and objective, or, say, the claims of knowledge to be dependent on or independent of the specific endowments—sensuous and intellectual—of the human being. And this in turn perhaps means a disappointment in the idea of taking the success of science, or what makes science possible, as an answer to the threat of skepticism, rather than a further expression of it. Romanticism's work here interprets itself, so I have suggested, as the task of bringing the world back, as to life. This may, in turn, present itself as the quest for a return to the ordinary, or of it, a new creation of our habitat; or as the quest, away from that, for the creation of a new inhabitation: Wordsworth and Coleridge would represent the former alternative; Blake and Shelley, I believe, the latter. (Thoreau's notion of "revising Mythology" suggests that these alternatives may not be so different.) But romanticism in either direction makes its own bargain with the concept of knowledge and the threat of skepticism, one which a philosopher may feel gives up the game, one that accepts something like animism, represented by what seems still to be called, when it is called, the pathetic fallacy.

This bargain seems simply to ignore Kant's companion effort, as determined as his effort to close off skepticism, to stave off dogmatism or superstition or fanaticism: his effort to make room for faith by, so to speak, limiting faith; to deny that you can experience the world as world, things as things; face to face, as it were, call this the life of things. I noted near the start of the preceding lecture that, about the victory Kant declared over skepticism in negotiating away the possibility of knowing the thing in itself, one will sometimes feel, Thanks for nothing. Yet someone with his or her Kantian conscience intact, if not unmodified—say, one's Enlightenment conscience—may feel precisely as strongly about this return of the thing in itself by negotiating for animism, Thanks for nothing (or more strictly, No thanks for everything).

I pause to note a characteristic difficulty in the way I find myself setting out to think. A philosopher will ask me what exactly I mean by "experiencing things as things face to face," and someone will ask how I define "the life of things." The answer to the former question is, Nothing technical; the answer to the latter is, I don't. Such words mean nothing whatever, or I have no interest in their meaning anything, apart from their accuracy in wording an intuition—here my intuitions concerning something like a prohibition of knowledge, a limitation of it as from outside. This wording of intuitions is essential to what I mean by such words as "letting oneself be read by a text." The text in question here is some fragment like "the thing in itself is off the limits of human knowledge." This noting, of course, says nothing about why one desires to be read, or why one takes that for an intellectual virtue, or beginning, or where it will end. (If experiencing the life of things is another expression for a feeling for what Kant calls the unconditioned, then it is an experience, in Kant's terms, of the sublime. Then another open question for me—a companion to the question whether knowledge or consciousness is the more fundamental or useful emphasis in understanding romanticism—is whether animism or sublimity is the more fundamental emphasis. While I am here following out the emphasis on knowledge as directed by the problematic of what I understand as skepticism, I assume that the alternatives in each question are inseparable.)

The price of animism is an aspect of the romantic settlement in terms of which I proceed to the main business of this lecture, the reading of four texts, the first and the last (*The Ancient Mariner* and Wordsworth's Intimations Ode) at greatest length, for they are the principal war-horses—beyond Emerson and Thoreau—in whose terms or paces my statements about romanticism here must find or lose support. The middle two texts, which I mostly glance at, are philosophical papers, one from each of the traditions of philosophy, the German and the English, whose mutual shunning—from the point of Kant's settlement and increasingly in this century (until perhaps a certain thaw of the past few years, in certain circles at any rate)—has helped to make satisfying public discussion of the issues most on my mind all but out of the question. The first of the philosophical papers is Heidegger's "Das Ding" ("The Thing"); the second, entitled "Gods," is by John Wisdom, one of Wittgenstein's first disciples.

The matter of animism is not going to be simple to state, because it has seemed badly misconceived (though perhaps it no longer is) as something romantics embrace—whereas Wordsworth's endlessly discussed remarks concerning poetic diction are in practice as much *against* the pathetic fallacy, against certain accessions to it, as in theory they are *for* the imitation of the rustic and the low, and perhaps the one because of the other. And in *The Ancient Mariner* the images of the animated, or rather reanimated, bodies I take as the equivalent in the realm of mind of what, in the realm of matter, or nature, the pathetic fallacy can accomplish. For an intellect such as Coleridge's, for which objects are now dead, they will not be enlivened by an infusion of some kind of animation from outside. (I think, further, of Coleridge's picture of animated bodies, the work in his poem of the figure of Life-in-Death, who has at that stage taken possession of the Mariner, as a parody of what a certain kind of philosopher, a person in a certain grip of thought, takes the human being, hence human society, to be. The Mariner says of his population, "We were a ghastly crew." I am thus reminded that in *The Concept of Mind,* less famous a book now than it was when I was in graduate school, when it represented what many took ordinary language philosophy to be, Gilbert Ryle called something like this the myth of the Ghost in the Machine, and attributed the myth to Descartes. Ryle did not spell out his myth in anything remotely like the detail Coleridge provides, but it is fairly clear that he meant something of the myth Descartes was at pains to *overcome* when, for example, in his Sixth Meditation, he denied that the soul is in the body as the pilot is in the ship.)

54

The issue, or specter, of animism makes a momentary, somewhat disguised or frightened appearance in a late speculation in the final part of *The Claim of Reason*. That part keeps coming upon ways in which skepticism with respect to so-called material objects or to the so-called external world, and skepticism with respect to so-called other minds—or as I might say for short, skepticism and solipsism—are reciprocals or counters of one another, opposing one another in a lengthening set of features: for example, on the constitution in each of "a best case" of knowledge, on the consequences that befall me when a best case fails me, on the ideal of knowledge that each projects, on the role of the figure I call the Outsider in each, or whether these skeptical fates are equally to be lived, equally open to avoidance, and so on. The late speculation I have in mind now concerns whether one or the other route of skepticism is the more fundamental; it arises from taking Othello's (other-minds) relation to Desdemona as an allegory (call it) of material-object skepticism. The consequent speculation is that this very possibility shows material-object skepticism to be derivable from other-minds skepticism, hence perhaps, on this line, less fundamental. But prompting this speculation had been the idea that solipsism may not be a genuine skepticism because of its livability: my capacity to doubt the existence of others seems, on this line, less fundamental than my doubt in the existence of the material world—indeed doubt of the existence of things seems impossible to live with, whereas doubt of others may seem to mark the way I live. A reasonable moral to draw from these opposite lines is that we do not know what constitutes living our skepticism.

I say in the passage about Othello that the speculation about the fundamentality of the two directions of skepticism anticipates further than my book actually goes. It is understandable that I shrank from that anticipation. It invites the thought that skeptical doubt is to be interpreted as jealousy and that our relation to the world that remains is as to something that has died at our hands. My new misgiving comes initially from the surmise consequent upon the surmise of jealousy, that we have killed the world, and specifically out of revenge.

Here there seems no shaking the sense that I have transformed the issue of skepticism into the issue of animism, exchanged one form of craziness for another. (As if this answer to skepticism has gone further than it meant to; as perhaps skepticism itself did.) Can this exchange be of intellectual profit? It may be intellectual profit enough if we come to see the idea of the jealousy of the world as bringing out an animism already implicit in the idea of doubting its existence—to the extent that the uncertainty created by this doubt is pictured less in terms of whether one's knowledge is well grounded (whether, for example, we can achieve assured knowledge of the world on the basis of the senses alone) than in terms of whether one's trust is well placed (whether we are well assured, for example, that we are not now dreaming that we are awake).

Turning to my first text, *The Rime of the Ancient Mariner,* I take the Mariner's shooting of the Albatross as the path I will follow through the poem, partly because that incident is in any case one that a fuller reading of the poem would be obliged to hazard, and partly because it confronts us, as I see it, almost immediately with the issue of animism, in the following way. Prominent candidates that critics have advanced as the Mariner's motive in the shooting have been a species of motive-less malignity and a kind of gratuitous violence meant to establish one's separate identity. It seems to me that the focus of the search for motive should be on the statement in the poem that "the bird . . . loved the man / Who shot him with his bow." Then the idea may be that the killing is to be understood as the denial of some claim upon him. In that case the moral of the poem is not well conceived as it is formulated by the Mariner himself: "He prayeth best who loveth best / All things both great and small," which generally leaves its readers somewhat dis-satisfied. But why should the Mariner—who still wanders in penance at the end—have the moral straight, or full? I take what might be called the poem's moral in something like the reverse direction from his: to let yourself *be loved* by all things both great and small. This is of course not to deny the Mariner's formulation; it is meant as a practical or, say, romantic interpretation of it.

May we regard my moral as comprehensible advice? I suppose an answer will depend on what we take the poem to be saying. It seems to me that what I take it to be saying tests that comprehensibility by speak-ing to the question of the source of a false animism, some mindless animation (as a kind of aberration of true poetry, or of true religion, in a self-derived place Coleridge calls, in chapter 9 of *Biographia Literaria,* a wilderness of doubt, "skirting the sandy deserts of unbelief"); show-ing this to be as much the enemy of genuine poetry (which resists it) as it is of science (which does not, since to science the difference between a false animation and the life of things may be irrelevant).

On the account I have to give of it, the centrality of the killing of the Albatross is, rather, put in question, as if it were both asserted and denied, as if it is both fundamental and derivative. I know of no better discussion of the question of this act, and its motive, than Robert Penn Warren's of some four decades ago.

Taking "the fable, in broadest and simplest terms, [as] a story of crime and punishment and repentance and reconciliation" Warren pertinently undertakes to characterize the nature of the crime ("the Mariner's transgression") that starts things, and he finds especially (and here I find myself most directly preceded by him) that the very feature of the shooting of the Albatross that other critics of the poem take as a failing (which they express by describing the killing as wanton, trivial, or unthinking) is, on the contrary, key to the poem's work: "The lack of motiviation, the perversity, . . . is exactly the significant thing about the Mariner's act. The act re-enacts the Fall, and the Fall has two qualities important here: it is a condition of will, as Coleridge says, 'out of time' and it is the result of no single human motive." If one bears in mind the idea that the Mariner's seascape is an image of the skeptic's temptation and progress past (what presents itself to him as) the merely conventional limits of knowledge, Warren's remarks fit my sense of the issue of skepticism as an issue of the human denial of the conditions of humanity for which there is no (single) motive. This suggests understanding the motive as the horror of being human itself—but then the fate of denying this condition, hence denying the possession of such a motive, would be the point of this motive. So like Kant's Categorical Imperative and its basis of respect, respect for the human (that is, for the possessors of Reason, of which the horror of the human is an opposite, a denial, or parody), the denial of the human signals not the absence of motive but the presence of a particular kind of motive; Kant calls it formal.

But the concept of "perverseness" will not take us far enough in assessing the Mariner's state; or it will itself require as much, perhaps the same, investigation as the Mariner's state will. Perverseness brings to mind, in conjunction with the suggestion of motivelessness, Coleridge's characterization of Iago; whereas Othello is equally to the point. In the way I have set up my initial path through the poem, the initiating act of transgression—that which for me evokes the Fall—is the act of "crossing the line." It may be—so I am suggesting—that killing the bird is derivative from the ensuing drift into the cold country, along with the other events of that realm; derivative both in itself being a consequence of transgression rather than an original transgression on its own, and in its interpretation being determined, or determinable, in terms of the interpretation of the crossing of the line. In the preceding chapter, I indicate its interpretation in terms of Wittgenstein's idea of speaking or attempting to speak "outside language games," an idea that *The Claim of Reason* works from in altering the intuition of Kant's critical "line."

What is the matter with attributing this crossing of the line—whatever actions that allegorical picture turns out to capture—to perverseness? At a certain juncture in the skeptic's progress he may say such a thing as that we can never see *all* of any material object. One who finds that claim to be paradoxical may call it perverse. But one who finds the claim true may call the *denial* of it perverse. One side here will be expected to perceive the other as the loggerhead; but is either closer in touch with the facts? (I present a series of examples in *The Claim of Reason,* pp. 194–99, designed to show that both sides are out of touch—roughly, because the word "all" has been driven outside its ordinary language game[s], hence its occurrences are out of our control, or rather, take control of us.) Given my use of the skeptical problematic as my opening into romanticism (and contrariwise), I am accordingly apt to be suspicious of the charge of perverseness. Applied to the Mariner, the charge seems to me in too great a hurry to declare him incomprehensible. Or is the claim on the contrary that the concept is exactly meant to make his conduct comprehensible? (The disputants about seeing *all* of something think they are explaining something too.) Then perhaps I should say: those who charge him with perverseness are in too great a hurry to declare the Mariner in some way different, in the grip of something special, a Jonah. That is, the charge would be more at home leveled by his fellow crew members, in a certain mood of their desperation.

The pang I feel in regard to this application may be made clearer if one considers that certain critics have objected to taking *The Ancient Mariner* as an interpretation of the Fall on the ground that it exhibits nothing to call disobedience. This would be decisively telling if the Fall must be imagined as, say, Milton imagined it. But what if the poem presents an alternative picture of the human outcastness from Eden, together with an alternative interpretation of succumbing to temptation, one in which it is a sense of going too far that produces a sense of prohibition, not the other way around?

In a section from the essay "Excuses" headed "Small distinctions, and big too," Austin cites as a result of failing to imagine ordinary cases (a consequence, he says here, of being "in the grip of thought") our subjection to a confusion he supposes Plato and after him Aristotle "fastened upon us," a confusion between succumbing to temptation and losing control of ourselves. (Wittgenstein's "language games" and Austin's "ordinary cases" do not coincide but they do overlap. Wittgenstein invents games that go beyond, in a sense, "what is said;" this is one sense in which he is not an ordinary language philosopher, or not an ordinary one. But they do not go beyond what, in a sense, "can be said" [with ordinary language]. My view is that without seeing the internal connections here, one will not know what Austin's cases are cases of.) Austin's example in the present instance goes as follows:

I am very partial to ice cream, and a bombe is divided into segments corresponding one to one with the persons at High Table: I am tempted to help myself to two pieces and do so, thus succumbing to temptation. . . . But do I lose control of myself? Do I raven, do I snatch the morsels from the dish and wolf them down, impervious to the consternation of my colleagues? Not a bit of it. We often succumb to temptation with calm and even with finesse. ["A Plea for Excuses," p. 198n]

Call us casual. Taking the plot of *The Ancient Mariner*, in its "having passed the line," to illustrate a spiritual transgression in which the first step is casual, as if always already taken, I see it as manifesting the idea of wishing to get outside language games, hence of tracing what Kant calls "dialectical illusions" (they may be taken as forms of spiritual derangement—Kant names them fanaticism, sorcery, superstition, and delusion). The idea of perverseness does not, to my mind, get at the condition of casualness. But apart from that condition, we are not considering the ordinariness of the idea (fundamental to my chart of skepticism) that it is natural to the human to wish to escape the human, if not from above then from below, toward the inhuman. The idea of perverseness here suggests defiance. It, so to speak, romanticizes skepticism. This is no better, no purer an accounting, and maybe no worse, than skepticism's self-portrait, which tends to soberize, or respectify, or scientize itself, claiming, for example, greater precision or accuracy or intellectual scrupulousness than, for practical purposes, we are forced to practice in our ordinary lives. (To see in some detail how the claim of perverseness may be assessed in this connection, I take up in Postscript B to chapter 5 certain of its classical locations in Edgar Allan Poe, from which Warren has assumed it.)

I have sometimes put the human effort to escape the human together with what I call our fear of inexpressiveness (something Wittgenstein's discussion of privacy takes on): "The wish underlying this fantasy [of necessary inexpressiveness] covers a wish that underlies skepticism, a wish for the connection between my claims of knowledge and the objects upon which the claims are to fall to occur without my intervention, apart from my agreements" (*The Claim of Reason*, pp. 351–52). I find this thought pertinent to the familiar thought that the Mariner somehow also represents the *poète maudit:* Coleridge's curse, like the Mariner's, was not alone to know that his suffering could not be communicated, as if it were in fact incomprehensible to others (anyway, to others so far), but to know that he was more radically incommunicado, a state he describes or identifies as inexpressiveness in his Ode on Dejection. It presents itself to me as a state of incomprehensibility, the state Wittgenstein's fantasy of a private language is meant to capture. But if the Mariner is a poet, then his actions must be those of a poet. Then what has killing a bird got to do with what a poet does?

What is his act? The Mariner says "With my cross-bow / I shot the bird." He knows the consequence was deadly, but that may not have been what he intended. He may just have wanted at once to silence the bird's claim upon him and to establish a connection with it closer, as it were, than his caring for it: a connection beyond the force of his human responsibilities, whether conventional or personal, either of which can seem arbitrary. In dreaming his solution, to pierce it with his arrow, he split off the knowledge that the consequences of his act would be the death of nature, this piece of nature.

The dissatisfaction with one's human powers of expression produces a sense that words, to reveal the world, must carry more deeply than our agreements or attunements in criteria will negotiate. How we first deprive words of their communal possession and then magically and fearfully attempt by ourselves to overcome this deprivation of ourselves by ourselves, is a way of telling the story of skepticism I tell in *The Claim of Reason*. I note here merely that "being driven to deny my agreement or attunement in criteria" is my lingo for being driven to deny my internal, or natural, connection with others, with the social as such. As if my reaction to the discovery of my separateness is to perpetuate it, radicalize it, interpreting finitude as a punishment, and converting the punishment into self-punishment.

The Mariner's shipmates, the remainder of the population of the ship of state, are dead to him before he shoots, as if just possibly the shooting should bring them back to life. If Coleridge's dream-poem were mine, had by me, I would take the shooting of the arrow to be a figuration for using words originally to name the world—winged words. Hence the poet may have cause to fear that his art is as fatal as science's; more fatal, because he had hoped to overcome (what has appeared to the likes of him as) science's or the intellect's murdering to dissect; whereas he now finds that he has murdered to connect, to stuff nature into his words, to make poems of it, which no further power can overcome, or nothing further in the way of power.

Then what is the crime in the act of shooting the bird? Warren says, at one point, that "the criminality is established" in such a way—namely through "a sacramental conception of the universe"—that "in the end we have . . . in the crime against nature a crime against God." Without denying Warren's findings here, let us take into consideration that the Mariner's acts in the cold country are self-absorbed, narcissistic, as if to parody that supposed self-reflection that some philosophers take to constitute one's possession of a mind. It would not be an allegory of skepticism otherwise, any recovery from which must—apparently—be made alone, in the absence of the assumption of others. Otherwise it is not skepticism you are recovering from. So there is nothing for the Mariner's act to be but self-absorbed. Most memorably, the Mariner sucks his own blood to free his thirst for speech and to enable himself to call a ship for rescue. And I think it is as clear that he identifies himself with the water-snakes, the loving and blessing of which precipitates the freeing of himself from the Albatross. This preparation depends on taking as a mark of identification the lines

> The many men, so beautiful!
> And they all dead did lie:
> And a thousand thousand slimy things
> Lived on; and so did I.

The gloss glosses (indicating a competition with, and in, the poetry): "He despiseth the creatures of the calm, And envieth that they should live, and so many lie dead." Then this for me means that he despises and envies his own being alive, as survivors may do. It is when, thereupon, he sees the snakes in a different light, in moonlight, that he accepts his participation as a being living with whatever is alive—accepts animals of the slime as also his others—that is, accepts the fact, or you may say the gift, of life. This begins his recovery from the death-in-life of inexpressible guilt. (My words just now imply that I take Warren successfully to have made his case for the relations between moonlight and sunlight in the poem, a case made substantially a few years earlier, it seems to me, by Kenneth Burke.)

Similarly, whatever else the Albatross may signify, to the Mariner it must present itself as a manifestation of himself. The gloss again glosses: "The shipmates, in their sore distress, would fain throw the whole guilt on the ancient Mariner; in sign whereof they hang the dead sea-bird round his neck." But the shipmates are no better, if no worse, at signs than sailors, and other blamers, may be. Their act of hanging guilt also realizes an idea of the Mariner's intimacy with the bird that my sense of his shooting wished for, and serves (especially if one takes it as physically impossible to hang in that place so large a bird) simply to identify them with one another—the bird (whose name alters, hence alludes to, a name for pelican) with the man (who bears his own kind of cross, or cross-bow), both of whom give their blood for the rescue of others. Then the shooting was a form of suicide, as the Crucifixion was.

The idea of suicide, further, combines with the idea of the breaking of attunement, the killing of one's connection with others, one's craving for exemption from human nature, to yield the crime of killing the humanity in oneself. It should seem to constitute its own punishment. Accordingly I do not see in the poem, as others wish to see, a reconciliation of the Mariner with society. Warren says that "it is by the Hermit . . . that the Mariner is received back into the world of men." But on what terms? He is not enabled to participate in that world on equal terms with others. To the extent that the Mariner is not recovered to the world of men, the country to which he returns (our world) *remains* dramatized, diagrammed, by the cold country he has survived. Otherwise, why would his penance be to proclaim to its inhabitants, ever and anon and from land to land, the identical moral he had to learn in order to survive his life-in-death? The difference in the countries is that above the line the inhabitants are able to conceal their rejection of the world, and for the most part or, say, for practical purposes, to adjust to their condition as if it were the ordinary condition of the world. To bring them back from their concealed life-in-death, accordingly, the Mariner has to break into their adjustments, to become a disturber of their peace, which is no peace. (He recognizes us as living our skepticism, or gives one sense to that surmise.)

The Mariner entreats the Hermit to "shrieve" him, which is to say, to hear his confession and to prescribe his penance. The Hermit asks him to say what manner of man he is, whereupon an agony forces him to begin his tale, of which the Mariner says: "And then it left me free." The timely utterance of his tale gives him relief. And the penance prescribed by the Hermit (which the gloss wonderfully glosses as "the penance of life [falling] on him") seems to be exactly to repeat this encounter endlessly—to tell his ghastly tale in obedience to his agony, which therefore will endlessly return, and "at an uncertain hour," which keeps him wandering, looking into the faces of strangers to know who must hear him.

That the cursed poet, the skeptic turned believer, is shrived by the Hermit, the other figure of isolation in the poem, I take as a Coleridgean joke: to shrive is to prescribe something, that is, to write something (in advance), so the poet is shrived, prepared for redemption, by a writer, call him an unacknowledged legislator. Writing is accordingly a kind of self-redemption, which fits the fact that the Hermit's prescription is of a confession the very telling of which constitutes penance.

This is not complete enough to explain the punishment in this telling. Here what I have in mind turns upon the differences between the persons, first and last, to whom the Mariner is depicted telling his tale, at first the Wedding-Guest, and at last the Hermit. What I have now to do is to imitate the Mariner, I mean obey him, by drawing my own moral from his story. (I leave open whether this should count as continuing to read it. I mean continuing to give a reading of it.)

62

Coleridge makes dramatically clear the decisive importance of who speaks first. In neither case of telling his story does the Mariner speak first, exactly; I mean he does not tell what he has to say until he is asked a question. Hence, as in *Walden*'s sentence about attracting its inhabitants by sitting quietly, by owning silence, the poet is so far claiming the posture of a certain kind of philosopher, a certain kind of teacher, say therapist. But in each of his cases there is an ambiguity about who is first. The Mariner asks the Hermit, in effect, to ask him to speak; so his speaking first is only to ask authorization to speak. The Hermit complies perfectly, responding to his request with a question that allows him to tell his tale through; so far it is the Hermit who behaves like a philosopher. Or rather, since his question prescribes a penance, it *forces* the Mariner to the tale. The Hermit thereupon is absent, presumably because he has no further instruction for his interlocutor and because the ensuing tale has had no instruction for him. From which it follows that he is not, after all, a philosopher. The Mariner is careful not to speak first to his initial interlocuter, the Wedding-Guest. He draws him aside from the round of life and thus prompts a question from him, but it is a question neither about himself nor about who or what the Mariner is, but only about why he has been interrupted. So again it is not an invitation to dialogue, and hence again philosophy is not present; the Mariner also is not that kind of teacher.

The Apostle, on the contrary, in Kierkegaard's view of him (in *On Authority and Revelation*), does find himself drawn from the round of life to speak first, but he does not, like an old sailor, speak about himself. So the Mariner wanders between Apostleship and Sagehood, as though it is too late for religion, because nothing is any longer common to our gods, and too soon for philosophy, because human beings are not interested in their new lives. (No wonder the writer's explicit autobiography will be written in continuous digression.) He knows what he has to say and he sees to whom he is to say it. But he does not know why he speaks and does not know why his hearer needs to hear him. Without knowing the good of his teaching he can make no end of it. The gloss describes the Mariner as "having his will" of the Wedding-Guest. This is neither how apostles nor how philosophers teach; he is more a patient than a doctor, more a symptom than a cure.

The gloss dictates that the ancient Mariner "teach, by his own example, love and reverence to all things that God made and loveth." But how would his example show this, unless he holds his past life as a bad example? Or is he an example to teach that no one is beyond redemption? How does his example hold the promise of redemption? The examples by which the Mariner teaches, apart from the telling of his tale, are, I gather, these two: first to show that "to walk together to the

63

kirk / And all together pray / While each to his great Father bends" is far "sweeter than the marriage-feast"; and specifically, second, to enforce the lesson by buttonholing Wedding-Guests, preferably next of kin, and leaving them stunned, so that they too "[turn] from the bridegroom's door." Why? Even if one ceremony is sweeter than the other, it does not yet follow that they are incompatible, that we must choose between them. Why is the marriage deserted, that is, why are *all* and *each* found place for while *a pair* or *a couple* are not? Does God, among all the things he made and loves, not love, or no longer make, marriages? And shall there be no more marriages? How does the Mariner's tale compete with marriage?

It is, to be sure, a tale of loneliness so absolute "that God himself / Scarce seemed there to be." Moreover, the characterization of the Wedding-Guest after the tale as like "one that hath been stunned" relates him to the Mariner's state as he successfuly dreamed of rescue, when "the ship suddenly sinketh" and he was "stunned . . . like one that hath been seven days drowned." Being stunned is the state Socrates is described by Plato as having produced in those who have sought confrontation with him, but the Mariner *leaves* the Wedding-Guest in this state, without, so far as I can see, further rescue; permanently, one may say, awaiting redemption. No doubt this can be justified—say, as preparation for philosophy. But it is not philosophy's progress, and neither, I think, is it poetry's or religion's. So again I ask: Why is this preferable to marriage?

The way I figure the moral follows from the way I have been led to line up the issues, in which the Mariner takes his tale to compete with the prospect of a marriage, to prefer either aloneness or else society in its totality to the splitting or pairing contracted in marriage, and to have the power of stunning but not of further rescuing his interlocuter. And since, moreover, I am not one who takes romanticism as the achievement of major celebrations of privacy, but rather, in these terms, as the achievement of the willingness for privacy, the survival of it until, if ever, genuine publicness is recognizably established, or reestablished, I figure this way:

However inviting the merry din of marriage, however essential to the hope of the social, it is no longer a sacrament, neither sponsored by God nor ratifiable by society as society stands, but is a new mystery to which outsiders, however close in kin, are irrelevant. Nor can the new bonds which must reconstitute a legitimate public, which means overcome our drifts into privacy, be secured by marriage as it stands. To marry now is to be willing to have a further adventure of aloneness, without solitude but also without society; as if marriage is a further investment of our narcissism, as children so typically are. If marriage is the name of our only present alternative to the desert-sea of skepticism, then for that very reason this intimacy cannot be celebrated, or sanctified; there is no outside to it. You may describe it as lacking its poetry; as if intimacy itself, or the new pressure upon it, lacked expression. No wonder you cannot tell who is married.

Then the Mariner's may in this way be a message of romanticism as such, that there is such an intimacy at large, and that poetry is responsible for giving it expression. (Then the question would arise: How did it get loose, as if disinvested? And why does not friendship demand it, as well as marriage? Or does it?) At all odds, not only does the Mariner's news for the Wedding-Guest make his tale more important than an outsider's attendance at a wedding-feast, but his news is singularly pertinent to that position: namely, that such a position is unnecessary, even empty; that the expression of our intimacies now exists only in the *search* for expression, not in assurances of it. (If marriage is the emblem of intimacy it is equally the emblem of institutions. So friendship does have some institution, if it takes place within marriage.) If marriage so conceived, say, as letting yourself be loved devotedly and reciprocating the devotion (as if love were a ring), is the poem's hope against a false animation; if this is the poem's hope for and its recommendation of the intimacy with the world that poetry (or what is to become poetry) seeks; then it will not be expected that we can yet say whether this projects a new animism, a truer one, or whether the concept of animism will fall away, as if outgrown. I would not call the poem an Antithalamion, but it is a fair enough warning about the stakes in play.

Since the stakes closely resemble those I find in the mysterious marriages, and their lacks of feasts, under observation in the best comedies of the Hollywood sound era, as well as the stakes in my preoccupations concerning skepticism, one may feel sometimes that such results about Coleridge's poem are rather too good to be true. Such a feeling may exactly signal resistance, from which conviction is a turn away.

THE SECOND OF THE SEQUENCE of four texts in which I propose to study the Kantian bargain with skepticism (buying back the knowledge of objects by giving up things in themselves) and romanticism's bargain with the Kantian (buying back the thing in itself by taking on animism) is Heidegger's "The Thing" ("Das Ding"), which I am taking as another effort, companion to Coleridge's, at the overcoming of the line in thinking, Kant's line to begin with.

Heidegger's essay gets us to Kant's question almost without our knowing it, over a Heideggerian path of questions that makes the Kantian seem simple in its familiarity. Heidegger's opening sentence is, "All distances in time and space are shrinking"; then further down the first page, "Yet the frantic abolition of all distances brings no nearness; for nearness does not consist in shortness of distance"; then on the next page, "How can we come to know . . . the nature [of nearness]? . . . Near to us are what we usually call things. But what is a thing?"; and on the third page, "What in the thing is thingly? What is the thing in itself? We shall not reach the thing in itself until our thinking has first reached the thing as a thing." This turns out to require "a step back" from the way we think to another way ("looking another way" Thoreau calls perhaps this). And close to the end the essay has: "Thinking in this way, we are called by the thing as the thing. In the strict sense of the german word *bedingt,* we are the be-thinged, the conditioned ones. We have left behind us the presumption of all unconditionedness."

What the essay is after is a return of human thinking around from Kant's turning of it upside down in his proud Copernican Revolution for philosophy: rather than saying that in order for there to be a world of objects of knowledge for us, a thing must satisfy the conditions—whatever they turn out under philosophical investigation to be—of human knowledge, Heidegger is saying that in order for us to recognize ourselves as mortals, in participation with earth and sky, we must satisfy the conditions of there being things of the world—whatever accordingly these turn out within philosophical thought to be. And this apparently means: The redemption of the things of the world is the redemption of human nature, and chiefly from its destructiveness of its own conditions of existence.

Is this a philosophy of romanticism? If it systematizes something like the task of romanticism in poetry, that is, if romanticism believes, and is right in its belief, that things need redemption from the way we human beings have come to think, and that this redemption can happen only poetically; then according to Heidegger's essay romanticism would be right in believing that it is thereby a redemption of human nature from the grip of itself. And in that case the activity of poetry is the possibility of human life; so it is understandable that poetry takes itself, its own possibility, as its proper subject.

This, by the way, sketches out a response to one of the earliest and latest charges against the romantics, to the effect that they prefer things to people. At a high level it is expressed in D'Alembert's rotten crack about Rousseau that he would not need so much to be by himself if he did not have something to hide. On a lower plane there is Irving Babbitt's Pastor Mandersish observation that "the hollowness of the Rousseauistic communion with nature" is one of romanticism's "substitutes for genuine communion" (*Rousseau and Romanticism,* p. 235).

(I note that the years in which Heidegger was beginning to write

66

his last essays, those after his so-called turn from *Being and Time*, were those in which John Crowe Ransom was writing *The World's Body*, another effort to link together the fate of poetry and that of the experience of the world. From time to time I wonder [or wonder if it makes sense to wonder] what American intellectual life would have had to be for Ransom to have had a literary-philosophical culture comparable to Heidegger's within which to write. It was that culture, in Europe, that logical positivism had been formed to combat. When positivism was forced to America it found certain affinities with pragmatism as well as certain more intimate enmities with it; and the native intellectual culture had to take positivism on, as it were, single-handedly, hardly knowing what it was in for, as in the case of Ransom. I do not credit Heidegger with a better touch for literature than Ransom's, or Kenneth Burke's, or R. P. Blackmur's, or Paul Goodman's, but the Americans compose their theoretical works in a kind of scrip, good for exchanges at the company store but worth next to nothing on the international market. It may seem a kind of private language. [To say of the New Critics that they composed their theory privately or locally seems to me truer than to say, as I hear it said, that they composed no theory, or little. And then one might look more fruitfully for the cause of what theory they produced.] In bad moments it seems we have had a choice only between this fate of privacy or that of fashion. But perhaps a better moral is a modification of the Mariner's: not everything is expressible in every country. [The case of England would of course be closer to that of America, though still quite distinct.])

Without lifting a finger now to lay out and to try to justify Heidegger's argument (roughly, that the recall of things is the recall, or calling on, of humanity), I point to the feature of it that poses to my mind, or let me say to the Enlightenment mind, the hardest barrier to this philosophical work, to our accepting this work as philosophy—its coming out with such propositions as the following:

> The thing stays—gathers and unites—the fourfold. The thing things world.

That was published in 1950, when it would still have been fashionable for an analytical philosopher, had he (or just possibly, then, she) come across such propositions excerpted some place or other, to call them meaningless. More serious, or significant, for us now, I believe, is that we can see that such a term of criticism would have been offered with, or as, a kind of nervous laugh. I am confident enough that the older charge of meaninglessness, directed toward such propositions, has become quite quaint in its intellectual isolation: for not only can the meaning of those propositions readily be explained in the terms the essay, and its companions, set up; but the fact that apart from those terms—say, in what might be called cognitive terms—they would be meaningless is not only not a charge against the propositions, but the very heart of the teaching of which they are part. Those who teach them, or anyway say them, may be deluded; they may be frauds; but they are not speaking meaninglessly.

Yet I find that such propositions do project a barrier for me. It comes from my still not understanding the nervous laughter they still may at any time—to the post-Enlightenment mind—inspire. I interpret the nervousness as responding to another apparent exchange of knowledge for animism. But if Heidegger's idea of the thing as thing, gathering and uniting something or other, must be seen as expressive of animism, then what was presenting itself as a philosophy of romanticism merely begs, it does not clarify, the questionable idea that keeps surfacing in romantic texts, that there is a life and death of the world, dependent on what we make of it.

Have we arrived here at the bound of a hermeneutical circle, which we should undertake either to enjoy or to quit? Let us see if we can widen its horizons by glancing at the third of my sequence of four texts, the only writing I know within the Anglo-American analytical tradition that offers, even in passing, something like a rational justification of the idea of animism, John Wisdom's "Gods," published five or six years before "The Thing." Like Heidegger's, Wisdom's justification is led to propose a new view of, as it were, rational justification.

Wisdom investigates the idea of animism, or what he calls the hypothesis of minds in flowers and trees, by considering the question "Do flowers feel?" He describes a context in which someone's treatment of flowers (one's caring for them, let us say) elicits from an observer the assertion, "You believe flowers feel." A year or two later Austin, in his much more influential essay "Other Minds," alludes to Wisdom's believer in the feelings of flowers as "holding a certain pointless belief" (p. 114); it is one of Austin's few very drab moments in a superbly rich piece of writing. Wisdom's claim is that when the skeptic says to a man, "You believe flowers feel," he feels that the man's treatment of flowers suggests an attitude inappropriate to them (though perhaps not to butterflies), even somewhat crazy, and he thus opens the question, I am sure deliberately, as to who is crazy. But why open it this way, by imagining it to be a liberal skeptic's description? It may be for just *that* reason that the man's treatment of the flowers is described in a way designed to invite, or incite, the suspicion of pathetic fallacy, because a skeptic can only imagine something like a projection of emotion in play, hence a suspicious projection, since *he* knows, so to speak, that flowers do *not* feel, or anyway that they are not animate, at least not as animals are, or not something.

Then let us hold off the explanatory hypothesis about believing that flowers feel (explanatory of what would make a certain way of treating them rational, anyway comprehensible) and instead imagine, if we can, someone's finding himself or herself struck by a treatment of flowers (a particularly nervous handling of them, or a special decorum in their presence, or a refusal to cut them, or perhaps a horror of cutting them, or a panic upon dropping them) in such a way that he is led to *consider* what flowers are, *what* it is he takes himself to know about what is and is not appropriate in our treatment of them. To consider, for example, that it is on the whole normal upon our meeting flowers to seek their odor; but on the whole not, with special exceptions, in the case of our meeting animals and persons; and on the whole not, it is worth adding, in the case of meeting stones and metals.

Wittgenstein says, in a famous passage, that if a lion could talk we could not understand him (*Investigations,* p. 223). Whatever one may wish to imagine about what a lion might, as it were, *say* if he talked, I take Wittgenstein's statement to mean that it is part of our understanding of human beings that (with understandable exceptions) they talk and part of our understanding of lions that (without exception) they do not, so that a lion's talking rather than roaring would not clarify for us, for example, why the lion is in discomfort. (It would, to say the least, perplex us in the extreme; in any case it would prevent our caring about his or her suffering then and there.) Recently an animal trainer and poet, Vicki Hearne, has published a remarkable account of some of her life with animals, "Talking with Dogs, Chimps, and Others," in which she alludes to my having said, in an early part of *The Claim of Reason,* that we can't talk to everyone about everything, and that we don't have to, but that there are some things we do have to talk about to everyone, if we are to talk to them at all. And then she goes further: "We have to talk to dogs about biting if we are to talk to them at all." Shall we say we are not really talking to the dog because the dog can give us no back talk? (Or can he? Let us grant for the moment that he cannot.) What else would you expect? If flowers could feel for us what we feel for them, we would not treat them as we treat flowers, for example, arrange them; not even lovingly.

In "Intimations of Immortality from Recollections of Early Childhood"—to turn to my final text—Wordsworth apparently claims to find not only that flowers feel but that they speak.

I preface what I can say about this poem here, dealing so briefly with so little of it, with three passages from Freud, as a kind of internal epigraph. I will say nothing about the relation of these passages to the poem's work, because either they will seem to be foreign material, in which case elaborating on them would make matters worse, or they will seem so native and pertinent that we could talk about them all night. The passages are from the case history, "Analysis of a Phobia in a Five-Year-Old Boy."

> Surely there must be a possibility of observing in children at first hand and in all the freshness of life the sexual impulses and wishes which we dig out so laboriously in adults from among their own debris—especially as it is also our belief that they are the common property of all men, a part of the human constitution, and merely exaggerated or distorted in the case of neurotics. [P. 6]

> Any one who, in analysing adults, has become convinced of the invariable presence of the castration complex, will of course find difficulty in ascribing its origin to a chance threat . . . ; he will be driven to assume that children construct this danger for themselves out of the slightest hints, which will never be wanting. [P. 8, n. 2]

> A few months ago—in the spring of 1922—a young man introduced himself to me and informed me that he was the "little Hans" whose infantile neurosis had been the subject of the paper which I published in 1909. . . . One piece of information given by little Hans struck me as particularly remarkable; nor do I venture to give any explanation of it. When he read his case history, he told me, the whole of it came to him as something unknown; he did not recognize himself; he could remember nothing; and it was only when he came upon the journey to Gmunden that there dawned on him a kind of glimmering recollection that it might have been he himself that it happened to. So the analysis had not preserved the events from amnesia, but had been overtaken by amnesia itself. [Pp. 148–49]

But I was about to speak of Wordsworth's listening to flowers.
Stanza 4 of the ode ends as follows:

> But there's a Tree, of many, one,
> A single Field which I have looked upon,
> Both of them speak of something that is gone:
>   The pansy at my feet
>   Doth the same tale repeat:
> Whither is fled the visionary gleam?
> Where is it now, the glory and the dream?

(The speaking of the tree and the field and the pansy have, evidently, to do with their having been singled out from their kinds. That you cannot know individuals beyond the last of the species they belong to is a point of Aristotle's that may be pertinent here; I am not focusing on it.) And

70

in the final stanza, 11, the poet is again present at their speaking. It opens:

> And O, ye Fountains, Meadows, Hills, and Groves,
> Forebode not any severing of our loves!

"Forebode" means foretell, or portend, so here speaking is interpreted as, let us say, bespeaking, forming an omen of something. And so the poet provides safer philosophical ground than we may have imagined for ourselves: it is easier for us—us English-speaking metaphysicians (to adapt the phrase Coleridge uses for himself)—to accept the idea of the earth as an omen, open to interpretation by us, than the idea, as in stanza 4, of the Earth as adorning herself, or, as in stanza 6, as filling her lap with pleasures of her own. Easier for an English-speaking poet as well, since this poem as a whole may be taken as a process of understanding and overcoming the unabashed pathetic fallacy that occurred in its opening stanzas, where the moon looks round her with delight, and land and sea give themselves up to jollity, and every beast keeps holiday. But in favor of what is this overcome, and why is it so hard? I mean, why is it, or why was it, when we were children, *natural* to us; an ordinariness which a new ordinariness must replace? (Or why does it, when we look back, present itself this way?) I note that the final stanza begins ("And O, ye Fountains . . . Groves . . ."), by speaking, for the first time in the poem, *to* preanimate nature.

Is this speaking to nature the replacement of taking nature to talk (back)? The idea should seem to us somewhat safer philosophically, I mean safer to take an interest in; but hardly perfectly safe, since our talking to nature ought to strike us as being nearly as crazy as being spoken to by it. Yet it seems to me worth trying philosophically to understand well, and to be part of understanding what Wordsworth meant, in the preface to the *Lyrical Ballads,* by "communicating with objects."

Coleridge will not allow Wordsworth to mean much, if anything, coherent by that phrase. In volume 2, chapter 17 of the *Biographia* he says, criticizing Wordsworth's preface: "If to communicate with an object implies such an acquaintance with it, as renders it capable of being discriminantly reflected on; the distinct knowledge of an uneducated rustic would furnish a very scanty vocabulary." This willfully takes Wordsworth to be praising the rustic's knowledge, say, of the paths through his woods, as superior to, *and in the same line as,* the knowledge that surveyors and cartographers could acquire of them. Not only does this refuse to interpret the preposition "with," pretending that what Wordsworth likes in his rustics is their ability to discourse in endless monologues about their belongings and neighborhood, as though they were veritable and boring Coleridges; but it perversely turns a deaf ear to Wordsworth's evident wish to speak of the kind of knowledge that is, let us say, wordless. Coleridge might have criticized Wordsworth for putting too much stock in such knowledge, or for aestheticizing, or we could say, romanticizing it, but that is not what he does. When in his tremendous chapter 22 he lists the "characteristic excellences" of Wordsworth's work, he cites "Fourth; the perfect truth of nature, as taken immediately from nature, and proving long and genial intimacy with the very spirit which gives the physionomic expression to all the works of nature." Here he has roughly glossed what Wordsworth, so far as I can judge, does mean by "communicating with objects," but instead of acknowledging this he persists in a view which takes Wordsworth, while having been granted by God an angel's capacity for singing, to have been allowed for theorizing the capacity of, let us say, a rustic. Coleridge thus romanticizes his own friend.

We might by now be able to think of the question of our communicating with objects as the question whether we and objects have access to one another; whether, perhaps like rooms that communicate with one another (or it may be caves), we are *near* one another, lead to one another, give ground.

A question for us becomes, Is there something we have to say to nature if we are to say some things at all? To say some poems, for example? I figure Wordsworth knows as much about such matters as anyone who ever wrote, and in concluding I indicate how I am approaching such writing, to ask it to speak again, to such a formulation of the question.

In the line I cited in which the poet speaks to things, what he speaks to them about is their speaking, their foreboding. He commands them, or beseeches them, not to be omens of severing, presumably because he knows that severing is a reasonable thing for them to foretell; but the child ("Mighty Prophet! Seer blest!") may foresee another way. In the closing pair of lines the poet takes the communciation further:

> To me the meanest flower that blows can give
> Thoughts that do often lie too deep for tears.

"Giving thoughts" is another formulation of bespeaking, and here what is foretold is something ambiguous about what can be expressed, or mourned for: are thoughts often deeper than grief, and would this mean as deep as joy? or do grief and joy have a depth that is inexpressible, or not fully expressible?

I will take in evidence mostly the single line: "Our birth is but a sleep and a forgetting." Since forgetting has to relate to the title idea of recollecting, which all will agree hearkens back to Plato's idea, or parable, of the preexistence, hence immortality, of the soul, let us take this statement philosophically, not (not merely, at any rate) as a description of a past event, indeed of the first event, in our biographies; but equally as a statement about the conditions of human birth, of the birth of the human, one that we, as we stand, might still suffer, sometimes called a second birth; a statement about the growth of the human mind after childhood. And let us put together with this the proposal that the child may take its life in terms of another major Platonic concept, buried in the sentimental stanza 7:

> The little Actor cons another part;
> . . . .
> As if his whole vocation
> Were endless imitation.

Imitation, in Plato, refers to *participation,* of things in their forms, or, say, of time in eternity, as I imagine it does when we are asked to imitate Christ. In this poem, about recovering from the loss of childhood by recovering something of, or in, childhood (in particular, recovering its forms of recovery), we are to recover it, participate in it, by imitating it, as it imitated us (so imitating its endless readiness for imitation). This will mean participating in it by participating in what it participated in, for instance in remembering what it remembered, and in forgetting what it forgets (even perhaps in allowing it to forget); so imitating ourselves, or what we might become. In the line in question we are to participate in childhood's birth; which means to participate in our birth, in the fact, I would like to say, that we are natal, that we "[keep] watch o'er man's mortality" by recollecting his natality. If I call the poem Wordsworth's natality ode, this is to remind us, or to let Frances Ferguson's *Wordsworth: Language as Counter-Spirit* caution me, to go back to Milton's Nativity Ode. The connection, to my mind, is through the idea of the birth of the human: that it is the birth of a world, and that in the process old oracles are fled.

I take it amiss that Coleridge refuses to try to determine why Wordsworth calls the child a philosopher. ("Thou best Philosopher, who yet dost keep / Thy heritage, . . . / Haunted for ever by the eternal mind.") I would like to answer in this way. The child is a philosopher because we are to learn from the fact of childhood, from the fact that we are the bearers of our childhood, Participation and Recollection; and initially by recollecting and participating in our own childhoods. These will be philosophical ways of letting childhood go, of bearing childhood as gone, as having become what we are, sharing our fate. Putting aside childish things becomes the achievement of intellect. It is the only path away from the sack of nostalgia, which we might think of, in opposition to remembering childhood, as the eternal reenactment (what Freud calls "acting-out") of the past. To thread through this difference between remembering and enactment I am taking as a task of Wordsworth's poem, call it a psychological task, or call it epistemological. It is a tract, or field, of instruction.

What we are instructed to recollect, to call back and to gather together, is a sleep and a forgetting. "Sleep" is characterized earlier as the region of fields from which the Winds come, which I take as pretty straight romantic code for creative inspiration. And later the child's play is described as constituting "some fragment from his dream of human life." Hence in this respect to participate in the child's work, in his inspiration toward life, is to recollect the dream of life, as from fragments, as if the whole vocation of becoming human, of suffering birth, were endless participation in such a dream, that human life will come to pass. Only so can we recollect that we as we are are not yet the fulfillment of this dream.

"Our birth" occurs to me as a kind of abandonment: the clouds are of glory, but we only trail them; not in utter nakedness do we come, but not fully protected either. In which context "not in entire forgetfulness," as well as suggesting a past setting that was home, to my mind suggests, something other readers apparently do not share, a grudge, anger, at being deprived of this home for a sojourn on this earth. I suppose that *all* our feelings for childhood lost are feelings to be found intimated in childhood itself ("all that is at enmity with joy"), angers as well as griefs. Then merely to long for childhood is to ignore what the joys of childhood come from, its separations, its anxieties. To capture that braver joy, to have a new birth, requires a new sleep, a new forgetting.

"A forgetting" names not a thing forgotten but an activity, a process of some kind; not a lapse of memory but a success of forgoing, of given something over. This is spiritually dangerous. Childish things can be put aside vengefully, which is not giving something over. The way recommended, so far as I have understood it, in the idea of a forgetting that constitutes a birth, lies in forgoing the grief and anger in abandonment, the one by God the Father, and the one by the Child who is father to the Man. (I do not mean to assume that this way is acceptable, as it stands, to the Child who is mother to the Woman; certainly not when following a poem about birth.) And the way lies in accepting relief such as timely utterance can give, lacking full depth, complete expression, as things of time will be lacking; and in willing nevertheless to say you are strong again, recovered as from an illness. In stanza 10:

> We will grieve not, rather find
> Strength in what remains behind.

Among other things, grief suggests grievance, as relief suggests legal remedy. To get a remedy for a grievance is to receive some recompense. This has a strength, but not the strength of birth. To get relief from the thought of grief is to know that nothing can "bring back the hour / Of splendour in the grass," to let time lapse so that there can exist a "new-born Day," hence to "find / Strength in what remains behind." What remains should not compensate, but it may yet suffice. Suffice, perhaps, for more present angers. The twin of grief, which I just called grievance, fails to bring relief, release; it ties us to pastness because it is a modification of vengefulness: it makes getting even a condition of being the odd one one is, one's having that to recollect and to imitate that one has; so it is always pitching one's battles on alien ground.

We moderns are likely to imagine that the giving up of the ground of revenge is the *effect* of therapy. I take the Intimations Ode to be saying on the contrary that this forgoing is the *cause*, or say the condition, of change. We do not know where the inspiration to give up revenge comes from. Much of its poet's energy has to be spent in a kind of reseduction (as does much of the energies of Heidegger, and of Wittgenstein, not to say Freud), because our powers of being drawn from elsewhere ("we come from afar"), of being interested, in heaven or in earth, are deadened. Otherwise we would not require birth, or poetry, or philosophy.

What remains of the "vision splendid" is that it "fades into the light of common day." Such is Wordsworth's construction of the ordinary. Shall we take this, as I suppose it commonly is taken, to be the same as a going out? But "fades into" does not *say* "fades out." It may propose some other mode of becoming, a happier disillusionment, so that the vision is preserved in the way in which it is forgone. Wordsworth's construction is to replace the ordinary in the light in which we live it, with its shades of the prison-house closing upon us young, and its custom lying upon us deep almost as life, a world of death, to which we are dead—replace it accordingly with freedom ("heaven-born freedom"); and with lively origination, or say birth; with interest. How far can the vision be preserved and lived? What remains of interest to us? What for us is remains? We must turn to that.

4

Recounting Gains, Showing Losses
(A Reading of The Winter's Tale*)*

APART FROM ANY MORE GENERAL indebtedness of the romantics to Shakespeare, *The Winter's Tale* is particularly apt in relation to the romantic themes I have emphasized of reawakening or revival, beginning with the figure of the six-year-old boy of Wordsworth's Intimations Ode and the ode's idea of the adult's world as "remains," as of corpses. In my preceding lecture I associate this figure, especially in view of his difficulties over remembering, with Freud's report of a phobia in a five-year-old boy, partly simply to commemorate Freud's acknowledgment that he was preceded in his perceptions by the poets, more specifically because of Freud's consequent perception, in this case, of adult human life struggling toward happiness from within its own "debris." Now here at the end of *The Winter's Tale* a dead five- or six-year-old boy remains unaccounted for.

Or is this prejudicial? Shall we say that the absent boy is meant to cast the shadow of finitude or doubt over the general air of reunion at the end of the play, to emblematize that no human reconciliation is uncompromised, not even one constructible by the powers of Shakespeare? Or shall we say that in acquiring a son-in-law the loss of the son is made up for? Would that be Hermione's—the son's mother's—view of the matter? Or shall we take the boy's death more simply symbolically, as standing for the inevitable loss of childhood? Then does Perdita's being found mean that there is a way in which childhood *can*, after all, be recovered? But the sixteen years that Perdita was, as it were, lost, are not recovered. Time may present itself as a good-humored old

76

man, but what he speaks about in his appearance as Chorus in this play is his lapse, his being spent, as if behind our backs. Then is the moral that we all require forgiveness and that forgiveness is always a miracle, taking time but beyond time? Any of these things can be said, but how can we establish or deliver the weight or gravity of any such answer?

Why did the boy die? The boy's father, Leontes, says on one occasion that the boy is languishing from

> nobleness!
> Conceiving the dishonor of his mother,
> He straight declined, drooped, took it deeply,
> Fastened, and fixed the shame on't in himself.
> (2.3.11–14)

But this sounds more like something Leontes himself has done, and so suggests an identification Leontes has projected between himself and his son. The lines at the same time project an identification with his wife, to the extent that one permits "conceiving" in that occurrence to carry on the play's ideas of pregnancy, given the line's emphasis on drooping, as under a weight. But I am getting ahead of my story. The servant who brings the report of Mamillius's death attributes it to anxiety over his mother's plight. But the timing of the play suggests something else. Mamillius disappears from our sight for good when he is ordered by his enraged father to be separated from his mother. "Bear the boy hence, he shall not come about her" (2.1.59). And theatrically, or visually, the father's rage had immediately entered, as if it was brought on, with Mamillius sitting on his mother's lap and whispering in her ear. What the boy and his mother interpret themselves to be doing is telling and listening to a winter's tale. What Leontes interprets them to be doing we must surmise from two facts: first, that both mother and son have got into this intimate position as a result of mutually seductive gestures, however well within the bounds, for all we know, of normal mental and sexual growth; second, that the idea of whispering has already twice been hit upon by Leontes' mind as it dashes into madness, once when it imagines people are gossiping about his cuckoldry, again as it cites evidence for the cuckoldry to the courtier Camillo in the astounding speech that begins "Is whispering nothing?" (1.2.284).

Naturally I shall not claim to know that Leontes imagines the son to be repeating such rumors to his mother, to the effect that he is not the son of, as it were, his own father. We are by now so accustomed to understanding insistence or protestation, perhaps in the form of rage, as modes of denial, that we will at least consider that the *negation* of this tale is the object of Leontes' fear, namely the fear that he *is* the father. As if whatever the son says, the very power of his speaking, of what it is he bespeaks, is fearful; as if his very existence is what perplexes his father's mind.

Why would the father fear being the true father of his children? One reason might be some problem of his with the idea that he has impregnated the mother, I mean of course the *son's* mother. Another might be that this would displace him in this mother's affection, and moreover that he would himself have to nurture that displacement. Another might be that this would ratify the displacement of his and his friend Polixenes' mutual love, his original separation from whom, which means the passing of youth and innocence, was marked, as Polixenes tells Hermione, by the appearance of the women they married. But for whatever reason, the idea of his fearing to be a father would make his jealousy of Polixenes suspicious—not merely because it makes the jealousy empirically baseless, but because it makes it psychologically derivative. This is worth saying because there are views that would take the jealousy between brothers as a rock-bottom level of human motivation. In taking it as derivative I do not have to deny that Leontes is jealous of Polixenes, only to leave open what that means, and how special a human relation it proposes.

To further the thought that disowning his issue is more fundamental than, or causes, his jealousy of his friend and brother, rather than the other way around, let us ask how what is called Leontes' "diseased opinion" (1.2.297) drops its disease.

It vanishes exactly upon his learning that his son is dead. The sequence is this: Leontes refuses the truth of Apollo's oracle; a servant enters, crying for the King. Leontes asks, "What's the business?" and is told the Prince is gone. Leontes questions the word and is told it means "is dead." Leontes' response at once is to relent: "Apollo's angry, and the heavens themselves / Do strike at my injustice;" whereupon Hermione faints. Of course you can say that the consequences of Leontes' folly have just built up too far for him to bear them any further and that he is shocked into the truth. This is in a general way undeniable, but it hardly suggests why it is *here* that he buckles, lets himself feel the shock. It would not be forced to imagine that he first extend his assertion of Mamillius's drooping from shame and accuse Hermione of Mamillius's murder, or at least that Shakespeare follow his primary source, the tale of jealousy as told in Robert Green's romance *Pandosto,* and let Leontes immediately believe the oracle, but still too late; so that news of his son's death and of Hermione's death upon that news comes during his recantation, as double punishment for his refusal of belief. Or again,

Shakespeare could have persisted in his idea that Leontes believes the oracle only after he sees that his disbelief has killed, and still have preserved the idea of the shock as the death of both his son and his wife. But the choice of *The Winter's Tale* is, rather, to make the cure perfectly coincide with the death of the son alone. How do we understand Shakespeare's reordering, or recounting?

Think of the boy whispering in his mother's ear, and think back to her having shown that her fantasy of having things told in her ear makes her feel full (1.2.91–92); that is, that her pregnancy itself is a cause of heightened erotic feeling in her (something that feeds her husband's confusion and strategy). Then the scene of the boy's telling a tale is explicitly one to cause jealousy (as accordingly was the earlier scene of telling between Hermione and Polixenes, which the present scene repeats, to Leontes' mind); hence the son's death reads like the satisfaction of the father's wish. The further implication is that Apollo is angry not, or not merely, because Leontes does not believe his oracle, but because the god has been outsmarted by Leontes, or rather by his theater of jealousy, tricked into taking Leontes' revenge *for* him, as if himself punished for believing that even a god could halt the progress of jealousy by a deliverance of reason. (Leontes' intimacy with riddles and prophecies would then not be his ability to solve them, but to anticipate them.)

Then look again at the "rest," the relief from restlessness of his brain, that Leontes has achieved at this stage of death and fainting. He says, as he asks Paulina and the ladies in attendance to remove and care for the stricken Hermione, "I have too much believed mine own suspicion" (3.2.148)—a fully suspicious statement, I mean one said from *within* his suspicion, not from having put it aside. The statement merely expresses his regret that he *believed* his suspicion too much. How much would have been just enough? And what would prevent this excess of belief in the future? The situation remains unstable. How could it not, given what we know of the condition from which he requires recovery?

He had described the condition in the following way, in the course of his speech upon discovering the mother and the son together:

> There may be in the cup
> A spider steeped, and one may drink, depart,
> And yet partake no venom, for his knowledge
> Is not infected; but if one present
> Th'abhorred ingredient to his eye, make known
> How he hath drunk, he cracks his gorge, his sides,
> With violent hefts. I have drunk, and seen the spider.
> (2.1.39–45)

Of the fabulous significance in these lines, I note here just the skeptic's sense, as for example voiced by David Hume, of being cursed, or sickened, in knowing more than his fellows about the fact of knowing itself, in having somehow peeked behind the scenes, or say conditions, of knowing. (Though what Shakespeare is revealing those conditions to be is something Hume, or Descartes, would doubtless have been astonished to learn.) And Leontes has manifested the collapse of the power of human knowing in the "Is whispering nothing?" speech, which ends:

> Why, then the world and all that's in't is nothing,
> The covering sky is nothing, Bohemia nothing,
> My wife is nothing, nor nothing have these nothings,
> If this be nothing.
>
> (1.2.293–96)

Chaos seems to have come again; and what chaos looks like is the inability to say what exists; to say whether, so to speak, language applies to anything.

These experiences of Leontes go rather beyond anything I find I might mean by speaking of believing my suspicions too much. So far I am suggesting merely that this insufficiency of recovery is what you would expect in tracking Leontes' progress by means of the map of skepticism. For here is where you discover the precipitousness of the move from next to nothing (say from the merest surmise that one may be dreaming, a repeated surmise in Leontes' case) into nothingness. Hume recovers from his knowledge of knowledge, or, let me say, learns to live with it, but what he calls its "malady" is never cured; and Descartes recovers only by depending (in a way I assume is no longer natural to the human spiritual repertory) on his detailed dependence on God. I assume it is unclear to what extent we have devised for ourselves late versions of these reparations. If *The Winter's Tale* is understandable as a study of skepticism—that is, as a response to what skepticism is a response to—then its second half must be understandable as a study of its search for recovery (after Leontes, for example, and before him Othello, have done their worst). That skepticism demands—Cartesian skepticism, Humian skepticism, the thing Kant calls a scandal to philosophy—efforts at recovery, is internal to it: it is inherently unstable, no one simply wants to be a (this kind of) skeptic. Skepticism's own sense of what recovery would consist in dictates efforts to refute it; yet refutation can only extend it, as Othello notably found out. True recovery lies in reconceiving it, in finding skepticism's source (its origin, say, if you can say it without supposing its origin is past).

To orient ourselves in finding how *The Winter's Tale* conceives of this search for recovery, let us question its title further. Several passages in the play are called tales or said to be like tales, but the only thing said to be a tale for winter is the tale begun by the boy Mamillius. I have heard it said, as if it is accepted wisdom, that the remainder of the play, after we no longer hear what Mamillius says, or would have said, *is* the tale as it unfolds. Supposing so, what would the point be? According to what I have so far found to be true of that narration, what we are given are events motivated by seduction, told in a whisper, having the effect of drawing on the vengeance of a husband and father who, therefore, has interpreted the tale as revealing something about him, and specifically something to do with the fact that his wife has or has not been faithful to him, where her faithfulness would be at least as bad as her faithlessness would be. (This is the match of my way of looking at *Othello,* in concluding *The Claim of Reason.*) Although I find these to be promising lines to follow out as characteristics of our play, they will any of them depend on some working sense of why a play is being called a tale. Is it simply that the play is about a tale, or the telling of a tale, as for instance the film *The Philadelphia Story* is, in a sense, about a magazine story, or the getting and the suppressing of a story? Does it matter that we do not know what the tale is that the play would on this account be about? Three times an assertion is said to sound like an old tale—that the king's daughter is found, that Antigonous was torn to pieces by a bear, and that Hermione is living—and each time the purpose is to say that one will have trouble believing these things without seeing them, that the experience of them "lames report," "undoes description," and lies beyond the capacity of "ballad-makers . . . to express it" (5.2.61–62, 26–27). It is uncontroversial that Shakespeare's late plays intensify his recurrent study of theater, so we may take it that he is here asserting the competition of poetic theater with nontheatrical romance as modes of narrative, and especially claiming the superiority of theater (over a work like his own "source" *Pandosto*) in securing full faith and credit in fiction. But what are the stakes in such a competition, if they go beyond the jealousies of one profession or craft toward another? Let us consider that Leontes' interruption of Mamillius's tale itself suggests a competition over the question *whose* tale the ensuing tale is, the son's or the father's, or somehow both, the one told in whispers and beckonings, under the voice, the other, at the same time, at the top of the voice, in commands and accusations.

While evidently I expect considerable agreement that in Leontes' intrusion we have an Oedipal conflict put before us, I am not assuming that we thereupon know how to work our way through the conflict.

Freud, I guess like Sophocles, seems to look at the conflict as initiated by the son's wish to remove or replace the father, whereas in *The Winter's Tale* the conflict, on the contrary, seems primarily generated by the father's wish to replace or remove the son. Perhaps this speaks of a difference between tragedy and romance—hence of their inner union—but in any case I do not wish to prejudge such a matter.

Let us for the moment separate two of the play's primary regions of ideas that intersect in Mamillius's whispering of a tale of generation, namely ideas concerning telling or relating and ideas concerning breeding and issue. These are the ideas I shall follow out here to the extent I can, and from which I derive the point of calling the play a tale, something told. To grasp initially how vast these regions are, consider that telling in the play belongs to its theme not alone of relating or recounting, but to its theme of counting generally, hence to its preoccupation with computation and business and the exchange of money. And consider that the theme of breeding or branching or issue or generation belongs to the play's themes of dividing or separation.

The regions may be seen as the poles or opposite faces of a world of partings, or parting's dual valence, as suggested in the paired ideas of participation and of separation, or in other words of the play, ideas of being fellow to and of dissevering. The play punctuates its language with literal "part"-words, as if words to the wise, words such as *depart, parting, departure, apart, party to, partner,* and of course, *bearing a part.* That last phrase, saying that parts are being born, itself suggests the level at which theater (here in a phrase from music) is being investigated in this play, hence suggests why theater is for Shakespeare an *endless* subject of study; and we are notified that no formulation of the ideas of participation and separation in this play will be complete that fails to account for their connection with theatrical parts, or put otherwise, to say why tales of parting produce plays of revenge, sometimes of revenge overcome.

Since the region of telling and counting (think of it as *relating;* I am naming it participation) is so ramified, and may yet remain incompletely realized, let me remind you of its range. Reading *The Winter's Tale* to study it, to find out my interest in it, was the second time in my literary experience in which I have felt engulfed by economic terms, I mean felt a text engulfed by them. The first time was in studying *Walden,* another work insistently about pastoral matters and the vanishing of worlds. In *The Winter's Tale,* beyond the terms *tell* and *count* themselves, and beyond *account* and *loss* and *lost* and *gain* and *pay* and *owe* and *debt* and *repay,* we have *money, coin, treasure, purchase, cheat, custom, commodity, exchange, dole, wages, recompense, labor, affairs, traffic, trades-*

men, borrow, save, credit, redeem, and—perhaps the most frequently repeated economic term in the play—*business.* But the sheer number of
such terms will not convey the dense saturation of the language of this
play—perhaps, it may seem, of language as such, or some perspective
toward language, or projection of it—in this realm of terms; not even
the occurrence within this realm of what one may take as the dominating thematic exchanges of the action, from suffering loss to being redeemed to paying back and getting even. The saturation seems more
deeply expressed by the interweavings of the words and the scope of
contexts—or, let us say, interests—over which they range. If one seeks
an initial guess for this saturation or shadowing of language by the
economic, or the computational, one might say that it has to do with
the thought that the very purpose of language is to communicate, to
inform, which is to say, to tell.

And you always tell more and tell less than you know. Wittgenstein's *Investigations* draws this most human predicament into philosophy, forever returning to philosophy's ambivalence, let me call it, as
between wanting to tell more than words can say and wanting to evade
telling altogether—an ambivalence epitomized in the idea of wishing to
speak "outside language games," a wish for (language to do, the mind
to be) everything and nothing. Here I think again of Emerson's wonderful saying in which he detects the breath of virtue and vice that our
character "emits" at every moment, words so to speak always before and
beyond themselves, essentially and unpredictably recurrent, say rhyth-
mic, fuller of meaning than can be exhausted. So that it may almost be
said of every word and phrase in the language what William Empson
has said of metaphors, that they are pregnant (or are they instead, or at
the same time, seminal?).

I was speaking of the thought that the very purpose of language,
it may be said, is to tell. It is therefore hardly surprising, as it were, that
an answer to the question "How do you know?" is provided by specifying how you can tell, and in two modes. Asked how you know there
is a goldfinch in the garden you may, for example, note some feature of
the goldfinch, such as its eye markings or the color of its head; or you
may explain how you are in a position to know, what your credentials
are, or whether someone told you. (I take this example from, and mean
it in homage to, J. L. Austin's unendingly useful study, "Other Minds.")
In the former case you begin a narrative of the object's differences from
other relevant objects; in the latter case a narrative of differences in your
position from other positions. (From such trivial cases one may glimpse
the following speculation arising: if a narrative is something told, and
telling is an answer to a claim to knowledge, then perhaps any narrative,

however elaborated, may be understood as an answer to some implied question of knowledge, perhaps in the form of some disclaiming of knowledge, or avoidance of it.)

But there is another route of answer to the question how you know (still confining our attention to what is called empirical knowledge), namely a claim to have experienced the thing, most particularly in the history of epistemology, to have seen it. This answer, as it occurs in classical investigations of human knowledge, is more fundamental than, or undercuts, the answers that consist of telling. What makes it more fundamental is suggested by two considerations. First, to claim to have seen is to claim, as it were, to have seen for oneself, to put one's general capacity as a knower on the line. Whereas one does not claim to tell by the eye markings for oneself, but for anyone interested in such information; hence what is at stake here is just a more or less specialized piece of expertise, which may for obvious reasons be lacking or in obvious ways need improvement. Second, knowing by telling, as suggested, goes by differences, say by citing identifying marks or features of a thing: you can for instance tell a goldfinch from a goldcrest because of their differences in eye markings. Whereas knowing by seeing does not require, and cannot employ, differences. (Unless the issue is one of difference in the mode or nature of seeing itself, call this the aesthetics of seeing. Epistemology is obliged to keep aesthetics under control, as if to guard against the thought that there is something more [and better] seeing can be, or provide, than evidence for claims to know, especially claims that particular objects exist.) You cannot tell (under ordinary circumstances; a proviso to be determined)—it makes no clear sense to speak of telling—a goldfinch from a peacock, or either from a telephone, or any from a phone call. To know a hawk from a handsaw—or a table from a chair—you simply have, as it were, to be able to say what is before your eyes; it would be suggestive of a lack (not of expertise but) of mental competence (for example suggestive of madness) to confuse one with the other. As if the problem of knowledge is now solely how it is that you, or anyone, know at all of the sheer existence of a thing. This is why epistemologists such as Descartes, in assessing our claims to know, have had, out of what seems to them a commitment to intellectual purity and seriousness, to consider possibilities that in various moods may seem frivolous or farfetched, such as that they may now be dreaming that they are awake—a possibility (unless it can be ruled out, explicitly) that at a stroke would put under a cloud any claim to know the world on the basis of our senses. (The difference between dreaming and reality is one of the great philosophical junctures, or jointures, that is not a function of differences; not to be settled by noting specific marks and features, say predicates. It is my claim for Wittgenstein's thought, that his criteria are meant not to settle the field of existence [in its disputes with dreams, imaginations, hallucinations, delusions] but to mark its bourn, say its conceptual space.) This is a long story, not to everyone's taste to pursue at length, and not to anyone's taste or profit to pursue at just any time (as Descartes is careful to say). What interests me here is to get at the intersection of the epistemologist's question of existence, say of the existence of the external world, and of what analytical philosophy calls other minds, with Leontes' perplexity about knowing whether his son is his.

Leontes' first question to his son is: "Art thou my boy?" And then he goes on to try to recognize the boy as his by their resemblance in certain marks and features, at first by comparing their noses. That speech, distracted, ends with a repetition of the earlier doubt: "Art thou my calf?" Already here we glimpse Shakespearean pathos, a sense that one may feel mere sadness enough to fill an empty world. Upon the repetition Leontes compares their heads. These efforts are of course to no avail. Then he rules out the value of the testimony of anyone else, as if testifying that he must know for himself; and as he proceeds he insists that his doubts are reasonable, and he is led to consider his dreams. It is all virtually an exercise out of Descartes's *Meditations*. But while Descartes suggests that his doubts may class him with madmen, he succeeds (for some of his readers) in neutralizing the accusation, that is, in sufficiently establishing the reasonableness of his doubts, at least provisionally. Whereas Leontes is, while in doubt, certainly a madman. What is their difference?

What Leontes is suffering has a cure, namely to acknowledge his child as his, to own it, something every normal parent will do, or seems to do, something it is the first obligation of parents to do (though, come to think about it, most of us lack the knock-down evidence we may take ourselves to possess, in this case as in the case of owning that the world exists). Still it is enough, it is the essence of the matter, to know it for ourselves, say to acknowledge the child. The cure in Descartes's case is not so readily describable; and perhaps it is not available. I mean, acknowledging that the world exists, that you know for yourself that it is yours, is not so clear a process. Descartes's discovery of skepticism shows, you might say, what makes Leontes' madness possible, or what makes his madness representative of the human need for acknowledgment.

The depth of this madness, or of its possibility, is revealed by *The Winter's Tale* to measure, in turn, the depth of drama, or of spectacle, or of showing itself, in its competition with telling or narrative, because, as suggested, even after believing the truth proclaimed by an oracle Leontes is not brought back to the world (supposing he ever is) except by the drama of revelation and resurrection at the end of this work for theater; by seeing something, beyond being told something.

This is confirmed as a matter of this drama's competition with narrative romance, by making the finding of a child who has been empirically lost, in *fact* rejected and abandoned, a matter swiftly dealt with by simple narration: the Gentlemen who share the telling of the story of the daughter found, say it is hard to believe, but in the event (especially given their use of the convention of increasing one's credibility by saying that what one will say will sound incredible), nothing proves easier. The matter for drama, by contrast, is to investigate the finding of a wife *not* in empirical fact lost, but, let me say, transcendentally lost, lost just because one is blind to her—as it were conceptually unprepared for her—because that one is blind to himself, lost to himself. Here is what, at some final stage, becomes of the great Shakespearean problematic of legitimate succession: always seen as a matter essential to the flourishing state, recognizing (legitimizing) one's child now appears as a matter essential to individual sanity, a discovery begun perhaps in Hamlet, and developed in Lear.

We are bound, it seems to me, at some point to feel that this theater is contesting the distinction between saying and showing. If the concluding scene of this theater is telling something, it is not something antecedently known; it is rather instituting knowledge, reconceiving, reconstituting knowledge, along with the world. Then there must be a use of the concept of telling more fundamental than, or explaining or grounding that of, its use to tell differences; a use of the concept of telling as fundamental as seeing for oneself. That there is such a use is a way of putting the results of my work on Wittgenstein's idea of a criterion. Wittgenstein uses that idea, in connection with his idea of grammar, to describe, in a sense to explain, how language relates (to) things, how things fall under our concepts, how we individuate things and name, settle on nameables, why we call things as we do—questions of how we determine what *counts* as instances of our concepts, this thing as a table, that as a chair, this other as a human, that other as a god. To speak is to say what counts.

This is not the time to try to interest anyone in why the concept of counting occurs in this intellectual space—I mean, to convince one unconvinced that its occurrence is not arbitrary and that it is the same concept of counting that goes with the concept of telling. (Something counts because it fits or *matters*. I think of the concept in this criterial occurrence as its nonnumerical use—it is not here tallying how much or how many, but establishing membership or belonging. This is a matter both of establishing what Wittgenstein speaks of as a grammatical kind of object, and also of attributing a certain value or interest to the object). But before moving from this region of parting to the other—that is, from the region of telling and imparting or relating and partaking, which I am calling the region of participation, to the region of departing or dividing, which I am calling the region of separation—I want to note two ways for further considering the question.

The first way is to ask whether it is chance that the concept of telling is used both to cover the progress of relating a story and to cover the progress of counting or numbering, as if counting numbers were our original for all further narration. Consider that counting by numbers contains within itself the difference between fiction and fact, since one learns both to count the numbers, that is to recite them, intransitively, and to count things, that is to relate, or coordinate, numerals and items, transitively; and counting by numbers contains the ideas that recitations have orders and weights and paces, that is, significant times and sizes of items and significant distances between them. In counting by numbers, intransitively or transitively, matters like order and size and pace of events are fixed ahead of time, whereas in telling a tale it is the tale's pleasure to work these things out as part of the telling, or as part of a mode or genre of telling—it is why what the teller of a story does is to recount, count *again*—so you needn't be making a mistake if you let lapse a space of sixteen years in your account of certain kinds of things.

The second way I note for considering the connection of counting by criteria with counting as telling (or tallying) concerns what I suppose is the major claim I make in *The Claim of Reason* about Wittgenstein's idea of a criterion, namely that while criteria provide conditions of (shared) speech they do not provide an answer to skeptical doubt. I express this by saying that criteria are disappointing, taking them to express, even to begin to account for, the human disappointment with human knowledge. Now when Leontes cannot convince himself that Mamillius is his son on the basis of criteria such as their having similar noses and heads, and then instead of recognizing criteria as insufficient for this knowledge, concludes that he may disown his child, not count him as his own, Leontes' punishment is that he loses the ability to count, to speak (consecutively), to account for the order and size and pace of his experiences, to tell anything. This is my initial approach to the "Is whispering nothing?" speech. Without now trying to penetrate to the meaning of that Shakespearean "nothing," trying rather to keep my head up under this onslaught of significance, I take the surface of the speech as asking whether anything counts: Does whispering count? Does it matter? Is it a criterion for what the world is? Is anything? And in that state no one can answer him, because it is exactly the state in which you have come to repudiate that attunement with others in our criteria on which language depends. So I take us here to be given a portrait of the skeptic at the moment of the world's withdrawal from his grasp, to match the portrait of Othello babbling and fainting, in comparison with which the philosopher's portrait of the skeptic as not *knowing* something, in the sense of being uncertain of something, shows as an intellectualization of some prior intimation.

And Shakespeare's portrait indicates what the intimation is of, of which the philosopher's portrait is the intellectualization. It is an intimation, as I keep coming back to putting it, of the failure of knowledge as a failure of acknowledgment, which means, whatever else it means, that the result of the failure is not an ignorance but an ignoring, not an opposable doubt but an unappeasable denial, a willful uncertainty that constitutes an annihilation. These formulations suggest that *The Winter's Tale* may be taken as painting the portrait of the skeptic as a fanatic. The inner connection between skepticism and fanaticism is a further discovery of *The Critique of Pure Reason*, which takes both skepticism and fanaticism as products of dialectical illusion (the one despairing over the absence of the unconditioned, the other claiming its presence), divided by perfect enmity with one another, united in their reciprocal enmities with human reason.

The Shakespearean portrait lets us see that the skeptic *wants* the annihilation that he is punished by, that it is his way of asserting the humanness of knowledge, since skepticism's negation of the human, its denial of satisfaction in the human (here in human conditions of knowing), is an essential feature of the human, as it were its birthright. It is the feature (call it the Christian feature) that Nietzsche wished to overcome by his *affirmations* of the human, which would, given our state, appear to us as the overcoming or surpassing of the human. I said that Leontes loses the ability to count, to tell, to recount his experiences, and now I am taking that as his point, his strategy—to turn this punishment into his victory. Before he is recovered, he *wants* not to count, not to own what is happening to him as his, wants for there to be no counting, which is to say, nothing. Why?

This takes us to that other region of parting, that of departure, dividing, branching, grafting, flowering, shearing, issuing, delivering, breeding: separation, parturition. Without partings in this region there is nothing, if nothing comes from nothing, and if something comes only from the seeds of the earth. Leontes is quite logical, in wanting there to be nothing, to want there to be no separation.

The action of the play is built on a pair of literal departures, in the first half (after a short introductory scene) a departure from Sicilia, and in the second (after the introductory scene of Time's soliloquy) a departure back from Bohemia. And the prologue, so to speak , of the play, the opening scene of act 1, is, among some other things, a recounting of the separation of Leontes and Polixenes. Against which, how are we to understand the range of Leontes', and the play's, final words:

> Good Paulina
> Lead us from hence, where we may leisurely
> Each one demand and answer to his part
> Performed in this wide gap of time since first
> We were dissevered. Hastily lead away.

When were we first dissevered? Who is we? Perhaps we think first of Leontes and Hermione; but Hermione thinks first of Perdita (she does not speak to Leontes in her only speech upon reviving, but says that she "preserved / [Herself] to see the issue" (5.3.127–28); and if Leontes is thinking of Polixenes when he says "first dissevered," does he mean sixteen years ago or at the time of their childhoods; and if he is thinking of Perdita he must mean when he had her carried off, but we will, perhaps, think of her delivery from her mother in prison; and perhaps we will think of Paulina's awakening Hermione by saying "come away," speaking of life's redemption of her, and of "bequeathing to death [her] numbness," as her leaving death, departing from it, as a being born (again). As if all disseverings are invoked in each; as if to say that life no less than death is a condition and process of dissevering; as if to see each of us "demanding and answering to our part" means seeing ourselves as apart from everything of which we are part, always already dissevered, which above all here means—and hence the idea of theater in this theater above all means—that each is part, only part, that no one is everything, that apart from this part that one has, there is never nothing, but always others. How could one fail to know this? I say that such thoughts are invoked in Leontes' concluding words, but to what extent in saying "Hastily lead away" is he, do we imagine, anxious to depart from them as well?

Let us go back to my claim that Leontes' wish for there to be nothing—the skeptic as nihilist—goes with his effort, at the cost of madness, not to count. The general idea of the connection is that counting implies multiplicity, differentiation. Then we could say that what he wants is for there to be nothing separate, hence nothing but plenitude. But he could also not just want this either, because plenitude, like nothingness, would mean the end of his (individual) existence. It may be that each of these fantasies comes to the wish never to have been born. Beyond suggesting a wish not to be natal, hence not mortal, the wish says on its face that suicide is no solution to the problem it sees. While some philosophers have taken the idea of never having been born as clearer than the idea of being dead, and as dissipating the fear of death, it does not at the moment strike me so, if for no other reason than that suicide effects the end of life but not the annihilation of its beginning. Leontes' nothingness was, as it were, to make room within plenitude for his sole existence, but it makes too much room, it lets the others in and out at the same time. So Leontes, I am taking it, wants neither to exist nor not to exist, neither for there to be a Leontes separate from Polixenes and Hermione and Mamillius nor for there not to be, neither for Polixenes to depart nor for him not to.

It is out of this dilemma that I understand Leontes to have come upon a more specific matter not to count. What specifically he does not want to count is the other face of what he does not want to own, the time of breeding, the fact of life that time is a father, that it has issue, even, as Time, the Chorus, says in this play, that it "brings forth" its issue, which suggests that time may also be, like nature, a mother. Of all the reasons there may be not to wish to count time, what is Leontes' reason?

The last word of the prologue is the word "one" (in that context a pronoun for "son"); and the opening word of the play proper, as it were, is "nine." It is the term of Hermione's pregnancy, which, as I suppose is by now predictable, I am taking as the dominating fact of the play. Let us have that opening speech of Polixenes before us.

> Nine changes of the wat'ry star hath been
> The shepherd's note since we have left our throne
> Without a burden: time as long again
> Would be filled up, my brother, with our thanks
> And yet we should for perpetuity
> Go hence in debt. And therefore, like a cipher,
> Yet standing in rich place, I multiply
> With one "We thank you," many thousands more
> That go before it.
> (1.2.1–9)

(For fun I note that it is a speech of nine lines, the last not [yet] complete, and that of Polixenes' seven speeches before he accedes to the command to stay, all but one are either nine lines or one line long.) Polixenes' opening speech speaks Leontes' mind, it contains everything Leontes' mind needs (which now means to me, since a working mind, a mind still in command of language, a mind that cannot simply not count), everything it needs to miscount, or discount, to misattribute, the thing it finds to be unbearable to count: the speech has the figure nine as the term at once of pregnancy and of Polixenes' sojourn in Sicilia; it has the contrast between being absent or empty (his throne without a burden) and being present and filled up ("standing in rich place," and especially *time* as filled up, about to issue in something); and it has the idea of nothing as breeding, that is, of a cipher multiplying, being fruitful, the Shakespearean nothing—as noting, as cipher, as naughtiness, as origin—from which everything comes (as Lear, for example, to his confusion, learned).

I observe in passing that the clause "like a cipher / Yet standing in rich place, I multiply" is a latent picture of sexual intercourse, by which I mean that it need not become explicit but lies in wait for a mind in a certain frame, as Leontes' is, the frame of mind in which the earth is seen as, or under the dominance of, in Leontes' phrase, a "bawdy planet." He uses the phrase later in the scene when he concludes, "No barricado for a belly; know't; / It will let in and out the enemy / With bag and baggage" (1.2.204–6) another latent fantasy of intercourse and ejaculation. The vision of our planet as bawdy is shared by Hamlet and Lear as a function of their disgust with it, and it is an instance of the way in which the world, in a phrase of Emerson's is asked to wear our color: Leontes' vision of the world sexualized is a possibility realized in *Antony and Cleopatra,* confronting in that play the vision of the world politicized, where those worlds intersect or become one another; in *The Winter's Tale* the intersection of sexualization is with the world, I would say, economicized.

In Polixenes' opening speech, economicization is expressed in the idea of his multiplying, which in that context means both that he is breeding and that numbers and words in general, like great nature and time, are breeding out of control; and it is expressed in that phrase he uses about filling up another nine months, making time pregnant with thanks, namely that he would still "for perpetuity / Go hence in debt." The ensuing computation by multiplication (adding an inseminating cipher) is meant not to overcome but to note the debt. What the unpayable debt is is sketched in the opening scene, the prologue. In this civilized, humorous exchange (in prose, out of the ordinary) between courtiers representing each of the two kings, each expresses his own king's wish to pay back something owed the other. The debt is discussed as a visiting and a receiving, but in the central speech of the scene, Camillo describes the issue between the kings as one in which an affection rooted between them in their childhoods has branched, that is, continued but divided. "Since their more mature dignities and royal necessities made separation of their society, their encounters though not personal, have been attorneyed with interchange of gifts, letters, loving embassies, that they have seemed to be together, though absent; shook hands as over a vast." In the ensuing play the vast opens, and the debt seems to be for the fact of separation itself, for having one's own life, one's own hands, for there being or there having to be substitutes for the personal, for the fact that visits are necessary, or possible; a debt owed, one might say, for the condition of indebtedness, relatedness, as such, payment of which could only increase it, have further issue.

So we already have sketched for us here an answer to the question why a play about the overcoming of revenge is a play of computation and economic exchange: the literal, that is economic, ideas of paying back and of getting even, allow us to see and formulate what revenge Leontes requires and suggest the transformations required if revenge is to be replaced by justice. Leontes wishes an evenness, or annihilation of debt, of owing, which would take place in a world without counting, apart from any evaluation of things, or commensuration of them, for example, any measuring of visits, of gifts, of exchanges, as of money for things, or punishments for offenses, or sisters or daughters for wives. Payment in such a case would do the reverse of what he wants, it would increase what he wishes to cease; it would imply the concept of indebtedness, hence of otherness. And this sense of the unpayable, the unforgivability of one's owing, as it were for being the one one is, for so to speak the gift of life, produces a wish to revenge oneself upon existence, on the fact, or facts, of life as such.

Nietzsche spotted us as taking revenge on Time, Time and its "It was," (*Zarathustra*, "On Redemption") as if we were locked in a death struggle with nostalgia. Leontes seems rather to want revenge on Time and its "It will be," not because of its threat of mutability, bringing change to present happiness, but for something like the reverse reason, that its change perpetuates the nightmare of the present, its changes, its issuing, the very fact of more time. This may mean that Leontes' case is hopeless, whereas Nietzsche is led to a proposal for reconceiving time; but then this also meant reconceiving human existence. Nietzsche's formulations will have helped produce some of mine; but a more interesting matter would be to understand what helped produce some of his—doubtless his work on tragedy went into it. This leaves open the question of the relation of telling and retaliation, the question whether narration as such is being proposed as the offspring of revenge, that it is out of revenge for the fact of issuing and unpayable indebtedness that words breed into tales in which evenness is sought, in which recounting, counting again, is imperative, either as retribution or as the overcoming of retribution we know as forgiveness and love.

The opening scene proper of *The Winter's Tale* raises the question why Polixenes, after a visit of nine months, chooses now to leave; it alerts us to consider that Polixenes gives no good answer to this question. He expresses a fear of what, in his absence, may "breed" (1.2.12); and when Hermione says that if he'll "tell he longs to see his son" she'll not only let him go but "thwack him hence with distaffs"—that is, to attend to his brood is a reason any woman will respect—but he does not claim this. Furthermore, the victory of her argument comes with saying that, since he offers no reason, as if leaving something unsaid, she'll be forced to keep him "as prisoner, / Not like a guest." When in the next act she is reported, in prison, to receive comfort from her babe, what she is reported saying is "My poor prisoner, I am innocent as you" (2.2.27–28). And Polixenes gives in to her with the words, "Your guest, then madam: / To be your prisoner should import offending" (1.2.54–55). Take this as something Leontes hears, or knows for himself, almost says for himself in his identification with Polixenes. The offense for *him* in being her prisoner, her child, would be a matter of *horror*, if she were having *his* child. His logic again, in denying this consequence, is therefore impeccable. This is not the only time, in noting Leontes' identification with Polixenes, that I allude to the psychic complexities this poses for Leontes. For a further consideration, if Polixenes is his brother, hence Hermione Polixenes' sister (in law), then imagining that they are adulterous may be imagining them incestuous as well. If you take Leontes either as horrified or as jealous of that, hence either as denying or craving it, then the implication is that he feels *himself* on that ground to be the illegitimate and incestuous brother. (This idea would be helped, perhaps signaled, by the emphatic lack of mention of the present situation of Polixenes' own wife.)

I am still asking why Polixenes has decided to part now. To the evidence I have been marshaling from his opening speech concerning breeding and time's being filled up and his multiplying and later his not being a prisoner, I add the repeated explanation with which he ends each of his succeeding two substantial speeches: "Besides, I have stayed / To tire your royalty" (1.2.14) and "My stay [is] . . . a charge and trouble" (1.2.25–26). Taken as pro forma, civilized excuses these must receive pro forma, civilized denials from his hosts; and for a long time it seemed to me that Polixenes was saying just the thing that would prompt his host and hostess to urge him civilly to say. Then the urging gets out of hand, and the leaving becomes no less suspicious than the urging. My better suggestion is by now clear enough, and is contained in Polixenes' word "nine."

He is departing because Hermione's filling up and approaching term seems to him to leave no more room and time for him in Sicilia. It is this, the implication of the fact of her pregnancy, that Polixenes' speech leaves unsaid; and it is this that Leontes in turn undertakes to deny, for, it seems to me, all kinds of reasons. First out of his love for Polixenes, to reassure him; again, because he feels the same way, that his room and time are being used up by Hermione's plenitude; again, with the very intensifying of his identification with Polixenes, the wish or push to exit, to depart, feels to him like abandonment, as does the imminent issuing, or exiting, or dissevering, of Hermione.

I regard it as a recommendation of this way of looking at the opening of the play that it leaves open the division, or economy, of Leontes' love (and loss) between its investment in Polixenes and in Hermione, and that it does not deny the sexual implication of the number nine that Shakespeare's telling carefully sets up in coordinating the beginning of Polixenes' visit with Hermione's conceiving. However fantastic it seems of Leontes to imagine that the first thing that happened upon Polixenes' arrival on his shores is that he impregnated his wife, it is not fantastic for him to relate that arrival to an access of his own desire; indeed, we have the amplest evidence of that access. Another recommendation of this way of taking things is that it does not require a choice between locating the onset of Leontes' jealousy as occurring only with the aside "Too hot, too hot" at the 108th line of the scene and as having been brought on the stage with him. This is now a matter of a given performance, of determining how you wish to conceive of Leontes' arrival at the conjunction of the events in Polixenes' opening speech: he would not have to hear them from Polixenes, for what Polixenes knows is not news for him. What matters is the conjunction itself, and its precipitousness. Taking the jealousy as derivative of the sense of revenge upon life, upon its issuing, or separating, or replication, I am taking it as, so to speak, the solution of a problem in computation or economy, one that at a stroke solves a chain of equations, in which sons and brothers are lovers, and lovers are fathers and sons, and wives and mothers become one another. It is a place—the companion to that of Othello and Desdemona—within which to investigate psychic violence, or torture, as a function both of skepticism's annihilation of the world and of the wounded intellect's efforts to annihilate skepticism. Hume's recommendation of distraction from the malady of philosophy is a philosophically crucial such place. Competitors of Hume's recommendation, as it were, are Heidegger's case against the violence of representative thinking and, as later in my sixth lecture, Thoreau's and Freud's acceptance of mourning. Other countermotions to the invitation of skepticism are, as in my third lecture, the Ancient Mariner's tropism in killing the bird; and in the lecture following this one, Poe's narrator's more elaborate designs on his reader and Emerson's counter-measures with his. It looks like the place of the exchange of violence with skepticism will come into some manifestation anywhere romanticism introduces what in the second lecture I called its bargain with skepticism, its offer to buy back the thing in itself—an offer I have more or less taken as a philosophical allegory of the quest for a better relation with the things of the world, say a better life with things—at the price of turning poetry and philosophy toward one another, on one another, risking the autonomy of each. This issue comes back somewhat more fully in the sixth lecture, on the uncanny.)

Still at the beginning of Shakespeare's play, it is nearing time to call a halt. I must reach its closing scene, since that will present this play's vision of a path of recovery, the search for which is, as I claimed earlier, imposed by the nature of skepticism itself. To prepare what I have to say about this vision of recovery—and as if in earnest of the intention one day to get further into the second part of the play, the Bohemian part, that which after all makes a romance out of a tragedy—I shall pick out two elements of that part that I shall need for a description of the final events: the elements of Autolycus and of the fabulous bear.

In the figure of Autolycus the play's preoccupations with deviousness (both in money and in words—his father or grandfather was Hermes) and with lawlessness and economy and sexuality and fertility and art are shown to live together with jollity, not fatality. They are together in his early line, "My traffic is sheets" (4.3.23), meaning that his business is stealing and bawdry; that he sells ballads and broadsheets; that he sells ballads about, let us say, birds that steal sheets; that he steals the ballads from which he makes a living; and that these exchanges have something to do with the providing of sexual satisfaction—all of which it seems reasonable to suppose that Shakespeare would be glad to say of his own art. I emphasize Autolycus as an artist figure, in balance with the solemnity of the Giulio Romano artistry at the play's close, as one of the contributions Bohemia makes to Sicilia, its recounting of existence. It is in Autolycus that, in this play of the play between art and nature, between artifice and issue, we see that the sheepshearing festival is also a business enterprise; it is not in itself, as one might have thought, the recovery from skepticism, or civilization; it celebrates the progress of nature no more than the exchange of money and custom, like the play to which it lends its great image. The Clown enters to Autolycus (it is our first view of him after his going off to perform the "good deed" of burying the remains of the bear's dinner of Antigonous) as follows:

Let me see: every 'leven wether tods; every tod yields pound and odd
shilling; fifteen hundred shorn, what comes the wool to? . . . I cannot
do't without counters. Let me see, what am I to buy for our sheepshearing feast?

(4.3.32–38)

The Clown's painful calculation reminds us that all the arithmetical operations—not alone multiplying, but dividing, adding, and subtract-
ing—are figures for breeding, or for its reciprocal, dying. If Thoreau
had asked the question, What comes the wool to?, I am sure he would
at the same time have been asking, What does wool mean? what does it
matter? what does it count for?—as if to declare that this piece of nature's issue is itself money and that the process of determining meaning
is a process of counting (that words are already "counters"); as if the
fullness of language shown in figuration has as sound a basis as the
issuing of language demonstrated in figuring. (I mention as a curiosity
that the idea of shearing or pruning, as well as that of summing up or
reckoning, is contained in the idea of computing.)

One of Autolycus's ballads he claims to have gotten from a mid-
wife named Mistress Taleporter, evidently a carrier of tales, about "how
a usurer's wife was brought to bed of twenty moneybags at a burden"
(4.4.263–65). It is agreed that Autolycus is mocking contemporary
ballads about monstrous births, and I hope it will equally be agreed
that this, while filling in the play with ideas of money being bred,
hence of art and nature as creating one another, is mocking Leontes'
idea that birth is as such monstrous; it seeks perspective on the idea.
Further perspective is sought in the following scene, of the sheepshearing itself, in the notorious debate between Perdita and Polixenes concerning bastards, which expresses the halves of Leontes' mind: Perdita,
like her conventional natural father, who called her a bastard and
shunned her, wants to shun bastards; Polixenes, in denying a flat distinction between nature and nature's mending art, benignly concludes
that all graftings are legitimate, as legitimate as nature; typically, he has
thus shown a possibility from which Leontes draws a malignant conclusion, here that no birth is legitimate, that the world *is* of bastards, to be
shunned and cast adrift.

This brings me to the bear, in whom nature seems to be reabsorb-
ing a guilty civilization. His dining on the roaring gentleman, mocking
him, is carefully coordinated in the Clown's report with the raging,
mocking storm, which is seen as having "swallowed" or "flapdragoned"
the roaring souls on the ship. But if the bear is nature's initial response
to Leontes' denials of it, is there a suggestion that the denial of nature

is also nature's work? I take it that the play concludes (explicitly, at any rate) not, or not always, that in its citing of "an art / Which does mend Nature, change it rather; but / The art itself is Nature" (4.4.95–96), the implication is that there is also an art that does not mend nature, but that instead changes it into something else, unnatural, or, say, lawful, or rather social, an art not born of nature but, hence, of the human or of something beyond.

This is one of the arguments of which the final scene is a function, summarized in Leontes' cry:

> Oh, she's warm!
> If this be magic, let it be an art
> Lawful as eating.
> (5.3.109–11)

In proposing that there is a lawful as well as an unlawful magic, which perhaps comes to the idea that religion is lawful magic (thus reversing an older idea), Leontes' words suggest that there is an unlawful as well as a lawful eating. A play like *Coriolanus* a few years earlier was in part built from the idea there is an unlawful, or prelawful, eating, a cannibalism, that Shakespeare names elsewhere as well as the relation of parents to children. (*Coriolanus,* on my view, goes so far as to suggest that there is even a lawful cannibalism, one necessary, at any rate, to the formation of the lawful, that is, to the social.) I note again that *The Winter's Tale* similarly presents lawful and unlawful versions of its ramifying idea of "paying back," with which the first two scenes of act 1 and the first and last scenes of act 5 open, revenge being the unlawful version of which justice would be the lawful. (I note further that in act 1 there was a suggestion that friendship has an unlawful counterpart: "To mingle friendship far is mingling bloods" [1.2.109].) I propose taking the final scene as, among other things, a marriage ceremony. This means taking Paulina's warning to her audience that hers may seem unlawful business and her invitation to them to leave, as a statement that she is ratifying a marriage that can seem unlawful, where the only unlawfulness in question would seem to be some forbidden degree of consanguinity. In Polixenes' statement to Perdita,

> You see, sweet maid, we marry
> A gentler scion to the wildest stock,
> And make conceive a bark of baser kind
> By bud of nobler race.
> (4.4.92–95)

(which names the convention of grafting as what marriage is, marriage of different stocks and buds), marriage is located as the art, the human invention, which changes nature, which gives birth to legitimacy, lawfulness, hence also to their negations. No wonder Shakespeare's investigation of marriage has no end.

Since I am not dealing very consecutively with the Shakespearean problematic of incestuousness, which haunts this play, and since I propose no theory of incest—wanting rather to keep the events of the play at the level of data for which any such theory would wish to account—let me register my sense here that we can hardly these days avoid the thought that a play in which the line between nature and law is blurred and questioned is a play preoccupied with incestuousness, taking the incest taboo, with Freud and Lévi-Strauss, as that event which created the social out of natural bonds. A reason for me not to hurry into this area is that this role attributed to the incest taboo is, in traditional philosophy, attributed, if ambiguously, to the social contract, which may help to explain why the existence of this contract and the new bonds it is said to have created have been the subject of confusion and joking in the history of political theory. It suggests itself that the tyranny of kings, from which the contract was to free us, was itself an expression or projection of something beyond divine right, namely that we require divorce from a contract already in effect, a kind of marriage bond; divorce from the tyranny of the parental or, say, the romance of the familial, a subjugation not by force but by love. Leontes was mad, but the problem he had fallen prey to is real, and remains without a perfect solution.

I said that the bear dining on the gentleman is the play's image of lawful eating, for, as the Clown observes, "They [viz., bears] are never curst [i.e., bad tempered (Arden ed.) or vicious (Signet ed.)] but when they are hungry" (3.3.129–30), so that, unlike mankind, things of nature are not insatiable. This is why this dinner can carry comically, why its expression of nature's violence seems the beginning of redemption, or rescue, from the shipwreck of human violence, with its unpayable debts. Near the end of the chapter entitled "Spring," just before the concluding chapter of *Walden,* Thoreau paints the violence of nature in sentences like the following:

> We need to witness our own limits transgressed, and some life pasturing freely where we never wander. We are cheered when we observe the vulture feeding on the carrion which disgusts and disheartens us and deriving health and strength from the repast. . . . I love to see that Nature is so rife with life that myriads can be afforded to be sacrificed, suffered to

prey on one another. . . . The impression made on a wise man is that of universal innocence.

In having already described the final scene as a study of theater and proposed it as a wedding ceremony, I am, it will be clear, not satisfied to think of it—as was once more familiar—as a translated moment of religious resurrection, with Paulina a figure for St. Paul, a figure justified by the appearance in the scene of the words *grace, graces, faith,* and *redeems*. It is, however, equally clear to me that an understanding of the scene will have to find its place for this translation. I look for it in a sense of this theater as in competition with religion, as if declaring itself religion's successor. It may be that I am too influenced here by some things I have recently said about *Coriolanus,* but it strikes me that the reason a reader like Santayana claimed to find everything in Shakespeare but religion was that religion is Shakespeare's pervasive, hence invisible, business. The resurrection of the woman is, theatrically, a claim that the composer of this play is in command of an art that brings words to life, or vice versa, and since the condition of this life is that her spectators awake their faith, we, as well as Leontes, awake, as it were, with her. A transformation is being asked of our conception of the audience of a play, perhaps a claim that we are no longer spectators, but something else, something more, say participants. But participants in what? Who is this woman, and on what terms is she brought to life?

She says she preserved herself "to see the issue" (5.3.128), meaning the issue of the oracle that gave hope Perdita was in being, and meaning Perdita as her issue, her daughter, to whom alone, as said, she speaks (except for the gods) as she returns to life. Does this mean that she does *not* forgive Leontes? Perdita is equally his issue, and does the odd naming of her as "the issue" accept or reject this? Perdita found is equally the issue of this play, called *The Winter's Tale,* as is Hermione awakened. Beyond this, in a general scene of issuing, of delivery, I find myself feeling in Hermione's awakening that the play itself is being brought forth, as from itself, that she *is* the play, something I first felt about Cleopatra and her play, in which her final nested acts of theater are also the staging of a wedding ceremony. Who knows what marriage is, or what a wedding ceremony should look like, after Luther and Henry VIII have done their work? And if we are created with Hermione, then we are equally, as an audience, her, and the play's, issue.

Paulina (with her echoing of St. Paul, the expounder both of marriage and of salvation by faith alone) I take as the muse of this ceremony, or stage director; she knows the facts; it is Leontes' faith that is at stake. And the ceremony takes place at his bidding and under his authority:

PAULINA.   Those that think it is unlawful business
                I am about, let them depart.
LEONTES.   Proceed.
                No foot shall stir.
                    (5.3.96–98)

So we, the eventual audience, are here under his authority as well. What happens from now on is also his issue, it is his production. To see what happens to this scene conceived as his creation, and the culmination of his creatings, I put this together with two other authorial moments of his in the early scenes in Sicilia. First with his aside upon sending off Hermione and Polixenes to dispose themselves according to their own bents:

> I am angling now,
> Though you perceive not how I give line.
> (1.2.180–81)

Taken as an author's revelation to his audience, he is cautioning us that what we do not perceive in his lines will work to betray ourselves. And I put his authority—compromised as authority is shown to be—together also with my seeing him as interrupting his son's tale of generation, another authorial self-identification. Leontes has found the voice in which to complete it, as it were a son's voice, as if he is accepting in himself the voices of father and son, commanding and whispering, hence multiplicity, accepting himself as having, and being, issue. What is the issue?

    I have said that not the play alone is the issue of the tale of romance, as from a source, but Hermione as the play. Can Hermione be understood as Leontes' issue? But this is the sense—is it not?—of the passage from Genesis in which theology has taken marriage to be legitimized, in which the origin of marriage is presented as the creation of the woman from the man. It is how they are one flesh. Then let us emphasize that this ceremony of union takes the form of a ceremony of separation, thus declaring that the question of two becoming one is just half the problem; the other half is how one becomes two. It is separation that Leontes' participation in parturition grants—that Hermione has, that there is, a life beyond his, and that she can create a life beyond his and hers, and beyond plenitude and nothingness. The final scene of *The Winter's Tale* interprets this creation as their creation by one another. Each awakens, each was stone, it remains unknown who stirs first, who makes the first move back. The first move of revenge it seems easy to determine; the first move to set aside revenge, impossible. Some good readers of this play who would like to believe in it further than they find they can, declare themselves unconvinced that this final scene "works" (as it is typically put). But I take some mode of uncertainty just here to be in the logic of the scene, as essential to its metaphysics as to the working of its theater. Its working is no more the cause of our conviction, or participation, than it is their result; and our capacity for participation is precisely a way of characterizing the method no less than the subject of this piece of theater.

Does the closing scene constitute forgiveness, Hermione's forgiveness of Leontes? At the beginning of act 5 Leontes was advised by one of his faithful Lords that he has "redeemed," "paid" more penitence than done trespass, and that he should "Do as the heavens have done, forget your evil; / With them, forgive yourself." This mysterious advice first of all implies that to be forgiven you must allow yourself to be forgiven, accept forgiveness. Has Leontes accomplished this? It seems to be the form in which the revenge against life (as Nietzsche almost said), the weddedness to nothingness, is forgone, forgotten. The romantics saw this revenge, as for example in *The Ancient Mariner,* as our carrying the death of the world in us, in our constructions of it. The final scene of issuing in *The Winter's Tale* shows what it may be to find in oneself the life of the world.

IS THE LIFE OF THE WORLD, supposing the world survives, a big responsibility? Its burden is not its size but its specificness. It is no bigger a burden than the responsibility for what Emerson and Thoreau might call the life of our words. We might think of the burden as holding, as it were, the mirror up to nature. Why assume just that Hamlet's picture urges us players to imitate, that is, copy or reproduce, (human) nature? His concern over those who "imitated humanity so abominably" is not alone that we not imitate human beings badly, but that we not become imitation members of the human species, abominations; as if to imitate, or represent—that is, to participate in—the species well is a condition of being human. Such is Shakespearean theater's stake in the acting, or playing, of humans. Then Hamlet's picture of the mirror held up to nature asks us to see if the mirror as it were clouds, to determine whether nature is breathing (still, again)—asks us to be things affected by the question.

At Stanford

CONFERENCE: RECONSTRUCTING INDIVIDUALISM (1984)

5

Being Odd, Getting Even
(Descartes, Emerson, Poe)

I N THE LOBBY OF WILLIAM James Hall at Harvard, across the
story-tall expanse of concrete above the bank of elevators facing
you as you enter, brass letters spell out the following pair of sentences,
attributed by further such letters to William James:

THE COMMUNITY STAGNATES WITHOUT THE IMPULSE
OF THE INDIVIDUAL

THE IMPULSE DIES AWAY WITHOUT THE SYMPATHY
OF THE COMMUNITY

The message may be taken as empirically directed to whoever stands
beneath and reads it, and thence either as a warning, or an exhortation,
or a description of a state of current affairs—or else it may be taken as
claiming a transcendental relation among the concepts of community
and individual as they have so far shown themselves. Does this multiplicity produce what certain literary theorists now speak of as the undecidable? Or is the brass indifference of this writing on the wall an apt
expression of our avoidance of decision, a refusal to apply our words to
ourselves, to take them on?

    This lecture is a kind of progress report on my philosophical jour-
ney to locate an inheritance of Wittgenstein and Heidegger, and of
Emerson and Thoreau before them, for all of whom there seems to be
some question whether the individual or the community as yet, or any

longer, exists. This question (or, you may say, this fantasy) gives ground equally for despair and for hope in the human as it now stands. It is also the question or fantasy in which I have been seeking instruction from certain Hollywood comedies of remarriage and, before them, from Shakespearean romance and tragedy. In this mood I do not wish to propose a solution to the riddle of whether society is the bane or the blessing of the individual, or to offer advice about whether a better state of the world must begin with a reformation of institutions or of persons, advice that would of course require me to define institutions and individuals and their modes of interpenetration. So I will pick up the twist in the story of the discovery of the individual where Descartes placed it in his *Meditations*—before, so to speak, either individual or institutional differences come into play. This twist is Descartes's discovery that my existence requires, hence permits, proof (you might say authentication)—more particularly, requires that if I am to exist I must name my existence, acknowledge it. This imperative entails that I am a thing with two foci, or in Emerson's image, two magnetic poles—say a positive and a negative, or an active and a passive.

Such a depiction may not seem to you right off to capture Descartes's cogito argument. But that something like it does capture that argument is what I understand the drift of Emerson's perhaps inaudibly familiar words in "Self-Reliance" to claim. My first task here will be to establish this about Emerson's essay; my second will be to say why I think Emerson is right, as right in his interpretation and inheritance of Descartes as any other philosophical descendant I know of. Following that, as a third principal task, I will take up a pair of tales by Edgar Allan Poe, primarily "The Imp of the Perverse" and subordinately "The Black Cat." These stories, I find, engage with the same imperative of human existence: that it must prove or declare itself. And since Poe's "The Imp of the Perverse" alludes more than once to *Hamlet,* it will bring us to my title, the idea of thinking about individuality (or the loss of it) under the spell of revenge, of getting even for oddness.

EMERSON'S INCORPORATION OF DESCARTES INTO "Self-Reliance" is anything but veiled. At the center of the essay is a paragraph that begins: "Man is timid and apologetic; he is no longer upright; he dares not say 'I think,' 'I am,' but quotes some saint or sage." It is my impression that readers of Emerson have not been impressed by this allusion, or repetition, perhaps because they have fallen into an old habit of condescending to Emerson (as if to pay for a love of his writing by conceding that he was hardly capable of consecutive thought, let alone capable of taking on Descartes), perhaps because they remember or assume the cogito always to be expressed in words that translate as "I think, *there-fore* I am." But in Descartes's Second Meditation, where I suppose it is most often actually encountered, the insight is expressed: "*I am, I exist,* is necessarily true every time that I pronounce it or conceive it in my mind." Emerson's emphasis on the *saying* of "I" is precisely faithful to this expression of Descartes's insight.

It is this feature of the cogito that is emphasized in some of the most productive thinking about Descartes in recent analytical philosophy, where the issue, associated with the names of Jaakko Hintikka and Bernard Williams, is phrased as the question whether the certainty of existence required and claimed by the cogito results from taking the claim "I think" as the basis (i.e., premise) for an inference, or as the expression of some kind of performance. Williams does not quite rest with saying, with Hintikka, that the cogito just is not an inference, and just is a performance of some kind, but Williams does insist that it is not an ordinary, or syllogistic, inference, as he insists, at the end of his intricate discussion, that the performance in play is no less peculiar of its kind, demanding further reflection. The cogito's peculiarity can be summarized as follows, according to Williams. On the one hand, the force of the first person pronoun is that it cannot fail to refer to the one using it, hence one who says "I exist" must exist; or, put negatively, "I exist" is undeniable, which is to say, "I do not exist" cannot coherently be said. On the other hand, to be said sensibly, "I" must distinguish the one saying it, to whom it cannot fail to refer, from others to whom it does not, at that saying, refer. But Descartes's use of it arises exactly in a context in which there are no others to distinguish himself (so to speak) from. So the force of the pronoun is in apparent conflict with its sense.

Compared with such considerations, Emerson's remark about our not daring to say "I think," "I am," seems somewhat literary. But why? Emerson is picking up a question, or a side of the question, that suc-ceeds the inferential or performance aspect of the cogito—namely, the question of what happens if I do *not* say (and of course do not say the negation of) "I am, I exist" or "conceive it in my mind." An analytical philosopher will hardly take much interest in this side of the question, since it will hardly seem worth arguing for or against the inference that if I do not say or perform the words "I am" or their equivalent (aloud or silently), therefore I perhaps do not exist. Surely the saying or think-ing of some words may be taken to bear on whether the sayer or thinker of them exists at most in the sense of determining whether he or she *knows* of his or her existence, but surely not in the sense that the saying or thinking may create that existence.

But this assurance seems contrary to Descartes's findings. He speculates a few paragraphs after announcing the cogito: "I am, I exist—that is certain; but for how long do I exist? For as long as I think; for it might perhaps happen, if I totally ceased thinking, that I would at the same time completely cease to be." This does not quite say that my ceasing to think would cause, or would be, my ceasing to exist. It may amount to saying so if I must think of myself as having a creator (hence, according to Descartes, a preserver) and if all candidates for this role other than myself dropped out. These assumptions seem faithful to Descartes's text, so that I am prepared to take it that the cogito is only half the battle concerning the relation of my thinking to my existing, or perhaps "I think, therefore I am" expresses only half the battle of the cogito: Descartes establishes to his satisfaction that I exist only while, or if *and only if,* I think. It is this, it seems, that leads him to claim that the mind always thinks, an idea Nietzsche and Freud will put to further use.

Emerson goes the whole way with Descartes's insight—that I exist only if I think—but he thereupon denies that I (mostly) do think, that the "I" mostly gets into my thinking, as it were. From this it follows that the skeptical possibility is realized—that I do not exist, that I as it were haunt the world, a realization perhaps expressed by saying that the life I live is the life of skepticism. Just before the end of the Second Meditation, Descartes observes that "if I judge that [anything, say the external world] exists because I see it, certainly it follows much more evidently that I exist myself because I see it." Since the existence of the world is more doubtful than my own existence, if I do not know that I exist, I so to speak even more evidently do not know that the things of the world exist. If, accordingly, Emerson is to be understood as describing the life left to me under skepticism—implying that I do not exist among the things of the world, that I haunt the world—and if for this reason he is to be called literary and not philosophical, we might well conclude, So much the worse for philosophy. Philosophy shrinks before a description of the very possibility it undertakes to refute, so it can never know of itself whether it has turned its nemesis aside.

But it seems to me that one can see how Emerson arrives at his conclusion by a continuing faithfulness to Descartes's own procedures, to the fact, as one might put it, that Descartes's procedures are themselves as essentially literary as they are philosophical and that it may even have become essential to philosophy to show as much. After arriving at the cogito, Descartes immediately raises the question of his metaphysical identity: "But I do not yet know sufficiently clearly what I am, I who am sure that I exist." He raises this question six or seven times over the ensuing seven or eight paragraphs, rejecting along the way such answers as that he is a rational animal, or that he is a body, or that his soul is "something very rarefied and subtle, such as a wind, a flame, or a very much expanded air . . . infused throughout my grosser components," before he settles on the answer that he is essentially a thing that thinks. There is nothing in these considerations to call argument or inference; indeed, the most obvious description of these passages is to say that they constitute an autobiographical narrative of some kind. If Descartes is philosophizing, and if these passages are essential to his philosophizing, it follows that philosophy is not exhausted in argumentation. And if the power of these passages is literary, then the literary is essential to the power of philosophy; at some stage the philosophical becomes, or turns into, the literary.

Now I think one can describe Emerson's progress as his having posed Descartes's question for himself and provided a fresh line of answer, one you might call a grammatical answer: I am a being who to exist must say I exist, or must acknowledge my existence—claim it, stake it, enact it.

The beauty of the answer lies in its weakness (you may say its emptiness)—indeed, in two weaknesses. First, it does not prejudge what the I or self or mind or soul may turn out to be, but only specifies a condition that whatever it is must meet. Second, the proof only works in the moment of its giving, for what I prove is the existence only of a creature who *can* enact its existence, as exemplified in actually giving the proof, not one who at all times does in fact enact it. The transience of the existence it proves and the transience of its manner of proof seem in the spirit of the *Meditations,* including Descartes's proofs for God; this transience would be the moral of Descartes's insistence on the presence of clear and distinct ideas as essential to, let me say, philosophical knowledge. Only in the vanishing presence of such ideas does proof take effect—as if there were nothing to rely on but reliance itself. This is perhaps why Emerson will say, "To talk of reliance is a poor external way of speaking."

That what I am is one who to exist enacts his existence is an answer Descartes might almost have given himself, since it is scarcely more than a literal transcript of what I set up as the further half of the cogito's battle. It is a way of envisioning roughly the view of so-called human existence taken by Heidegger in *Being and Time:* that Dasein's being is such that its being is an issue for it (p. 68). But for Descartes to have given such an answer would have threatened the first declared purpose of his *Meditations,* which was to offer proof of God's existence. If I am one who can enact my existence, God's role in the enactment is compromised. Descartes's word for what I call "enacting"—or "claiming" or "staking" or "acknowledging"—is "authoring." In the Third Meditation:

> I wish to pass on now to consider whether I myself, who have the idea of God, could exist if there had been no God. And I ask, from what source would I have derived my existence? Possibly from myself, or from my parents. . . . But if I were . . . the author of my own being, I would doubt nothing, I would experience no desires, and finally I would lack no perfection . . . I would be God (himself). . . . Even if I could suppose that possibly I have always been as I am now . . . it would not follow that no author of my existence need then be sought and I would still have to recognize that it is necessary that God is the author of my existence.

Apparently it is the very sense of my need for a human proof of my human existence—some authentication—that is the source of the idea that I need an author. ("Need for proof" will be what becomes of my intuition of my transience, or dependence, or incompleteness, or unfinishedness, or unsponsoredness—of the intuition that I am unauthorized.)

But surely the idea of self-authorizing is merely metaphorical, the merest exploitation of the coincidence that the Latin word for author is also the word for creating, nothing more than the by now fully discredited romantic picture of the author or artist as incomprehensibly original, as a world-creating and self-creating genius. It is true that the problematic of enacting one's existence skirts the edge of metaphysical nonsense. It asks us, in effect, to move from the consideration that we may sensibly disclaim certain actions as ours (ones done, as we may say, against our wills), and hence from the consideration that we may disclaim certain of our thoughts as ours (ones, it may be, we would not dream of acting on, though the terrain here gets philosophically and psychologically more dangerous), to the possibility that none of my actions and thoughts are mine—as if, if I am not a ghost, I am, I would like to say, *worked,* from inside or outside. This move to the metaphysical is like saying that since it makes sense to suppose that I might lack any or all of my limbs I might lack a body altogether, or that since I never see all of any object and hence may not know that a given object exists I may not know that the external world as such exists. Ordinary language philosophy, most notably in the teaching of Austin and of Wittgenstein, has discredited such moves to the metaphysical, as a way of discrediting the conclusions of skepticism. But in my interpretation of Wittgenstein, what is discredited is not the appeal or the threat of skepticism as such, but only skepticism's own pictures of its accomplishments. Similarly, what is discredited in the romantic's knowledge about self-authoring is only a partial picture of authoring and of creation, a picture of human creation as a literalized anthropomorphism of God's creation—as if to create myself I were required to begin with the dust of the ground and magic breath, rather than with, say, an uncreated human being and the power of thinking.

That human clay and the human capacity for thought are enough to inspire the authoring of myself is, at any rate, what I take Emerson's "Self-Reliance," as a reading of Descartes's cogito argument, to claim. I take his underlying turning of Descartes to be something like this: there is a sense of being the author of oneself that does not require me to imagine myself God (that may just be the name of the particular picture of the self as a self-present substance), a sense in which the absence of doubt and desire of which Descartes speaks in proving that God, not he, is the author of himself is a continuing task, not a property, a task in which the goal, or the product of the process, is not a state of being but a moment of change, say of becoming—a transience of being, a being of transience. (Emerson notes: "This one fact the world hates; that the soul *becomes*.") To make sense of this turn, Emerson needs a view of the world, a perspective on its fallenness, in which the *uncreatedness* of the individual manifests itself, in which human life appears as the individual's failure at self-creation, as a continuous loss of individual possibility in the face of some overpowering competitor. This is to say that, if my gloss of Emerson's reading of Descartes is right, the cogito's need arises at particular historical moments in the life of the individual and in the life of the culture.

Emerson calls the mode of uncreated life "conformity." But each of the modern prophets seems to have been driven to find some way of characterizing the threat to individual existence, to individuation, posed by the life to which their society is bringing itself. John Stuart Mill (in *On Liberty*) called it the despotism of opinion, and he characterized being human in his period in terms of deformity; he speaks of us as withered and starved, and as dwarfs (pp. 58–59). Nietzsche called the threat: the world of the last man ("Zarathustra's Prologue," §5), the world of the murderers of God (*Gay Science*, §125). Marx thinks of it rather as the preexistence of the human. Freud's discovery of the uncomprehended meaningfulness of human expression belongs in the line of such prophecy. Emerson's philosophical distinction here lies in his diagnosis of this moment and in his recommended therapy.

It is as a diagnosis of this state of the world that Emerson announces that Descartes's proof of self-existence (the foundation, Descartes named it, of the edifice of his former opinions, the fixed and immovable fulcrum on which to reposition the earth) cannot, or can no longer, be given, thus asking us to conclude (such is the nature of this peculiar proof) that man, the human, does not, or does no longer, exist. Here is Emerson's sentence again, together with the sentence and a half following it: "Man is timid and apologetic; he is no longer upright; he dares not say 'I think,' 'I am,' but quotes some saint or sage. He is ashamed before the blade of grass or the blowing rose . . . they are for what they are; they exist with God today." We can locate Emerson's proposed therapy in this vision of so-called man's loss of existence if we take the successive notations of this vision as in apposition, as interpretations of one another: being apologetic; being no longer upright; daring not to say, but only quoting; being ashamed, as if for not existing today. There are, as Wittgenstein is once moved to express himself (§525), a multitude of familiar paths leading off from these words in all directions. Let us take, or at least point down, two or three such paths.

To begin with, the idea that something about our mode of existence removes us from nature, and that this has to do with being ashamed, of course alludes to the romantic problematic of self-consciousness (or the post-Kantian interpretation of that problematic), a particular interpretation of the Fall of Man. But put Emerson's invocation of shame in apposition to his invocation of our loss of up-rightness, and he may be taken as challenging, not passing on, the romantic interpretation of the Fall as self-consciousness, refusing to regard our shame as a metaphysically irrecoverable loss of innocence but seeing it instead as an unnecessary acquiescence (or necessary only as history is necessary) in, let me say, poor posture, a posture he calls timidity and apologeticness. I will simply claim, without citing textual evidence (preeminently the contexts in which the word "shame" and its inflections are deployed throughout Emerson's essay), that the proposed therapy is to become ashamed of our shame, to find our ashamed posture more shameful than anything it could be reacting to. One might say that he calls for more, not less, self-consciousness; but it would be better to say that he shows self-consciousness not to be the issue it seems. It, or our view of it, is itself a function of poor posture.

But really everything so far said about existence, preexistence, and so forth may be some function of poor posture—including, of course, our view of what poor posture may be. Bad posture Emerson variously names, in one passage, as peeping or stealing or skulking up and down "with the air of a charity-boy, a bastard, or an interloper in the world which exists for him"; in another, he finds men behaving as if their acts were fines they paid "in expiation of daily non-appearance on parade," done "as an apology or extenuation of their living in the world—as invalids and the insane pay a high board. Their virtues are penances." This vision of human beings as in postures of perpetual penance or self-mortification will remind readers of *Walden* of that book's opening pages (not to mention Nietzsche's *Genealogy of Morals*).

Good posture has two principal names or modes in "Self-Reliance": standing and sitting. The idea behind both modes is that of finding and taking and staying in a place. What is good in these postures is whatever makes them necessary to the acknowledgment, or the assumption, of individual existence, to the capacity to say "I." That this takes daring is what standing (up) pictures; that it takes claiming what belongs to you and disclaiming what does not belong to you is what sitting pictures. Sitting is thus the posture of being at home in the world (not peeping, stealing, skulking, or, as he also says, leaning), of owning or taking possession. This portrayal of the posture of sitting is, again, drawn out in *Walden*, at the opening of the second chapter ("Where I Lived, and What I Lived For") where what Thoreau calls acquiring property is what most people would consider passing it by. Resisting the temptation to follow the turnings of these paths, I put them at once in apposition to the notation that in not daring to say something what we do instead is to quote.

There is a gag here that especially appeals to contemporary sensibilities. Emerson writes, "Man dares not say . . . but quotes." But since at that moment he quotes Descartes, isn't he confessing that he too cannot say but can only quote? Then should we conclude that he is taking back or dismantling (or something) the entire guiding idea of "Self-Reliance"? Or is he rather suggesting that we are to overcome the binary opposition between saying and quoting, recognizing that each is always both, or that the difference is undecidable? That difference seems to me roughly the difference between what Thoreau calls the mother tongue and the father tongue, hence perhaps makes the difference between language and literariness. And since I am taking the difference between saying and quoting as one of posture, the proposal of undecidability strikes me as the taking of a posture, and a poor one. I imagine being told that the difference in posture partakes of the same undecidability. My reply is that you can decide to say so. My decision is otherwise. (It is helped by my intuition that a guiding remark of Freud's is conceivable this way: Where thought takes place in me, there shall I take myself.)

Emerson's gag, suggesting that saying is quoting, condenses a number of ideas. First, language is an inheritance. Words are before I am; they are common. Second, the question whether I am saying them or quoting them—saying them firsthand or secondhand, as it were—which means whether I am thinking or imitating, is the same as the question whether I do or do not exist as a human being and is a matter demanding proof. Third, the writing, of which the gag is part,

113

is an expression of the proof of saying "I," hence of the claim that writing is a matter, say the decision, of life and death, and that what this comes to is the inheriting of language, an owning of words, which does not remove them from circulation but rather returns them, as to life.

That the claim to existence requires returning words to language, as if making them common to us, is suggested by the fourth sentence of "Self-Reliance": "To believe your own thought, to believe that what is true for you in your private heart is true for all men,—that is genius." (One path from these words leads to the transformation of the romantics' idea of genius: Genius is not a special endowment, like virtuosity, but a stance toward whatever endowment you discover is yours, as if life itself were a gift, and remarkable.) Genius is accordingly the name of the promise that the private and the social will be achieved together, hence of the perception that our lives now take place in the absence of either.

So Emerson is dedicating his writing to that promise when he says: "I shun father and mother and wife and brother when my genius calls me. I would write on the lintels of the door-post, *Whim*." (I will not repeat what I have said elsewhere concerning Emerson's marking of Whim in the place of God and thus staking his writing as a whole as having the power to turn aside the angel of death.) The point I emphasize here is only that the life-giving power of words, of saying "I," is your readiness to subject your desire to words (call it Whim), to become intelligible, with no assurance that you will be taken up. ("I hope it may be better than Whim at last, but we cannot spend the day in explanation.") Emerson's dedication is a fantasy of finding your own voice, so that others, among them mothers and fathers, may shun you. This dedication enacts a posture toward, or response to, language as such, as if most men's words as a whole cried out for redemption: "Conformity makes them not false in a few particulars, authors of a few lies, but false in all particulars . . . so that every word they say chagrins us and we know not where to begin to set them right."

Citing authorship as the office of all users of language, a thing as commonly distributed as genius, is the plainest justification for seeing the enactment or acknowledgment of one's existence as the authoring of it and in particular for what we may take as Emerson's dominating claims for his writing: first, that it proves his human existence (i.e., establishes his right to say "I," to tell himself from and to others); second, that what he has proven on his behalf, others are capable of proving on theirs.

These claims come together in such a statement as "I will stand for humanity," which we will recognize as marking a number of paths: that Emerson's writing is in an upright posture; that what it says represents the human, meaning both that his portrait of himself is accurate only insofar as it portrays his fellows and that he is writing on their behalf (both as they stand, and as they stand for the eventual, what humanity may become); that he will for the time being stand humanity, bear it, as it is; and that he will stand up for it, protect it, guard it, presumably against itself. But to protect and guard someone by writing to and for that same one means to provide them instruction, or tuition.

The path I am not taking at this point leads from Emerson's speaking of "primary wisdom as Intuition," to which he adds, "All later teachings are tuitions." I note this path to commemorate my annoyance at having to stand the repeated, conforming description of Emerson as a philosopher of intuition, a description that uniformly fails to add that he is simultaneously the teacher of tuition, as though his speaking of all later teachings as tuitions were a devaluing of the teachings rather than a direction for deriving their necessary value. Take the calling of his genius as a name for intuition. Marking *Whim* on his doorpost was intuition's tuition; an enactment of the obligation to remark the calling, or access, of genius; to run the risk (or, as Thoreau puts it, to sit the risk) of noting what happens to you, of making this happenstance notable, remarkable, thinkable—of subjecting yourself, as said, to intelligibility.

How could we test the claim Emerson's writing makes to be such enactment, its claim to enact or acknowledge itself, to take on its existence, or, in Nietzsche's words, or rather Zarathustra's (which I imagine are more or less quoting Emerson's), to show that Emerson "does not say 'I' but performs 'I'" ("On the Despisers of the Body," p. 34)? (The mere complication of self-reference, the stock-in-trade of certain modernizers, may amount to nothing more than the rumor of my existence.) How else but by letting the writing teach us how to test it, word by word?

"Self-Reliance" as a whole presents a theory—I wish we knew how to call it an aesthetics—of reading. Its opening words are "I read the other day," and four paragraphs before Emerson cites the cogito he remarks, "Our reading is mendicant and sycophantic," which is to say that he finds us reading the way he finds us doing everything else. How can we read his theory of reading in order to learn how to read him? We would already have to understand it in order to understand it. I have elsewhere called this the (apparent) paradox of reading; it might just as well be called the paradox of writing, since of writing meant with such ambitions we can say that only after it has done its work of creating a writer (which may amount to sloughing or shaking off voices) can one know what it is to write. But you never know. I mean, you never know when someone will learn the posture, as for themselves, that will make sense of a field of movement, it may be writing, or dancing, or passing a ball, or sitting at a keyboard, or free associating. So the sense of paradox expresses our not understanding how such learning happens. What we wish to learn here is nothing less than whether Emerson exists, hence could exist for us; whether, to begin with, his writing performs the cogito he preaches.

He explicitly claims that it does, as he must. But before noting that, let me pause a little longer before this new major path, or branching of paths: the essay's theory of reading, hence of writing or speaking, hence of seeing and hearing. The theory, not surprisingly, is a theory of communication, hence of expression, hence of character—character conceived, as Emerson always conceives it, as naming at once, as faces of one another, the human individual and human language. The writing side of the theory is epitomized in the remark: "Character teaches above our wills. Men imagine that they communicate their virtue or vice only by overt actions, and do not see that virtue or vice emit a breath every moment." The reading side of the theory is epitomized in: "To talk of reliance is a poor external way of speaking. Who has more obedience than I masters me, though he should not raise his finger."

On the reading side, the idea of mastering Emerson is not that of controlling him, exactly (though it will be related to monitoring him), but rather that of coming into command of him, as of a difficult text, or instrument, or practice. That this mastery happens by obedience, which is to say, by a mode of listening, relates the process to his dedicating of his writing as heeding the call of his genius, which to begin with he is able to note as Whim. It follows that mastering his text is a matter of discerning the whim from which at each word it follows. On the writing side, the idea of communicating as emitting a breath every moment (as if a natural risk of writing were transmitting disease) means that with every word you utter you say more than you know you say (here genteel Emerson's idea is that you cannot smell your own breath), which means in part that you do not know in the moment the extent to which your saying is quoting.

(Let me attract attention to another untaken path here, on which one becomes exquisitely sensible of the causes of Nietzsche's love of Emerson's writing. I am thinking now of Nietzsche's *Ecce Homo,* a book about writing that bears the subtitle *How One Becomes What One Is.* Its preface opens with the declaration that the author finds it indispensable to say who he is because in his conversations with the educated he becomes convinced that he is not alive; the preface continues by claiming or warning that to read him is to breathe a strong air. This book's opening part, "Why I Am So Wise," closes by saying that one of its author's traits that causes difficulty in his contacts with others is the uncanny sensitivity of his instinct for cleanliness: the innermost parts, the entrails, of every soul are *smelled* by him [pp. 233–34].)

So the question Emerson's theory of reading and writing is designed to answer is not "What does a text mean?" (and one may accordingly not wish to call it a theory of interpretation) but rather "How is it that a text we care about in a certain way (expressed perhaps as our being drawn to read it with the obedience that masters) invariably says more than its writer knows, so that writers and readers write and read beyond themselves?" This might be summarized as "What does a text know?" or, in Emerson's term, "What is the genius of the text?"

Here I note what strikes me as a congenial and fruitful conjunction with what I feel I have understood so far of the practices of Derrida and of Lacan. Others may find my conjunction with these practices uncongenial if, for example, they take it to imply that what I termed the genius of the text, perhaps I should say its engendering, is fatal to or incompatible with the idea of an author and of an author's intention. This incompatibility ought to seem unlikely since both genius and intending have to do with inclination, hence with caring about something and with posture. Austin, in a seminar discussion at Harvard in 1955, once compared the role of intending with the role of headlights (on a miner's helmet? on an automobile?). (This material is published under the title "Three Ways of Spilling Ink.") An implication he may have had in mind is that driving somewhere (getting something done intentionally) does not on the whole happen by hanging a pair of headlights from your shoulders, sitting in an armchair, picking up an unattached steering wheel, and imagining a destination. (Though this is not unlike situations in which W. C. Fields has found himself.) Much else has to be in place—further mechanisms and systems (transmission, fuel, electrical), roads, the industries that produce and are produced by each, and so on—in order for headlights and a steering mechanism to do their work, even to be what they are. Even if some theorists speak as though intention were everything there is to meaning, is that a sensible reason for opposite theorists to assert that intention is nothing, counts for nothing in meaning? Is W. C. Fields our only alternative to Humpty Dumpty?[1]

---

1. In linking W. C. Fields's suffering of convention with Humpty Dumpty's claim to be master, by his very wishes, of what words shall mean (and thinking of his fate), I find I have not forgotten a passage during the discussions of "Must We Mean What We Say?" the day I delivered it in 1957 (at Stanford, it happens). Against a certain claim in my paper, one philosopher cited Humpty Dumpty's view of meaning (by name) as obviously, in all solemnity, the correct one. This was, I think, the first time I realized the possibility that parody is no longer a distinguishable intellectual tone since nothing can any longer be counted on to strike us in common as outrageous.

But I was about to locate Emerson's explicit statement, or performance, of his cogito. In his eighth paragraph he writes: "Few and mean as my gifts may be, I actually am, and do not need for my own assurance or the assurance of my fellows any secondary testimony." Earlier in the paragraph he had said: "My life is for itself and not for a spectacle. . . . I ask primary evidence that you are a man, and refuse this appeal from the man to his actions." And two paragraphs later he will promise: "But do your work, and I shall know you."

In refusing the evidence of actions, or say behavior, Emerson is refusing, as it were before the fact, the thrashing of empiricist philosophy to prove the existence of other minds by analogy with one's own case, which essentially involves an appeal to others' behavior (and its similarity to our own) as all we can know of them with certainty. But how does Emerson evade and counter the picture on which such a philosophical drift repeatedly comes to grief, namely the picture according to which we cannot literally or directly have the experiences of others, cannot have what it is he apparently calls "primary evidence" of their existence? Emerson's counter is contained in the idea of what I called his promise: "But do your work, and I shall know you." Your work, what is yours to do, is exemplified, when you are confronted with Emerson's words, by reading those words—which means mastering them, obeying and hence following them, subjecting yourself to them as the writer has by undertaking to enact his existence in saying them. The test of following them is, according to Emerson's promise, that you will find yourself known by them, that you will take yourself on in them. It is what Thoreau calls conviction, calls being convicted by his words, read by them, sentenced. To acknowledge that I am known by what this text knows does not amount to agreeing with it, in the sense of believing it, as if it were a bunch of assertions or as if it contained a doctrine. To be known by it is to find thinking in it that confronts you. That would prove that a human existence is authored in it. But how will you prove thinking? How will you show your conviction?

One possibility Emerson presents as follows: "The virtue in most request is conformity. Self-reliance is its aversion." This almost says, and nearly means, that you find your existence in conversion, by converting to it, that thinking is a kind of turning oneself around. But what it directly says is that the world of conformity must turn from what Emerson says as he must turn from it and that since the process is never over while we live—since, that is, we are never finally free of one another—his reader's life with him will be a turning from, and returning from, his words, a moving on from them, by them. In "Fate," Emerson will call this aversion "antagonism": "Man is a stupendous antagonism," he says there. I can testify that when you stop struggling with Emerson's words they become insupportable.

But why does self-reliance insist that it will know its other, even create its other, meaning authorize the other's self-authorization, or auto-creation? Because it turns out that to gain the assurance, as Descartes had put it, that I am not alone in the world has turned out to require that I allow myself to be known. (I have called this requirement subjecting myself to intelligibility, or, say, legibility.) But doesn't this beg the question whether there *are* others there to do this knowing?

I would say rather that it orders the question. The fantasy of aloneness in the world may be read as saying that the step out of aloneness, or self-absorption, has to come without the assurance of others. (Not, perhaps, without their help.) "No one comes" is a tragedy for a child. For a grown-up it means the time has come to be the one who goes first (to offer oneself, allow oneself, to be, let us say, known). To this way of thinking, politics ought to have provided conditions for companionship, call it fraternity; but the price of companionship has been the suppression, not the affirmation, of otherness, that is to say, of difference and sameness, call these liberty and equality. A mission of Emerson's thinking is never to let politics forget this.

In declaring that his life is not for a spectacle but for itself, Emerson is not denying that it is a spectacle, and he thus inflects and recrosses his running themes of being seen, of shame, and of consciousness. A last citation on this subject will join "Self-Reliance" with Poe's "Imp of the Perverse."

In his fifth paragraph, Emerson says: "The man is as it were clapped into jail by his consciousness. As soon as he has once acted or spoken with *éclat* he is a committed person, watched by the sympathy or the hatred of hundreds, whose affections must now enter into his account. There is no Lethe for this." The idea is that we have become permanently and unforgettably visible to one another, in a state of perpetual theater. To turn aside consciousness, supposing that were possible, would accordingly only serve to distract us from this fact of our mutual confinement under one another's guard. The solution must then be to alter what it is we show, which requires turning even more watchfully to what it is we are conscious of and altering our posture toward it.

For example: "A man should learn to detect and watch that gleam of light which flashes across his mind from within, more than the lustre of the firmament of bards and sages. Yet he dismisses without notice his own thought, because it is his. In every work of genius we recognize our own rejected thoughts; they come back to us with a certain alienated majesty." Here I find a specification of finding myself known in this text; in it certain rejected thoughts of mine do seem to come back with what I am prepared to call alienated majesty (including the thought itself of my rejected thoughts). Then presumably this writer has managed not to dismiss his own thoughts but to call them together, to keep them on parade, at attention. ("Tuition" speaks differently of being guarded; and unguarded.)

Yet he speaks from the condition of being a grown-up within the circumstances of civil (or uncivil) obedience he describes, so he says all he says clapped into jail by his consciousness—a decade before Thoreau was clapped into jail, and for the same reason, for obeying rejected things. How is he released? If, going on with Emerson's words, there were Lethe for our bondage to the attention of others, to their sympathy or hatred, we would utter opinions that would be "seen to be not private but necessary, would sink like darts into the ear of men and put them in fear"—that is, my visibility would then frighten my watchers, not the other way around, and my privacy would no longer present confinement but instead the conditions necessary for freedom. But as long as these conditions are not known to be achieved, the writer cannot know that I am known in his utterances, hence that he and I have each assumed our separate existences. So he cannot know but that in taking assurance from the promise of knowing my existence he is only assuming my existence and his role in its affirmation, hence perhaps shifting the burden of proof from himself and still awaiting me to release him from his jail of consciousness, the consciousness of the consciousness of others. When is writing *done?*

THAT "SELF-RELIANCE" MAY ACCORDINGLY be understood to show writing as a message from prison forms its inner connection with Poe's "Imp of the Perverse." (The thought of such a message, of course, forms other connections as well—for example, with Rousseau's *Social Contract,* whose early line, "Man is born free and everywhere he is in chains," names a condition from which the writer cannot be exempting his writing, especially if his interpretation of his writing's enchainment is to afford a step toward the freedom it is compelled, by its intuition of chains, to imagine.) I can hardly do more here than give some directions for how I think Poe's tale should, or anyway can, be read. This is just as well, because the validation of the reading requires from first to last that one take the time to try the claims on oneself. The claims have generally to do with the sound of Poe's prose, with what Emerson and Nietzsche would call its air or its smell. Poe's tale is essentially about the breath it gives off.

The sound of Poe's prose, of its incessant and perverse brilliance, is uncannily like the sound of philosophy as established in Descartes, as if Poe's prose were a parody of philosophy's. It strikes me that in Poe's tales the thought is being worked out that, now anyway, philosophy exists only as a parody of philosophy, or rather as something indistinguishable from the perversion of philosophy, as if to overthrow the reign of reason, the reason that philosophy was born to establish, is not alone the task of, let us say, poetry but is now openly the genius or mission of philosophy itself. As if the task of disestablishing reason were the task of reconceiving it, of exacting a transformation or reversal of what we think of as thinking and so of what we think of as establishing the reign of thinking. A natural effect of reading such writing is to be unsure whether the writer is perfectly serious. I dare say that the writer may himself or herself be unsure, and that this may be a good sign that the writing is doing its work, taking its course. Then Poe's peculiar brilliance is to have discovered a sound, or the condition, of intelligence in which neither the reader nor the writer knows whether he or she is philosophizing, is thinking to some end. This is an insight, a philosophical insight, about philosophy: namely, that it is as difficult to stop philosophizing as it is to start. (As difficult, in Wittgenstein's words, as to bring philosophy peace [§133]. Most people I know who care about philosophy either do not see this as a philosophical problem or do not believe that it has a solution.)

A convenient way of establishing the sound of Poe's tales is to juxtapose the opening sentences of "The Black Cat" with some early sentences from Descartes's *Meditations*. Here is Descartes:

> There is no novelty to me in the reflection that, from my earliest years, I have accepted many false opinions as true, and that what I have concluded from such badly assured premises could not but be highly doubtful and uncertain. . . . I have found a serene retreat in peaceful solitude. I will therefore make a serious and unimpeded effort to destroy generally all my former opinions. . . . Everything which I have thus far accepted as entirely true and assured has been acquired from the senses or by means of the senses. But I have learned by experience that these senses sometimes mislead me, and it is prudent never to trust wholly those things which have once deceived us. . . . But it is possible that, even though the senses occasionally deceive us . . . there are many other things which we cannot reasonably doubt . . . —as, for example, that I am here, seated by the fire, wearing a winter dressing gown, holding this paper in my hands, and other things of this nature. And how could I deny that these hands and this body are mine, unless I am to compare myself with certain lunatics . . . [who] imagine that their head is made of clay, or that they are

121

gourds, or that their body is glass? . . . Nevertheless, I must remember
that I am a man, and that consequently I am accustomed to sleep and in
my dreams to imagine the same things that lunatics imagine when
awake. . . . I realize so clearly that there are no conclusive indications by
which waking life can be distinguished from sleep that I am quite astonished, and my bewilderment is such that it is almost able to convince me
that I am sleeping.

Now listen to Poe:

For the most wild, yet almost homely narrative which I am about to pen,
I neither expect nor solicit belief. Mad indeed would I be to expect it, in
a case where my very senses reject their own evidence. Yet, mad am I
not—and very surely do I not dream. But to-morrow I die, and today I
would unburthen my soul. My immediate purpose is to place before the
world, plainly, succinctly, and without comment, a series of mere household events. In their consequences, these events have terrified—have tor-
tured—have destroyed me. Yet I will not attempt to expound them.

The juxtaposition works both ways: to bring out at once Poe's brilliance
(and what is more, his argumentative soundness) and Descartes's
creepy, perverse calm (given the subjects his light of reason rakes
across), his air of a mad diarist.

Moreover, the *Meditations* appear within the content of "The Imp
of the Perverse," as indelibly, to my mind, as in "Self-Reliance." Before
noting how, let me briefly describe this lesser-known tale. It is divided
into two parts, each more or less eight paragraphs in length. The first
half is, as Poe says about certain of Hawthorne's tales, not a tale at all
but an essay. The essay argues for the existence of perverseness as a
radical, primitive, irreducible faculty or sentiment of the soul, the propensity to do wrong for the wrong's sake, promptings to act for the
reason that we should not—something it finds overlooked by phrenologists, moralists, and in great measure "all metaphysicianism," through
"the pure arrogance of the reason." This phrase "the pure arrogance of
the reason," to my ear, signals that Poe is writing a *Critique* of the
arrogance of pure reason—as if the task, even after Kant, were essentially incomplete, even unbegun. (This characterization is not incompatible with the appreciation of Poe as a psychologist, but only with a
certain idea of what psychology may be.) The second half of "The Imp
of the Perverse," which tells the tale proper, begins:

I have said thus much, that in some measure I may answer your question—that I may explain to you why I am here—that I may assign to you
something that shall have at least the faint aspect of a cause for my wear-

ing these fetters, and for my tenanting this cell of the condemned. Had I not been thus prolix, you might either have misunderstood me altogether, or, with the rabble, have fancied me mad. As it is, you will easily perceive that I am one of the many uncounted victims of the Imp of the Perverse.

Since we have not been depicted as asking, or having, a question, the narrator's explanation insinuates that we ought to have one about his presence; thus it raises more questions than it formulates.

The tale turns out to be a Poe-ish matter about the deliberately wrought murder of someone for the apparent motive of inheriting his estate, a deed that goes undetected until some years later the writer perversely gives himself away. As for the means of the murder: "I knew my victim's habit of reading in bed. . . . I substituted, in his bed-room candlestand, a [poisoned] wax-light of my own making, for the one which I there found." The self-betrayal comes about when, as he puts it, "I arrested myself in the act." That act is murmuring, half-aloud, "I am safe," and then adding, "yes, if I be not fool enough to make open confession." But "I felt a maddening desire to shriek aloud. . . . Alas! I well, too well understand that, to *think*, in my situation, was to be lost. . . . I bounded like a madman through the crowded thoroughfare. At length, the populace took the alarm, and pursued me."

To the first of my directions for reading "The Imp" I expect nowadays little resistance: both the fiction of the writer's arresting himself and wearing fetters and tenanting the cell of the condemned and the fiction of providing a poisonous wax light for reading are descriptions or fantasies of writing, modeled by the writing before us. There is, or at least we need imagine, no actual imprisoning and no crime but the act of the writing itself. What does it mean to fantasize that words are fetters and cells and that to read them, to be awake to their meaning, or effect, is to be poisoned? Are we being told that writer and reader are one another's victims? Or is the suggestion that to arrive at the truth something in the reader as well as something in the writer must die? Does writing ward off or invite in the angel of death?

I expect more resistance to, or puzzlement at, the further proposal that the fiction of words that are in themselves unremarkable ("I am safe"), but whose saying annihilates the sayer, specifies the claim that "I well, too well understand that, to *think*, in my situation, was to be lost"—which is a kind of negation or perversion of the cogito. Rather than proving and preserving me, as in Descartes, thinking precipitates my destruction. A little earlier Poe's narrator makes this even clearer: "There is no passion in nature so demoniacally impatient, as that of him, who shuddering on the edge of a precipice, thus meditates a plunge. To indulge for a moment, in any attempt at *thought,* is to be inevitably lost; for reflection but urges us to forbear, and *therefore* it is, I say, that we *cannot* . . . we plunge, and are destroyed." If the Whim drawing on Emerson's "Self-Reliance" is to say "I do not think, therefore I do not exist," that of Poe's Imp is to say, "I think, therefore I am destroyed." This connection is reinforced, in this brief pasage, by the words "meditates" and "demoniacally." Poe's undetected, poisoned wax light may even substitute for, or allude to, Descartes's most famous example (of materiality) in the *Meditations,* the piece of melting wax whose identity cannot be determined empirically, but only by an innate conception in the understanding. (That in Poe's tale the act of thinking destroys by alarming the populace and turning them against the thinker and that perverseness is noted as the confessing of a crime, not the committing of it—as if the confessing and the committing were figurations of one another—mark paths of parody and perverseness I cannot trace here. That thinking will out, that it inherently betrays the thinker— [th]inker—is a grounding theme of *Walden.* Its writer declares in the opening chapter, "Economy," that what he prints must in each character "thus unblushingly publish my guilt." He says this upon listing the costs of what he ate for the year. It is as if his guilt consists exactly in keeping himself alive ("getting a living," he says) in his existing, as he exists, and his preserving himself, for example, by writing.)

My third suggestion for reading Poe's tale is that the presiding image collecting the ideas I have cited and setting them in play is given in its title. The title names and illustrates a common fact about language, even invokes what one might think of as an Emersonian theory of language: the possession of language as the subjection of oneself to the intelligible. The fact of language it illustrates is registered in the series of imp words that pop up throughout the sixteen paragraphs of the tale: *impulse* (several times), *impels* (several times), *impatient* (twice), *important, impertinent, imperceptible, impossible, unimpressive, imprisoned,* and, of course, *Imp.* Moreover, *imp.* is an abbreviation in English for *imperative, imperfect, imperial, import, imprimatur, impersonal, implement, improper,* and *improvement.* And *Imp.* is an abbreviation for *Emperor* and *Empress.* Now if to speak of the imp of the perverse is to name the imp in English, namely as the initial sounds of a number of characteristically Poe-ish terms, then to speak of something called the perverse as containing this imp is to speak of language itself, specifically of English, as the perverse. But what is it about the imp of English that is perverse, hence presumably helps to produce, as users of language, us imps?

It may well be the prefix *im-* that is initially felt to be perverse, since, like the prefix *in-,* it has opposite meanings. With adjectives it is a negation or privative, as in *immediate, immaculate, imperfect, imprecise, improper, implacable, impious, impecunious;* with verbs it is an affirmation or intensive, as in *imprison, impinge, imbue, implant, impulse, implicate, impersonate.* (It is not impossible that *per-verse,* applied to language, should be followed out as meaning poetic through and through.) In plain air we keep the privative and the intensive well enough apart, but in certain circumstances (say in dreams, in which, according to Freud, logical operations like negation cannot be registered or pictured but must be supplied later by the dreamer's interpretation) we might grow confused about whether, for example, *immuring* means putting something into a wall or letting something out of one, or whether *impotence* means powerlessness or a special power directed to something special, or whether *implanting* is the giving or the removing of life, or whether *impersonate* means putting on another personality or being without personhood.

But the fact or idea of imp words is not a function of just that sequence of three letters. "Word imps" could name any of the recurrent combinations of letters of which the words of a language are composed. They are part of the way words have their familiar looks and sounds, and their familiarity depends upon our mostly not noticing the particles (or cells) and their laws, which constitute words and their imps—on our not noticing their necessary recurrences, which is perhaps only to say that recurrence constitutes familiarity. This necessity, the most familiar property of language there could be—that if there is to be language, words and their cells must recur, as if fettered in their orbits, that language is grammatical (to say the least)—insures the self-referentiality of language. When we do note these cells or molecules, these little moles of language (perhaps in thinking, perhaps in derangement), what we discover are word imps—the initial, or it may be medial or final, movements, the implanted origins or constituents of words, leading lives of their own, staring back at us, calling upon one another, giving us away, alarming—because to note them is to see that they live in front of our eyes, within earshot, at every moment.

But the perverseness of language, working without, even against, our thought and its autonomy, is a function not just of necessarily recurring imps of words but of the necessity for us speakers of language (us authors of it, or imps, or Emperors and Empresses of it) to mean something in and by our words, to desire to say something, certain things rather than others, in certain ways rather than in others, or else to work to avoid meaning them. Call these necessities the impulses and the implications of the saying of our words. There is—as in saying "I am safe," which destroyed safety and defeats what is said—a question whether in speaking one is affirming something or negating it. In particular, in such writing as Poe's has the impulse to self-destruction, to giving oneself away or betraying oneself, become the only way of preserving the individual? And does it succeed? Is authoring the obliteration or the apotheosis of the writer?

In the passage I cited earlier from "The Black Cat," the writer does not speak of being in fetters and in a cell, but he does name his activity as penning; since the activity at hand is autobiography, he is penning himself. Is this release or incarceration? He enforces the question by going on to say that he will not expound—that is, will not remove something (presumably himself) from a pound, or pen. But this may mean that he awaits expounding by the reader. Would this be shifting the burden of his existence onto some other? And who might we be to bear such a burden? Mustn't we also seek to shift it? Granted that we need one another's acknowledgment, isn't there in this very necessity a mutual victimization, one that our powers of mutual redemption cannot overcome? Is this undecidable? Or is deciding this question exactly as urgent as deciding to exist?

I WILL DRAW TO A close by forming three questions invited by the texts I have put together.

First, what does it betoken about the relation of philosophy and literature that a piece of writing can be seen to consist of what is for all the world a philosophical essay preceding, even turning into, a fictional tale—as it happens, a fictional confession from a prison cell? To answer this would require a meditation on the paragraph, cited earlier, in which Poe pivots from the essay to the tale, insinuating that we are failing to ask a question about the origin of the writing and claiming that without the philosophical preface—which means without the hinging of essay and tale, philosophy and fiction—the reader might, "with the rabble, have fancied me mad," not perceiving that he is "one of the many uncounted victims of the Imp of the Perverse." The meditation would thus enter, or center, on the idea of counting, and it is one I have in fact undertaken, under somewhat different circumstances, as part 1 of *The Claim of Reason.*

There I interpret Wittgenstein's *Philosophical Investigations,* or its guiding idea of a criterion, hence of grammar, as providing in its responsiveness to skepticism the means by which the concepts of our language are *of* anything, as showing what it means to have concepts, how it is that we are able to word the world together. The idea of a criterion I emphasize is that of a way of counting something as something, and I put this together with accounting and recounting, hence projecting a connection between telling as numbering or computing and telling as

relating or narrating. Poe's (or, if you insist, Poe's narrator's) speaking
pivotally of being an uncounted victim accordingly suggests to me that
philosophy and literature have come together (for him, but who is he?)
at the need for recounting, for counting again, and first at counting the
human beings there are, for reconceiving them—a recounting beginning from the circumstances that it is I, some I or other, who counts,
who is able to do the thing of counting, of conceiving a world, that it
is I who, taking others into account, establish criteria for what is worth
saying, hence for the intelligible. But this is only on the condition that
I count, that I matter, that it matters that I count in my agreement or
attunement with those with whom I maintain my language, from
whom this inheritance—language as the condition of counting—
comes, so that it matters not only what some I or other says but that it
is some particular I who desires in some specific place to say it. If my
counting fails to matter, I am mad. It is being uncounted—being left
out, as if my story were untellable—that makes what I say (seem) perverse, that makes me odd. The surmise that we have become unable to
count one another, to count for one another, is philosophically a surmise that we have lost the capacity to think, that we are stupefied.[2] I call
this condition living our skepticism.

Second, what does it betoken about fact and fiction that Poe's
writing of the Imp simultaneously tells two tales of imprisonment—in
one of which he is absent, in the other present—as if they are fables of
one another? Can we know whether one is the more fundamental? Here
is the relevance I see in Poe's tale's invoking the situation of Hamlet, the
figure of our culture who most famously enacts a question of undecidability, in particular, an undecidability over the question whether to
believe a tale of poisoning. (By the way, Hamlet at the end, like his
father's ghost at the beginning, claims to have a tale that is untellable—
it is what makes both of them ghosts.) In Poe's tale, the invocation of
Hamlet is heard, for example, in the two appearances of a ghost, who
the first time disappears upon the crowing of a cock. And it is fully
marked in the second of the three philosophical examples of perversity
that Poe's narrator offers in order to convince any reader, in his words,
"who trustingly consults and thoroughly questions his own soul" of
"the entire radicalness of the propensity in question":

2. I find it hard not to imagine that this surmise has to do with the history of
the frantic collection of statistical tables cited in Ian Hacking's "Making Up People," and
"Prussian Statistics." Emerson's essay "Fate" self-consciously invokes the new science of
statistics as a new image of human fate—a new way in which others are finding us captured by knowledge and which Emerson finds a further occasion for ignorance.

The most important crisis of our life calls, trumpet-tongued, for immediate energy and action. We glow, we are consumed with eagerness to
commence the work. . . . It must, it shall be undertaken today, and yet
we put it off until to-morrow; and why? There is no answer, except that
we feel *perverse,* using the word with no comprehension of the principle.
To-morrow arrives, and with it a more impatient anxiety to do our duty,
but with this very increase of anxiety arrives, also, a nameless, a positively
fearful because unfathomable, craving for delay.

These words invoke Hamlet along lines suspiciously like those in which
I have recently been thinking about what I call Hamlet's burden of
proof—but no more suspiciously, surely, than my beginning to study
Poe while thinking about Hamlet.

Hamlet studies the impulse to take revenge, usurping thought as
a response to being asked to assume the burden of another's existence,
as if that were the burden, or price, of assuming one's own, a burden
that denies one's own. Hamlet is asked to make a father's life work out
successfully, to come out even, by taking his revenge for him. The emphasis in the question "to be or not" seems not on whether to die but
on whether to be born, on whether to affirm or deny the fact of natality,
as a way of enacting, or not, one's existence. To accept birth is to participate in a world of revenge, of mutual victimization, of shifting and
substitution. But to refuse to partake in it is to poison everyone who
touches you, as if taking your own revenge. This is why if the choice is
unacceptable the cause is not metaphysics but history—say, a posture
toward the discovery that there is no getting even for the oddity of
being born, hence of being and becoming the one poor creature it is
given to you to be. The alternative to affirming this condition is, as
Descartes's *Meditations* shows, world-consuming doubt, which is hence
a standing threat to, or say condition of, human existence. (I imagine
that the appearance of the cogito at its historical moment is a sign that
some conditions were becoming ones for which getting even, or anyway overcoming, was coming to seem in order: for example, the belief
in God and the rule of kings.) That there is something like a choice or
decision about our natality is what I take Freud's idea of the diphasic
structure of human sexual development (in "Three Essays") to show—a
provision of, so to speak, the condition of the possibility of such a decision. The condition is that of adolescence, considered as the period in
which, in preparation for becoming an adult, one recapitulates, as suffering rebirth, one's knowledge of satisfactions. This is why, it seems to
me, one speculates about Hamlet's age but thinks of him as adolescent.
These matters are represented in political thought under the heading of

consent, about which, understandably, there has from the outset been a question of proof.

Finally, what does it betoken about American philosophy that Emerson and Poe may be seen as taking upon themselves the problematic of the cogito (Emerson by denying or negating it, Poe by perverting or subverting it) and as sharing the perception that authoring—philosophical writing, anyway, writing as thinking—is such that to exist it must assume, or acknowledge, the proof of its own existence? I have in effect said that to my mind this betokens their claim to be discovering or rediscovering the origin of modern philosophy, as sketched in Descartes's *Meditations*, as if literature in America were forgiving philosophy, not without punishing it, for having thought that it could live only in the banishing of literature. What does it mean that such apparent opposites as Emerson and Poe enter such a claim within half a dozen years of one another?

Let us ask what the connection is between Emerson's ecstasies (together with Thoreau's) and Poe's horrors (together with Hawthorne's). The connection must be some function of the fact that Poe's and Hawthorne's worlds, or houses and rooms, have other people in them, typically marriages, and typically show these people's violent shunning, whereas Emerson's and Thoreau's worlds begin with or after the shunning of others ("I shun father and mother and wife and brother when my genius calls me") and typically depict the "I" just beside itself. The interest of the connection is that all undertake to imagine domestication, or inhabitation—as well, being Americans, they might. For Emerson and Thoreau you must learn to sit at home or to sit still in some attractive spot in the woods, as if to marry the world, before, if ever, you take on the burden of others; for Poe and Hawthorne even America came too late, or perhaps too close, for that priority.

A more particular interest I have in the connection among these American writers is a function of taking their concepts or portrayals of domestication and inhabitation (with their air of ecstasy and of horror turned just out of sight) to be developments called for by the concepts of the ordinary and the everyday as these enter into the ordinary language philosopher's undertaking to turn aside skepticism, in the pains Austin and Wittgenstein take to lay out what it is that skepticism threatens. In the work of these philosophers, in their stubborn, accurate superficiality, perhaps for the first time in recognizable philosophy this threat of world-consuming doubt is interpreted in all its uncanny homeliness, not merely in isolated examples but, in Poe's words, as "a series of mere household events."

I end with the following prospect. If some image of marriage, as an interpretation of domestication, in these writers is the fictional equivalent of what these philosophers understand to be the ordinary, or the everyday, then the threat to the ordinary named skepticism should show up in fiction's favorite threat to forms of marriage, namely, in forms of melodrama. Accordingly, melodrama may be seen as an interpretation of Descartes's cogito, and, contrariwise, the cogito can be seen as an interpretation of the advent of melodrama—of the moment (private and public) at which the theatricalization of the self becomes the sole proof of its freedom and its existence. This is said on tiptoe.

POSTSCRIPT A
Skepticism and a Word concerning Deconstruction

During the discussion period at Stanford, Professor David Wellbery asked about how I conceive the relation of what I have been doing over the years to what deconstructionists have been doing. It is not the first time I have been asked something like this. Indeed the issue first arose in 1969, in the months after the publication of my *Must We Mean What We Say?* when a friend who had spent a decade and more of sabbatical leaves and summer vacations in Germany and France studying philosophy announced that what I wrote bore surprising and specific resemblances to the writing of Jacques Derrida, a name that I was hearing for the first time. Mostly, I guess, I feel that to locate and trace out these resemblances, along with their companion disparities, is not my business, that if this work of contrast has profit in it, others are better placed to realize it than I. But Professor Wellbery's full and detailed question was so courteous, and so clear and specific, that I have recalled it several times in the months since the conference, each time with regret at how little I was able to say in response. I take the occasion of these printed proceedings to acknowledge that fact and to give at least a better account of the poverty of my answer.

Careful not to deny the immeasurable, perhaps incommensurable, distance of provenance and style between such work as Derrida's and such work as my present essay, Wellbery noted certain affinities between them: for example, as I recall them, affinities in turning philosophy upon philosophy, especially by refusing to favor the philosophical or the literary over one another, in content or in form; in attending to the endlessness of language's responsiveness to (even origin in) language, a responsiveness pervading bits and pieces of words; and, not least, in my

130

having found my way to Poe, whom Wellbery informed me Derrida has also taken up with philosophical respect. In the light of these and other affinities, Wellbery asked about my impatience with the idea of the "undecidable" at several points in my paper.

If impatience is what it was, it was directed not toward Derrida but toward a conjunction of writings by those who adopt his terms and whose papers and chapters I characteristically find myself unable to finish. I am not proud of this, any more than of how difficult I find it to study Derrida. It perfects my bafflement that those who follow him seem to find what he writes *easy* to follow and summarize and assess. I feel subjected to a family discussion, not mine, yet mine, impertinent and pertinent (as Thoreau almost characterizes his neighbors at the opening of *Walden*), the prevailing issues of which, too many of the voices of which, are not among the rumors of my past, not up to me to turn; someone is refusing, and someone is getting, satisfactions that I am not alive to. This certainty alone is apt to make one impatient, to make one look for an exit. At the conference I responded by saying that the deconstructionist use of the term "undecidable," so far as I have encountered it, tends to sound like a soft literary pretension to hard philosophy, to be invoking Gödel's world-historical proof of unprovability only to (mis)describe issues concerning discontinuities or undercontinuities between grammar and rhetoric, or supercontinuities between narrations of fact and of fiction, or of reality and of dreams. ("The coffee is hot" may be an observation, a hint, a request, an explanation, an excuse, a warning—or hallucinated. So—in each case—what?)

This kind of objection—to the soft putting on hard clothing—might play itself out otherwise in terms of differences between what I say about Emerson's accusation of quotation and what I know, or must guess, of deconstructionist accounts of the matter. This is for another occasion, perhaps. But the issue, if I understand, promises to be a pretty one. It turns on a shared sense of the fatefulness of the fact that language is inherited, learned, always already there for every human. This sense can prompt divergent responses or emphases. One (I take it the deconstructionist emphasis) will see the fact of inheritance as undermining the distinction between quoted words and their originals: since all words are learned, you may say all are imitated or quoted; but then none are quoted, since there are no originals for them to contrast with. The other emphasis (represented by Wittgenstein, but also, I take it, by Emerson and Thoreau) will not wish to deny the truth in the first emphasis, but it will see that emphasis as deflecting attention, as rushing too quickly away, from the act or encounter entailed in the historical and individual process of inheriting. This second, practical emphasis falls not on the acquisition of the grammar or structure of a language but on the scene of instruction in words. The *Philosophical Investigations* opens with a (quoted) scene of instruction from Augustine's *Confessions,* and the ensuing 693 sections constituting part 1 of the *Investigations* can be understood as following out implications of that scene. The scene is explicitly, repeatedly invoked with each recurrence in the *Investigations* of the figure of the child. I sometimes find this figure to represent the most distinctive of all Wittgenstein's departures in philosophy. Something the recurring figure means to me is that the inheritance of language is essentially never over and done with— though any number of accidents, or say fixations, inner or outer, may put an end to it. The play of the literary is one field on which the contest of inheritance is shown to be continued, or continuable, within each breast, each text; the play of philosophy, as in the humor or frivolity of Austin and of Wittgenstein, is another—as if the inheriting of language is itself formed of the willingness for play, and continues as long as the willingness continues. (It is an essential piece of the inheritance I seek of Wittgenstein and Austin.) By contrast, the play in deconstructionist flights more often feels, to my ear or for my taste, somewhat forced, willful, as if in reaction to a picture of a completed inheritance, as if to undo its trauma. (A comparatively unforced text, perhaps, to work with here is Derrida's marvelously interesting "Coming into One's Own," which contains a study of the "Fort/Da" scene in the second section of Freud's *Beyond the Pleasure Principle,* another scene of instruction, inheritance of language, and a game.)

When Emerson notices, in "Self-Reliance," that "every word they say chagrins us," he is responding to the sound of quotation, imitation, repetition (conformity, confinement, etc.), but for him this sound sets a task of practice, not (merely) a routine for metaphysics—rather, it criticizes metaphysics not as a necessary defeat of thought but as a historical defeat of practice. (This sounds familiar. But Emerson may call undefeated practice, as he calls undefeated thought, "abandonment," which should not sound familiar; it combines bereavement and ecstasy.) And when Wittgenstein finds the task of philosophy to be the bringing of our words back to (everyday) life, he in effect discerns two grades of quotation, imitation, repetition. In one we imitatively declare our uniqueness (the theme of skepticism); in the other, we originally declare our commonness (the theme of acknowledgment). (Individuality, always to be found, is always at the risk of loss.) What you might call philosophy can be in service of either possibility; hence philosophy is never at peace with itself. Too often deconstructive procedures (like analytical procedures) seem to me readily used to bring philosophy a false peace, which may well present itself in the form of bustling activity.

This sense of philosophy's opposite possibilities is, at any rate, why I am drawn (and take the likes of Emerson and Wittgenstein to be drawn) not to undermine but to underline such distinctions as that between quoting and saying. I can imagine that this might be said of deconstruction too. Then style and its obligations become the issue—what I might call the address of language, or the assumption of it, perhaps the stake in it. I have most consecutively followed the consequences of (something like) the distinction between saying and quoting in my *The Senses of Walden,* which can as a whole be taken as a meditation on Thoreau's distinction between what he calls the mother tongue and the father tongue (see *Senses,* pp. 14–16). (This is something like—and nothing like—the distinction between speaking and writing. In *The Claim of Reason* it is at one point registered as the difference between what I call the first and the second inheritance of language [p. 189]. By the fourth and last part of that book the pressure of this question takes precedence over the presiding theme of the earlier parts, which is, within the first inheritance, how and when one speaks inside and outside language games.) Because the mother and the father are not two tongues but name two addresses to or assumptions of or stakes in whatever language we have, and because the father tongue is said by Thoreau to be a "reserved and select expression," which is the "maturity and experience" of the mother, it follows that the father tongue is both later and at the same time more original than the mother tongue. Accordingly there is a locale in which quotation becomes more original than its original. Does this deconstruct the distinction between words as quoted and as originally said? It seems to me (rather?) to invite the question whether words such as "quotation" and "original" are being used in the mother or in the father tongue; hence of course to invite the further question whether the differences of the mother and the father (in us) are to be erased or erected.

Go back once more to my sense of literary softness posing as philosophical hardness. We may postpone the question whether that distinction is itself soft or hard by taking particular cases. What harm would be done if someone wished to characterize the shifting duck-rabbit as undecidably a duck or else a rabbit? This might be harmless, even charming, so long as it did not rule out wishing (with straightforward accuracy) to describe the same figure as *decidably* a duck or else a rabbit. But unless the concept rules something out, what is the point of applying it? What harm if one wishes, taking an even colder cliché, to characterize Duchamp's exhibited urinal, entitled "Fountain," as undecidably a work of art or else not a work of art? Although this might do less harm than the arguments that Duchamp's nasty brilliance has so far inspired, it might do worse harm, since it would instill the thought that the idolized urinal is decidably art or the reverse. (I do not claim that this is impossible for some minds to think, but I expect they will be ones who would like to decide whether others are human or not.) But isn't the characterization "undecidable" at minimum a helpful antidote to the philosophical craving for essence? Now I wish to take on Wittgenstein's suggestion that "essence is expressed by grammar" (*Investigations*, §371), that in other words the philosophical craving for essence has been not so much directed to the wrong goal (seeing an explanation to its end somewhere) as wrongly addressing the goal (seeing the somewhere all explanations end). Have I just decided something?

Where, then, in a constellation of duplicitous objects and layered intentions shall we locate Poe's "Imp of the Perverse?" In my paper I said that the two readings, one focusing on the narrator, the other on the writer, are not on a par: the fictional prisoner is unmistakable, the actual writer is not; the narrator of this story may not exist apart from this story, but the writer must. So what sense is there in saying that there is duplicity here at all? In what sense are there two prisoners, two poisonings, two confessions, two disappearances? If we say that one is an allegory of the other, would that constitute an answer? Would it repudiate the question? I imagine someone might wish to say that the difference between one and two is undecidable. You might as well tell me that the existence of marriage is undecidable (on roughly the same ground, that it is undecidable whether two have become one). I would not wish to deny the conclusion, but I would feel that you are theorizing in the wrong place. And how can I, as a reader of the writer of *Walden*, remembering him describing himself as "caged in the woods"— which is to say, as penned in America—take the view that whether this is fiction or fact, allegory or event, is undecidable? Such a claim seems to me the place of what there is to decide. If it is allegory then he (who?) *is* penned; that is, he is whatever (else) his being caged allegorizes. Here I must come to a decision about what this makes me, his reader. Am I a visitor or a spectator? His keeper? Is he my adornment? Who domesticated him? Can I threaten to let him loose? Upon whom? What is his difference from me?

I use the doubleness of the Poe stories, as interpreting the structure of skepticism, to ask, to begin, investigations: of the extent to which writing as telling allegorizes our apparent fate of projecting ourselves as fictions, of appealing to others by theatricalizing ourselves, so that I can never be satisfied that their response is to *me* (Poe's world has advanced beyond Descartes's in having to consider that the author of myself and the narrator of myself may no longer be different persons, if still different selves); hence of the extent to which the resulting dissatisfaction may be a function, or price, of the satisfaction of projecting imaginary characters as real; and finally of what writing as penning is, what there is in it that can be represented as imprisonment, as deserving confinement, even as accepting it (perhaps all too easily).

I end this postscript by relating its issues more generally to the work my paper is intended to extend.

Whether when you say "I'll see you at home" you mean your words as a prediction, an agreement, a promise, an aspiration, or a decision is not a matter for decision, but a matter of the responsibility you bear—or take, or find, or disclaim—for your words. To call the matter undecidable may be just a way of affirming that the words "can" be taken these various ways (which is important, but not news) or a way of denying that you have this responsibility (which is not a fact; it may be a blindness, a posture, or perhaps a decision). In a more radical vein, "There is my home" may be said while pointing to your home or in a dream of pointing to your home (which may or may not resemble anything you now say is home). Nothing in the words will distinguish the real (referential?) from the dream (nonreferential?) occasion, and this difference is again not up for decision. (If it were up for decision, it would follow that life is as a matter of fact a dream, because only in a dream can you *decide* whether you are dreaming or awake.)

That such a thing is not up for decision is the pivot on which skepticism turns. In *The Claim of Reason* I describe this pivot as the limit of criteria, as criteria coming to an end (too soon, as it were), as there being no criteria (say marks or features) for distinguishing dreams from reality (or the animate from the inanimate, or the natural from the artificial). Knowing one from the other is not a matter of telling differences between them. To conclude that such issues are undecidable would be to decide that the conclusion of skepticism is true, that we never know so certainly but that we can doubt. This, to my mind, trivializes the claim of the skeptic, whose power lies not in some decision, but in his apparent discovery of the ineluctable fact that we cannot know; at the same time it theatricalizes the threat, or the truth, of skepticism: that it names our wish (and the possibility of our wishing) to strip ourselves of the responsibility we have in meaning (or in failing to mean) one thing, or one way, rather than another. Perhaps our most practical courses against the impositions of philosophy are indeed either to trivialize or to theatricalize them. But to me such courses seem to give up the game; they do not achieve what freedom, what useful idea of myself, there may be for me, but seem as self-imposed as the grandest philosophy—or, as Heidegger might almost have put it, as unself-imposed.

To indicate how far down the road a satisfying allocation of these matters is likely to take us, I would like to quote the last paragraph of part 2 ("Skepticism and the Existence of the World") of *The Claim of Reason*. The paragraph invokes the issue of logical positivism's abusive or prejudicial idea of decision, which I had thematically taken to task in a section of "The Availability of Wittgenstein's Later Philosophy," written about the same time. It suggests accordingly that today's advanced literary use of the idea of the undecidable is produced by the same distortion or prejudice as yesterday's advanced philosophical use of the decidable. So to me it appears that I am fighting the same battle, but now on an opposite flank.

> If the existence of the world, and our knowledge of its existence, becomes a real, a sensed problem, is it enough to say, with Carnap, "To accept the thing-world means nothing more than to accept a certain form of language, in other words, to accept rules for forming statements and for testing, accepting, or rejecting them?" ("Empiricism, Semantics, and Ontology," p. 211.) We might feel, Accepting the "thing-world" is just accepting the world, and what kind of choice do we have about that? (I don't say there isn't one.) And what kind of choice do we have about accepting a form of language? We can accept or reject whatever in language *we* can construct. . . . If we can't *decide* that (we will say that) the things of our world exist, shall we say that we *believe* they exist? That is something a philosopher will say in the course of that rehearsal of our beliefs with which he begins his investigation of their validity as a whole. But that rehearsal does not *express* belief in anything; it contains no claims. Or shall we say that we have *faith* that the things of our world exist? But how is that faith achieved, how expressed, how maintained, how deepened, how threatened, how lost? [Pp. 242–43]

I have been made aware that although *The Claim of Reason* is long it is still compressed. Let me, then, briefly decompress the final sentence I have quoted from it. The sentence is not vaguely rhetorical or vaguely psychological. It asks for particular opening pieces of the grammar (in Wittgenstein's sense) of "faith." (It is part of the grammar of "faith" that *this* is what we call "to lose one's faith," etc.) The implication is: if these pieces of grammar have no clear application to the case of the existence of the things of the world, then the concept of faith has no clear application to this case. Then what is our relation to the case of the world's existence? Or should we now see that there is nothing that constitutes this relation? Or see that there is no one something? What would it be to see such things?

POSTSCRIPT B
Poe's Perversity and the Imp(ulse) of Skepticism

Looking back at Robert Penn Warren's essay on *The Ancient Mariner,* I see I had forgotten that he adduces the following paragraph from Poe's "The Black Cat."

> In the meantime the cat slowly recovered. The socket of the lost eye presented, it is true, a frightful appearance, but he no longer appeared to suffer any pain. He went about the house as usual, but, as might be expected, fled in extreme terror at my approach. I had so much of my old heart left, as to be at first grieved by the evident dislike on the part of a creature which had once so loved me. But this feeling soon gave place to irritation. And then came, as if to my final and irrevocable overthrow, the spirit of Perverseness. Of this spirit philosophy takes no account. Yet I am not more sure that my soul lives, than I am that perverseness is one of the primitive impulses of the human heart—one of the indivisible primary faculties, or sentiments, which give direction to the character of Man. Who has not, a hundred times, found himself committing a vile or a silly action, for no other reason than because he knows he should *not?* Have we not a perpetual inclination, in the teeth of our best judgment, to violate that which is *Law,* merely because we understand it to be such? This spirit of perverseness, I say, came to my final overthrow. It was the unfathomable longing of the soul *to vex itself*—to offer violence to its own nature—to do wrong for the wrong's sake only—that urged me to continue and finally to consummate the injury I had inflicted upon the unoffending brute. One morning, in cold blood, I slipped a noose about its neck and hung it to the limb of a tree;—hung it with the tears streaming from my eyes, and with the bitterest remorse at my heart;—hung it *because* I knew that in so doing I was committing a sin—a deadly sin that would so jeopardize my immortal soul as to place it—if such a thing were possible—even beyond the reach of the infinite mercy of the Most Merciful and Most Terrible God.

Some of this can indeed sound similar, should, to the view I have taken of the Mariner's killing of the bird. Poe's view and mine both assert some relation between the wish to be loved and the fear of it, and between this conflict and the sense that one's existence lies under some metaphysical suspicion. The views also seem opposite, since mine takes the moral to demand that one accept the claim of others as the price of knowing or having one's existence, whereas Poe—rather, Poe's narrator—asserts the denial or annihilation of the other as that price. I might

137

try to fix the distance between these views by noting my having said (in the closing pages of *The Claim of Reason*) that Othello kills Desdemona not because she is faithless and disperses love but on the contrary because she is faithful, because the very reciprocity of the thing he has elicited from her is what makes him feel sullied. Poe's words are, "hung it because I knew that it *had loved* me" (my emphasis), which, if this means that the love has now been withdrawn, however understandable the cause, would be a reasonably understandable case of rage and vengefulness.

But then again, are these views so different? Poe's (narrator's) revenge would still be taken because he was loved, perhaps because he feels the love was too little, or because love is too little. Whereas to murder or abandon as Othello does, because the love of you persists, is hardly an acceptable return of love, perhaps feeling that the love was too much, or because love is too much. The views seem closer and more distant than this makes out.

I have claimed that skepticism is our philosophical access to the human wish to deny the conditions of humanity, relating this, as well as to Kant's vision, both to Christianity's and to Nietzsche's hopes for the human to be overcome. Along this line we might understand Poe as asserting that skepticism itself is the best assurance of existence, as if skepticism's very will to emptiness should draw us to it. This apparently perverse account of skepticism (turning its effect into its cause) bears to familiar philosophical accounts of skepticism something like the relation Poe's paragraph from "The Black Cat," in its arrangement of sin and law and the Most Merciful and Most Terrible God, bears to St. Paul's account of such things. As if it reads Paul's saying that there were no sin but for the law, and reads it to advise, Break the law. One may take this as an insight into Christianity or as a parody of it.

What I am calling Poe's perverse account of skepticism does, I think, capture an essential perverseness in skepticism, at once granting an insight into skepticism and enacting a parody of it. The insight is that skepticism, the thing I mean by skepticism, is, or becomes, necessarily paradoxical, the apparent denial of what is for all the world undeniable. I take skepticism not as the moral of a cautious science laboring to bring light into a superstitious, fanatical world, but as the recoil of a demonic reason, irrationally thinking to dominate the earth. I take it to begin as a wish not to reject the world but rather to establish it. The parody is to deny this, to conceal the longing for assurance under an allegedly more original wish for self-vexation. This concealment is revealed at the end of the confessional stories, when the walls (inner or outer) are broken open and the repressed returns. But if the murder of the world (or the soul) will out, in these stories the end is as perverse as the beginning, or rather the perversity is still unmoved, still original, and tragedy and its recognition are still deflected into inscrutably multiplied ironies. (G. R. Thompson, in introducing his selection of Poe's short works speaks of Poe's writing "as the work of one of the greatest ironists of world literature.")

Poe's view, so characterized, is a materialization, no doubt ironic, of the most familiar understanding I used to hear of philosophical skepticism in school, and one that I believe retains a certain currency yet. It is the view, roughly, that skepticism's repudiation of knowledge is merely a function of having set the sights of knowledge too high: *of course* if you impose the idea of absolute certainty on knowledge, you will not find that we know anything (except perhaps mathematics, together with what, if anything, is given to the senses); *of course* if you try to turn induction into deduction, induction will seem wanting; *of course* if you demand that in order to see an object you have to see *all* of the object, then we can never really or directly or immediately *see* an object. (I give other examples of this pattern, especially with respect to the question whether a critical paraphrase, say of a metaphor, is really a paraphrase, in "Aesthetic Problems of Modern Philosophy," pp. 76–77.) So skepticism is just the cause of the disappointments of which it complains. People have said this about philosophy as a whole. And earlier I alluded to a similar understanding of romanticism, as wanting in its disappointments (say, in melancholy or withdrawal) exactly what cannot exist.

I had not understood how a philosopher could claim to be satisfied with such an understanding of skepticism, in the absence of an understanding of how, and by what, a human being, call him or her a philosopher, would be drawn to "set the sights" so, drawn to just *this* form of self-defeat. Now, however, as a version of Poe's discrimination of perversity, it begins to make sense to me. What I am to conceive is that the self-defeat of skepticism is precisely the point of it. —But does this finally make sense to me? Or is its *not* exactly making sense something I should further regard as precisely its point?

I do not, as I said, object to the idea of perversity as a description of the skeptic's outcome; I accept it as a kind of translation of the paradoxicality which is an essential feature of the skepticism I mean. It is, as elsewhere, the attitude that rings false to me, or forced. (But does attitude much matter where what is at stake is the truth?) As I do not take the owner of Pluto—for that was the cat's name—to feel about the wife into whose head he buried an axe just the way Othello feels about the wife he suffocated, so I do not take the narrator committing and confessing his denials to be the Cartesian or the Humean or the Kantian thinker bringing himself back from, or giving himself up for, his deeds of doubt, back to the brink of the common world.

The attitude I am pointing to is one typically presented upon the promulgation of a paradox. When Pythagoras proved what has been called the incommensurability of the long side of a right triangle with the other (equal) sides, also called its measurement by an irrational number, some were frightened, some tried to keep the secret confined to an institution of intellectuals, some, I dare say right at the beginning, took it as a cosmic joke on humankind. Something similar will have happened in this century when Gödel's proof of formally undecidable propositions became known. So some seem to find these attitudes appropriate toward the discovery that there are no marks or features by which to distinguish dreams from waking life, of fiction from fact, literature from life, as though this kind of indistinguishability made them identical—as though literature and life were known to be familiar objects and the issue remaining were to decide whether they are to be counted as one or as two. —Well, if not a sense of absurdity, or of ironic pleasure or pain, at the dashable hopes of humankind, what attitude would you recommend? —None.

I might describe the attitude I find myself resisting, the posture I would alter toward the events of horror in Poe's stories, as one in which the narrator is "acting-out" a fantasy or an unconscious impulse, as opposed (as Freud does typically oppose "acting-out," thus partially defining it) to remembering something, an opposite way of bringing the past into the present, a way that brings the promise of a freedom from the violence and the alienatedness of the impulsion to repeat.[1]

Since remembering is the organ of that way of philosophizing to which I am drawn, naturally I am distrustful of what would oppose it. Sometimes you could call this the merely literary, or impulsive playfulness, which may sometimes take the form of a technical and seemingly rigorous discourse. Far be it from me either to take it for granted that psychoanalysis has made sufficiently clear Freud's distinction between repeating and remembering (in "Remembering, Repeating, and Working Through"), or to take Poe the writer as sufficiently like his narrator to be indistinguishable intellectually from him. But whether Poe is sufficiently unlike his narrator to draw on our (of course I mean my) philosophical interest, is a function of how interesting and convincing an account his discourse provides by way of grounding the notion of per-

---

1. See the entry under "Acting-out" in J. Laplanche and J.-B. Pontalis, *The Language of Psycho-Analysis*.

versity; of, that is to say, accounting for the human temptation to deny the conditions of humanity, or in other words, the will to be monstrous.

The question as to the existence of myself, or creation of myself, is modeled by Poe as the existence of a writer, who exists simultaneously with the writing, only as it is being written, uttered. Users of language, humans are creatures of language, exist only from it, as equally it exists only from us. If one is perverse so is the other. If we cannot speak (if, e.g., we have something so terrible to say that it either cannot be said or cannot be believed) we are inhuman. If the responsibility for speech is suffocating, you might think of enacting a deed so horrible that speech seems impossible; you might choose to become a monster. (Here it may be worth comparing Wittgenstein's speculation concerning what a private language would be.)

When the narrator of "The Imp of the Perverse" asks us to question our own soul in order to find undeniably "the entire radicalness of the propensity [viz., perverseness] in question," the example he thereupon appeals to is the torment "by an earnest desire to tantalize a listener by circumlocution," which is to say, the torment of the desire to tell stories, even (as this tale manifests) the torment of the desire to write a certain kind of philosophy—thus using himself (whom else would a skeptic invoke?) as the image or scapegoat of mankind. I mention one further region of the unsayable in Poe's tale, a region that is not a function of the imps in language but of ourselves as its imp and image: our power of affirmation (without which there is no assertion), hence of denial.

Years after the narrator has committed a perfect crime, impossible to detect, the narrator's imp presented itself and made detection possible.

> I would perpetually catch myself pondering upon my security, and repeating, in a low undertone, the phrase, "I am safe." One day, whilst sauntering along the streets, I arrested myself in the act of murmuring, half aloud, these customary syllables. In a fit of petulance, I remodelled them thus:—"I am safe—I am safe—yes—if I be not fool enough to make open confession!"

That is, "I am safe" is true as long as it is not said; saying refutes it. More famous sayings whose saying refutes them are "This statement is not true" and "I do not exist." (It may thereupon occur to you that [therefore] "I exist" is necessarily true, or undeniably true each time it is said.) But you equally cannot safely say, in Poe's depicted circumstances, "I am not safe." (Hence this example is unlike other unsayables, like "I am not here" and "I am asleep." These are pleasantries, and their negations are, in certain circumstances, informative.) One's safety, or lack of it, is unknowable. What can be known is the fact of one's existence, and whatever follows from that. Philosophers such as Descartes and Kant and Heidegger and Wittgenstein may agree on this point, and vary completely in what it is they find to follow. One may further try out the thought that the knowledge philosophers such as Marx and Kierkegaard and Nietzsche (and you may say Freud) begin from is that we do *not* exist, and vary in what they find follows from that.

It seems reasonably clear that Poe's (narrator's) search for a proof of his (her?) existence (in the confessional tales I was citing) is for a proof that he breathes, that is, that he is alive. "I am not more certain that I breathe, than that the assurance of the wrong or error of any action is often the one unconquerable *force* which impels us, and alone impels us, to its prosecution." Assume that he is betraying here an uncertainty that he breathes; and then turn around his comparison of certainties. The imp of himself here apparently gives him to think that he is not *less* certain that he breathes than that there is the impulsion in question. So his certainty of breathing becomes dependent on his impulse to wrongdoing. In Descartes the capacity for "the wrong or error of any action" is the proof of the possession of free will. For Descartes it follows that we are responsible for our error because we are free not to refrain from it (in particular, free to judge beyond the knowable). For Poe we are responsible metaphysically for our errors exactly because we are not morally responsible for them. I *am* the one who cannot refrain. Some moralists are of the view that when I do what I am impelled to do, the action is not exactly mine. Poe's view seems to be that in such case the responsibility is never discharged—it sticks to me forever. Of course not all actions are of such a kind but only ones that show what I have been calling the inhuman in the human, the monstrousness of it, ones that, I would like to say, come before and after morality: an example Poe gives of the former is the desire to tantalize in telling a good tale; examples of the latter are the more baroque Poe-behaviors, gouging out the eye of the cat, axing your wife, almost without provocation. The implication is that morality is stumped at certain points in judging human nature, a fact that should illuminate both those points "before" and those "after" morality. If there is a target of satire here, it is those who say they believe in determinism, who do not appreciate how free we are (capable of things it is hard to imagine) and how far from free (incapable of resisting this imagination).

"The Imp of the Perverse" opens with an explanation for our having overlooked perversity as a *primum mobile* of the human soul—all of us, the "phrenologists" and "all the moralists who have preceded them." The explanation is: "We saw no *need* for the impulse—for the propensity. We could not perceive its necessity. We could not understand, that is to say, we could not have understood, had the notion of this *primum mobile* ever obtruded itself;—we could not have understood in what manner it might be made to further the objects of humanity." And a little further on:

> It will be said, I am aware, that when we persist in acts because we feel we should *not* persist in them, our conduct springs from the *combativeness* of phrenologists. But combativeness is our safeguard against injury. Its principle regards our well-being. . . . It follows, that the desire to be well must be excited simultaneously with any principle which shall be a modification of combativeness, but in the case of that something which I term *perverseness,* the desire to be well is not only not aroused, but a strongly antagonistical sentiment exists.

Is this antagonistical sentiment a sentiment to be ill, which here must mean a desire to be injured? Say if you like (G. R. Thompson says it in the introduction to his edition of Poe cited earlier) that "the 'The Imp of the Perverse' clearly spells out Poe's fundamental conception that it is man's fate to act against his own best interests." But I see no original desire for self-injury in the tale, however much self-injury results from the events. True, the imp may have to forfeit perverseness as a "safeguard against injury;" that is not the kind of need that the evolution of perverseness can be understood to serve. But perhaps it is a safeguard against something else, something more original, even humanly more needful—a safeguard against annihilation, the loss of (the proof of) identity or existence altogether. (I am perhaps cagily masking the question as to what the proof of human life would primarily be directed to, to its existence or to its identity. To say both are in question is easy, if doubtless true. The question is about priorities.) God's existence has been said to follow from God's identity. Human existence no more follows from its identity than the existence of a stone is assured from a description of a stone. But unlike a stone, a human identity is not assured, as certain existentialists used to like to say, from the fact that a human being exists. Romantics are brave in noting the possibility of life-in-death and of what you might call death-in-life. My favorite romantics are the ones (I think the bravest ones) who do not attempt to escape these conditions by taking revenge on existence. But this means willing to continue to be born, to be natal, hence mortal.

One has to distinguish *what* it is that proofs of my existence are supposed to, or do, prove; what question it is one has to answer. Descartes's proof proves my existence as mind, it answers the question "Am I a mind or a body?" Psychoanalysis has distinguished the question

143

"Am I a woman or am I a man?" from the question "Am I alive or dead?"—the former as the hysterical question, the latter as the obsessional. Obviously I am taking the latter as Poe's question. But I earlier complicated what this will mean by in effect also giving him the question "Am I a human being or a monster?" (I have said a few words about these questions in "On Makavejev On Bergman," in relation to *The Claim of Reason*.)

The desire to be well is preceded by the desire to be. And against annihilation, ceasing to exist as the one I am, there is no safeguard, none suppliable by the individual, not even God's hand in our creation; its safeguard is the recognition of and by others. (So saying "I am safe" may in a sense save you after all.) If at the same time this recognition of and by others strikes you as threatening your life, you will be perplexed. I think we all more or less know of this perplexity. But to struggle with it by impulsively or obsessionally proposing that to gain proof you have to create (to be the author of) what there is to confess, as though there is nothing to acknowledge but in such confession, is comparatively trivial. It is trivial in comparison with the effort to acknowledge your unauthorized life as it is, taking an interest in it. Some will, I think, wish to say that there is no way one's life is; to me this betokens a refusal to try putting it into (provisional) words (a refusal to struggle for its authorship).

Poe's Perverseness may be seen as a parody of the vulnerability, the dropping of safeguard, in the placing of interest, in Poe's cases, the investment of love, the inevitable risks in its improbabilities. The truth of the parody is its measure of the pain these risks run, of how far our lives take on and maintain their forms by their need to ward off abandonment.

POSTSCRIPT C
The Skeptical and the Metaphorical

I had cause to be grateful to Robert Mankin's study "An Introduction to *The Claim of Reason*" from the moment I first read it, a few years ago, as I was preparing "Emerson, Coleridge, Kant," chapter 2 of the present volume. Looking over the chapter now, I am struck by its responsivness to what Mankin has to say, and I am glad for the occasion to say so and thank him. That essay of mine is inflected by two especially of Mankin's lines of inquiry, which I might formulate in something like the following questions: (1) What does it betoken about what I mean when I say "literature" that my instances of the concept are so often works of Shakespeare or of what is called romanticism; and in particular how do these instances bear on the more or less implicit theme of the relation (if that is the word) between philosophy and literature that recurs, even builds, in *The Claim of Reason*? (2) What causes the repeated, perhaps not uniformly important or accurate, confessions or accusations in the book to the effect that one is "forced" or "driven" to certain (modifications of?) concepts?

About (1). In "Emerson, Coleridge, Kant," I take romanticism to mark the (modern) struggle of philosophy and poetry for and against one another, for and against their own continued existence. Why there is, or comes to be, such a struggle is, it is implied, a philosophical and a poetic, no less than a historical, issue. The cause is something to which I assign, or extend, the name skepticism. The later lecture of mine, "Being Odd, Getting Even," to which this note is a postscript, extends further this way of looking at things. It finds in Poe (and suggests that it may be found in Hawthorne), on some other side of the American romantic mind from the side of Emerson and Thoreau, that philosophy undergoes something I describe as "turning into" literature. (Then what becomes of literature?) While such limited forays as I have reported will hardly count as answers to questions concerning the bearing of philosophy and literature on one another, I expect them to count as preparations for such answers.

About (2). "Emerson, Coleridge, Kant" rather features a discussion of being "forced" or "driven," through its discussions of Emerson's "Fate" and of Kant's and Coleridge's stories in which a "line" is transgressed. "Being Odd, Getting Even" furthers the discussion by aligning this issue of transgression with certain of Poe's words concerning "perverseness," as interpreted through a concept I construct from Poe's practice with what I call word imps. What perhaps interests me most, in this light, in the Poe material, apart from the alignment itself, is my suggestion that to take Poe as it were psychologically (I suppose the most familiar way of taking him) is to eclipse taking Poe as it were philosophically. Psychologically speaking, it seems that Poe is singling out certain rather extreme human types, his first person first among them, who are subject to sudden fits of violence that set them apart from the race of ordinary human souls; whereas philosophically Poe is singling out his first person as representative of an unnaturalness natural to the human soul, a thing whose violence is as casual as it is inevitable. If not, Poe would not pertain to skepticism, as I see it.

Again, I do not wish to imply that I think these extensions (as of invitations) of my interest are sufficient answers to Mankin's queries. His essay brings forth many issues with a seriousness that I very much appreciate. Some of his formulations I do not feel I as yet understand sufficiently well to do much with directly, as for example his remark that "the most deeply social of experiences may thus transcend our human forms of life and deserve other names like myth or literature or psychosis." Other contributions I gratefully accept as directly in the spirit, and opening out the range, of an issue as I broached it, for example the adducing of Laplanche's discussion of Freud's concept of "deferred action" in connection with what I had to say concerning Wittgenstein's "vision of (learning and teaching) language."

I should like to mention, in this connection, for future reference, a possible point of disagreement that may be worth pursuing in some earnest. Mankin asks at one point: "Is metaphor less essential to language than its generality?" as though I had rather suggested that metaphor was indeed less essential. His question is prompted by my discussion of what I call projecting a word, in chapter 7 ("Excursus on Wittgenstein's Vision of Language") of *The Claim of Reason*. I do not find my discussion to devalue metaphor's essentiality. The discussion is meant to gloss Wittgenstein's implied attack in traditional philosophical "explanations" of the generality of language which invoke what was called "universals." Mankin says of the discussion: "Metaphor has no place in this account, for Cavell, because it is always conceived as . . . 'unnatural.'" But in ending my chapter with the thought that metaphorical "transfer" is, in contrast with nonmetaphorical "projection," aptly describable as unnatural, I rather imagined that making, or showing, metaphor's "place" in language is just what I was about. It is true that the moral of this passage is that the metaphorical is implicitly shunned as an explanation of the generality of language; but this is hardly a slighting of the metaphorical, since my claim is that nothing (philosophical) will constitute such an explanation. Nor does it follow from this that the metaphorical is not "essential" to what we think of as language.

Perhaps my use of "unnatural" in this, as in other contexts, was unintuitive or, at any rate, confusing in conjunction with what I repeatedly say about the naturalness of natural language, especially about the way this naturalness is at once appealed to and repudiated in the skeptic's assault on our "knowledge" of the existence of things. It is this conjunction that leads Mankin to speculate that "Cavell may be reserved about discussing figurative language just to the extent that it points to the forcing element (and generality) in all conventions." I am not sure that I recognize myself under this description. If I am reserved about discussing figurative language in *The Claim of Reason*, the cause is more immediately, I would say, my dissatisfaction with the identifications and theories of figurative language that I have come across, and perhaps above all with my sense that the importance of the figurative in those theories seems somehow to go without saying, as if it held the key to language, to literariness, to the (destructive) ambitions of philosophy, etc. Perhaps the figurative strikes me as of no more importance than whatever it is supposed to exist in contrast with, say the literal. Now, of course, you can take the issue of the literal to have to do with the letters of language in such a way that it does not contrast with, but conceivably becomes an instance of, the figurative. But how do you tell that this does not simply change the subject? In any case, while my animus in the passage about the unnaturalness of metaphorical transfer was to signal that I had accounted for the "generality," or say conceptuality, in language in such a way that metaphoricality can be seen as the derivative issue (in opposition to claims or rumors that the reverse must be the correct relation), the issue is evidently at once standing and shifting, begging more study.

Failing that here, I will conclude these introductory words by beginning to clarify the ambiguity, in case it has been harmful, in my invoking the concept of the (un)natural in considering both the path of skepticism and the path of the metaphorical.

What makes skepticism unnatural is its occasion for coming to repudiate our criteria for applying the concepts of our language to anything; repudiating, I call this, our attunement with one another, a repudiation Wittgenstein calls our (being led to be) speaking outside language games. This begins in casualness but it continues in drivenness and hauntedness, finding rest (such as it will be) in a particular structure (of absolute "see-ables," fixed perspectives, decontextualized, or depersonalized, "meanings") from within which language seems a prison, or wasteland. This is not the rest, or rather the peace, that Wittgenstein declares he wishes to bring philosophy. Skepticism's rest looks more like a parody than like a renunciation of philosophy's mad ambitions. Wittgenstein's claim to bring peace may well elicit a knowing smile—as if this is in our time the way a gadfly likes to speak. But it might also strike one as a healthy hint for reading the work of the *Investigations,* a hint that the wish to bring peace is at all times to be seen as a search for philosophy's silence, a philosophical silence of whatever kind an unappeasable and embattled creature is capable of, say an end to meaningless wars, to wars of meaninglessness. The idea would be of the therapeutic not as a place but as a path. It is in this spirit that I emphasize skepticism's inherent "instability"—both of its beginning and of its ending moments.

What makes metaphor unnatural is its occasion to transcend our criteria; not as if to repudiate them, as if they are arbitrary; but to expand them, as though they are contracted. (The ordinary [or Wittgensteinian] grammar of "sun" must be preserved if the metaphorical application of it to Juliet is to carry; for example, the criteria for its rising and setting and its being obscured or eclipsed and its causing growth and thirst, and for its shining as something that, in creating day, hence night, lights the moon as well as the earth.) And metaphor transcends criteria not as if to repudiate our mutual attunement but as if to pressure this attunement (under which pressure certain of our attunements with others will fail; but with certain others the attunement will be intensified and refined). In the realm of the figurative, our words are not felt as confining but as releasing, or not as binding but as bonding. (This realm is neither outside nor inside language games.)

In response to these descriptions it may be felt, it may be true, that what I mean by "unnatural" concerning the metaphorical is captured by, say, the term "personal." Similarly, it may be that what I mean by "unnatural" concerning the skeptical is, say, "private." I would not deny these possibilities, but they would not of themselves lead me to give up the idea of the unnatural in the two cases, for two reasons: (1) using the same word for both cases marks a connection between them, even a direction for investigating the connection, that might otherwise be missed; (2) the ideas of the personal and of the private are no less in need of investigation than the idea of the (un)natural—and in particular an investigation of their tendency to insinuate themselves as our given condition of existence, one might say as the condition *natural* to us.

In portraying opposite directions of unnaturalness in the routes to the skeptical and to the metaphorical situations of language, I do not deny pertinence to Mankin's speculation about some reserve I harbor toward figurative language, a reserve toward the figurative as "[pointing] to the forcing element (and generality) in all convention." Now "portraying an opposite direction from" may be regarded conceptually as a "pointing to" (as with a psychological symptom). This would suggest that I take the sense of release in figuration to be bound to the sense of confinement or bondage in skepticism, from both of which, or from the opposition of which, I seek release. It may be.

Both routes of the unnatural are—as I habitually put the matter—natural to the human being; parts of the nature or fate of a creature complex enough for, or fated to, language. Here are ways of trying to hit off the experience of the human aspiration to knowledge of existence as essentially unsatisfiable—an aspiration to knowledge for which neither the claim to certainty nor the disclaiming of certainty is stable. (I have sometimes referred to this aspiration as the human desire to have God's knowledge; hence, doubtless, to be God.) This perpetual instability is what I call the threat of skepticism, which *The Claim of Reason* claims to be humanly definitive.

The ambiguity in the idea of the unnatural matches an ambiguity in the idea of the ordinary as what the natural (in language) reveals. The ambiguity concerns whether the ordinary, or say the human habitat, is something that thinking is to take us back to (as Wittgenstein seems to imagine) or something thinking is to take us onward to (as Heidegger seems to imagine). My sense of one phase in the thinking of Emerson and Thoreau is that it finds these alternatives to be interpretations of one another.

It is part of the sense of the unavoidability of both routes of the unnatural (up to metaphor, down to skepticism) that neither requires expertise. And this is part of the sense that both routes are natural to the human, all but inescapable for creatures with the capacity to converse, to subject themselves to intelligibility, to make themselves readable. But there is this apparent difference between the routes, that one *can* get along in the everyday world without exercizing the capacity for the figurative, while one can *only* get along in that world (can only "have" that world) if one does *not* exercize the capacity to skepticism. This latter absence will deprive you of access to certain philosophical fears and ambitions; the former absence will debar you from certain other intimacies. If the everyday world is inherently, unpredictably subject to the presence of both capacities, then it is inherently, unpredictably subject to conceiving of itself as limited, as implying a world elsewhere, as beyond a line, against which it is itself something less in depth or in intimacy of existence; an elsewhere, or an otherwise, which, for better or for worse, its inhabitants are drawn to inhabit. So the ordinary is always the subject of a quest and the object of an inquest.

At Stanford

THE TANNER
LECTURE (1986)

6

The Uncanniness of the Ordinary

THE PROSPECT OF DELIVERING THE Tanner Lecture inclined me and encouraged me to attempt to fit together into some reasonable, or say convivial, circle a collection of the main beasts in my jungle or wilderness of interests. An obvious opening or pilot beast is that of the concept of the ordinary, since the first essay I published that I still use (the title essay of the collection *Must We Mean What We Say?*) was begun as a defense of the work of my teacher J. L. Austin, the purest representative of so-called ordinary language philosophy. In anticipation of this attempt, I scheduled last year at Harvard a set of courses designed to bring myself before myself. In that fall I offered a course entitled The Philosophy of the Ordinary, in which I lectured for the first time in six or seven years on certain texts of Austin's and on Wittgenstein's *Philosophical Investigations,* with an increasing sense at once of my continuing indebtedness to this body of thought and practice, and at the same time with a sense of its relative neglect in contemporary intellectual life—a neglect at any rate of the aspect of this thought and practice that engages me most, namely the devotion to the so-called ordinariness or everydayness of language. In the spring semester I turned to one seminar on recent psychoanalytic literary criticism and to another on some late essays of Heidegger's, in both of which bodies of work desperate fresh antagonisms seem to be set up against the ideas of ordinary language philosophy. What I propose to do here is mostly to sketch a topography of certain texts and concepts from that year of courses in which these fresh antagonisms may serve to test the resources of the views in question.

Before entering the topography I must say something about the title I have given this material—the uncanniness of the ordinary. When I hit on this phrase I remembered it as occurring in Freud's essay "The Uncanny," but when I checked the text I learned that it does not. I had at the same time forgotten that the phrase more or less does occur in Heidegger, in "The Origin of the Work of Art" (p. 54). Its occurrence in Heidegger is pertinent, but my intuition of the ordinariness of human life, and of human life's avoidance of the ordinary, is not Heidegger's. For him the extraordinariness of the ordinary has to do with forces in play that constitute our common habitual world; it is a constitution he describes as part of his account of the technological, of which what we accept as the ordinary is as it were one consequence; it is thus to be seen as a symptom of what Nietzsche prophesied, or diagnosed, in declaring that for us "the wasteland grows," a phrase Heidegger recurrently invokes in *What Is Called Thinking?* Whereas for me the uncanniness of the ordinary is epitomized by the possibility or threat of what philosophy has called skepticism, understood (as in my studies of Austin and of the later Wittgenstein I have come to understand it) as the capacity, even desire, of ordinary language to repudiate itself, specifically to repudiate its power to word the world, to apply to the things we have in common, or to pass them by. (By "the desire of ordinary language to repudiate itself" I mean—doesn't it go without saying?—a desire on the part of speakers of a native or mastered tongue who desire to assert themselves, and despair of it.) An affinity between these views of the ordinary, suggesting the possibility of mutual derivation, is that both Heidegger's view and mine respond to the fantastic in what human beings will accustom themselves to, call this the surrealism of the habitual—as if to be human is forever to be prey to turning your corner of the human race, hence perhaps all of it, into some new species of the genus of humanity, for the better or for the worst. I might describe my philosophical task as one of outlining the necessity, and the lack of necessity, in the sense of the human as inherently strange, say unstable, its quotidian as forever fantastic. In what follows I am rather at pains to record variations of this sense in certain writers not customarily or habitually, say institutionally, called philosophers. What all of this comes from and leads to is largely what the five hundred pages of *The Claim of Reason* is about. I hope enough of it will get through in this lecture to capture a sense of what I take to be at stake.

One general caution. I am not here going to make a move toward deriving the skeptical threat philosophically. My idea is that what in philosophy is known as skepticism (for example, as in Descartes and

Hume and Kant) is a relation to the world, and to others, and to myself, and to language, that is known to what you might call literature, or anyway responded to in literature, in uncounted other guises—in Shakespeare's tragic heroes, in Emerson's and Thoreau's "silent melancholy" and "quiet desperation," in Wordsworth's perception of us as without "interest," in Poe's "perverseness." Why philosophy and literature do not know this about one another—and to that extent remain unknown to themselves—has been my theme it seems to me forever.

It may help give a feel for what is at stake for me if I spell out a little my response to discovering that the phrase "the uncanniness of the ordinary" is not in Freud's text. My response was, a little oddly and roughly, to think: "That's not my fault, but Freud's; he hadn't grasped his own subject." A cause of my response has to do with a pair of denials, or rather with one denial and one error, in Freud's reading of the E. T. A. Hoffmann story called "The Sandman" with which the essay on the uncanny occupies itself. Freud introduces the Hoffmann story by citing its treatment in the only discussion in German in the "medico-psychological" literature Freud had found on the subject of the uncanny, an article from 1906 by a certain Jentsch. Jentsch attributes the sense of the uncanny to the recognition of an uncertainty in our ability to distinguish the animate from the inanimate. Hoffmann's story features the beautiful automaton Olympia with whom the hero falls in love (precipitated by his viewing her through a magic spyglass constructed by one of her constructors). At first this love serves for the amusement of others who are certain they see right through the inanimateness of the machine; but then the memory of the love serves to feed their anxiety that they may be making the same error with their own beloveds—quite as though this anxiety about other minds, or other bodies, is a datable event in human history. (As in Hoffmann's story, "A horrible distrust of human figures in general arose.") The hero Nathaniel goes mad when he sees the automaton pulled apart by its two fathers, or makers. He is, before the final catastrophe, nursed back to health by his childhood sweetheart Clara, whom he had forgotten in favor of Olympia.

Now Freud denies, no fewer than four times, that the inability to distinguish the animate from the inanimate is what causes the sense of the uncanny, insisting instead that the cause of the undoubted feeling of the uncanny in Hoffmann's tale is the threat of castration. I find Freud's denial in this context to be itself uncanny, I mean to bear a taint of the mechanical or the compulsive and of the return of the repressed familiar, since there is no intellectual incompatibility between Freud's explanation and Jentsch's. One would have expected Freud, otherwise claiming his inheritance of the poets and creative writers of his culture,

to invoke the castration complex precisely as a new explanation or interpretation of the particular uncertainty in question, that is, to suggest
that Hoffmann's insight is that one does not resolve the uncertainty, or
achieve the clear distinction, between the animate and the inanimate,
until the Oedipal drama is resolved under the threat of castration. Put
otherwise: until that resolution one does not see others as other, know
and acknowledge their (separate, animate, opposed) human existence.
So put, this issue of the other's automatonity shows itself as a form of
the skeptical problem concerning the existence of (what Anglo-American philosophy calls) other minds. And this opening of philosophy in
the Hoffmann story suggests a way to understand Freud's as it were
instinctive denial of the problem of animatedness as key to it. It is
a striking and useful instance of Freud's repeated dissociation of
psychoanalysis from philosophy: a dissociation, as I have argued elsewhere, in which Freud seems to me to be protesting too much, as
though he knows his own uncertainty about how, even whether, psychoanalysis and philosophy can be distinguished without fatal damage
to each of them. (This is a guiding topic of my essay "Psychoanalysis
and Cinema.")[1]

Freud's insistent denial that the uncanny is unsurmountable (that
is, his denial that it is a standing philosophical threat) is perhaps what
causes (or is caused by) the straightforward error he makes in reading
(or remembering) the closing moments of Hoffmann's tale.[2] Freud recounts as follows:

> From the top [of the tower] Clara's attention is drawn to a curious object
> moving along the street. Nathaniel looks at this thing through Coppola's
> spy-glass, which he finds in his pocket, and falls into a new attack of
> madness. . . . Among the people who begin to gather below there comes
> forward the figure of the lawyer Coppelius, who has suddenly returned.
> We may suppose that it was his approach, seen through the spy-glass,
> which threw Nathaniel into his fit of madness.

It is true that one *expects* Nathaniel—and doubtless so does he—as he
takes out the glass, to direct it to whatever had caught Clara's attention,
and the ending suggests that this would have been his father. But in fact
(that is to say, in Hoffmann's tale) what happens is something else:
"Nathaniel . . . found Coppola's spy-glass and looked to one side. Clara

---

1. Further specific (implied or ambivalent) denials by Freud of the development
of philosophy in psychoanalysis are recorded in my essay "Psychoanalysis and Cinema:
The Melodrama of the Unknown Woman."

2. Samuel Weber, in "The Sideshow, or: Remarks on a Canny Moment," notes
the error but interprets it differently.

was standing in front of the glass. There was convulsive throbbing in his pulse. . . ." What we are, accordingly, climactically asked to think about is not why a close spotting of Coppelius (whom Nathaniel never finds in the glass), but rather a chance vision of Clara, causes Nathaniel's reentry into madness. (We are asked to think indeed of the significance that the woman has come between Nathaniel and the object he sought, call this his father; rather than, as Freud claims, of the father coming between the man and his desire. The divided pairs of fathers would then signify not the father's power but his impotence, or resignation.) Then the leap from the tower is to the father, in accusation and appeal. Freud is awfully casual about the power of the father's gift (or curse) of vision: what we know about the father's glass until the climax on the tower is that, in the glass, inanimate, constructed Olympia achieves animation for Nathaniel. So let us continue at the end to grant the glass that power. But how? Since Clara is—is she not?—animate, shall we reverse the direction of the power of the glass and say that it transforms Clara into an automaton? This is not unimaginable, but the irony of reversal seems too pat, too tame, to call upon the complexity of issues released in Hoffmann's text.

I recall that Nathaniel had, in an early outrage at Clara's rejection of his poetry, called her a "damned lifeless automaton," and from the opening of the tale he expresses impatience with her refusal to credit lower and hence higher realms of being—impatience with, let me say, her ordinariness. (He has something of Heidegger's sense of the ordinary, the sense of it in one form of romanticism.) Then when Nathaniel glimpses Clara in his glass we might glimpse that again something has come to life for him—Clara as she is, as it were, in her ordinariness, together with the knowledge that he could not bear this ordinariness, her flesh-and-bloodness, since it means bearing her separateness, her existence as other to him, exactly what his craving for the automaton permitted him to escape, one way or the other (either by demanding no response to the human or by making him an automaton). The concluding paragraph of the tale passes on a report that many years later Clara "had been seen in a remote district sitting hand in hand with a pleasant-looking man in front of the door of a splendid country house, two merry boys playing around her . . . that quiet, domestic happiness . . . which Nathaniel, with his lacerated soul, could never have provided her." My reading in effect takes this description as of the image Nathaniel came upon in the spyglass on the tower.

The glass is a death-dealing rhetoric machine, producing or expressing the consciousness of life in one case (Olympia's) by figuration, in the other (Clara's) by literalization, or say defiguration. One might also think of it as a machine of incessant animation, the parody of a certain romantic writing; and surely not unconnectedly as an uncanny anticipation of a movie camera. The moral of the machine I would draw provisionally this way: There is a repetition necessary to what we call life, or the animate, necessary for example to the human; and a repetition necessary to what we call death, or the inanimate, necessary for example to the mechanical; and there are no marks or features or criteria or rhetoric by means of which to tell the difference between them. From which, let me simply claim, it does not follow that the difference is unknowable or undecidable. On the contrary, the difference is the basis of everything there is for human beings to know, or say decide (like deciding to live), and to decide on no basis beyond or beside or beneath ourselves. Within the philosophical procedure of radical skepticism, the feature specifically allegorized by the machine of the spyglass is skepticism's happening all at once, the world's vanishing at the touch, perhaps, of the thought that you may be asleep dreaming that you are awake, the feature Descartes expresses in his "astonishment."

The essay of mine I mentioned a moment ago, in which I press the case of Freud's inheritance of philosophy against his fervent dissociation of his work from it, is framed by a reading of Max Ophuls's film *Letter from an Unknown Woman* focused on the melodramatic gesture of horror elicited from the man who is sent the depicted letter, as he completes its reading. My reading of his death-dealing vision is very much along the lines of the one I have just given of Nathaniel's horror on looking through (or reading the images offered by) the spyglass—a horrified vision of ordinariness, of the unremarkable other seen as just that unremarkable other. You may feel, accordingly, that I wish to force every romantic melodrama to yield the same result. Or you may, I hope, feel that I have honestly come upon a matter that romantic tales of horror, and certain films that incorporate them, have in fact and in genre taken as among their fundamental subjects for investigation, say the acknowledgment of otherness, specifically as a spiritual task, one demanding a willingness for the experience of horror, and as a datable event in the unfolding of philosophical skepticism in the West.

Now let us turn to those courses I mentioned and their topography, associated with Austin's and Wittgenstein's ideas of the ordinary, and with the name of Heidegger, and with psychoanalytic literary criticism.

Wittgenstein says in the *Investigations,* "When I talk about language (words, sentences, etc.) I must speak the language of every day. Is this language somehow too coarse and material for what we want to say? *Then how is another one to be constructed?*—And how strange [*merkwürdig*] that we should be able to do anything at all with the one we have!" ($120). Strange, I expect Wittgenstein means immediately to imply, that we can formulate so precise and sophisticated a charge within and against our language as to find it "coarse" and "material." Are these terms of criticism themselves coarse and material?

Now listen to words from two texts of Heidegger's, from the essay "Das Ding" ("The Thing") and from his set of lectures *Was Heisst Denken?* (translated as *What is Called Thinking?*), both published within three years before the publication of the *Investigations* in 1953. From "The Thing:" "Today everything present is equally near and far. The distanceless prevails." And again: "Is not this merging [or lumping] of everything [into uniform distancelessness] more unearthly than everything bursting apart? Man stares at what the atom bomb could bring with it. He does not see that the atom bomb and its explosion are the mere final emission of what has long since taken place, has already happened." What has already happened according to Heidegger is the shrinking or disintegration of the human in the growing dominion of a particular brand of thinking, a growing violence in our demand to grasp or explain the world. (I put aside for the moment my distrust, almost contempt, at the tone of Heidegger's observation, its attitude of seeming to exempt itself from the common need to behave under a threat whose absoluteness makes it [appear to us] unlike any earlier.) A connection with ordinary language of the fate of violent thinking and of distancelessness comes out in *What Is Called Thinking?*, where Heidegger says:

> A symptom, at first sight quite superficial, of the growing power of one-track thinking is the increase everywhere of designations consisting of abbreviations of words, or combinations of their initials. Presumably no one here has ever given serious thought to what has already come to pass when you, instead of University, simply say "Uni." "Uni"—that is like "Kino" ["Movie"]. True, the moving picture theater continues to be different from the academy of the sciences. [Does this suggest that one day they will not be different? How would this matter? How to Heidegger?] Still, the designation "Uni" is not accidental, let alone harmless. [P. 34]

Reading this I ask myself: When I use the word "movies" (instead of "motion pictures?" "cinema?") am I really exemplifying, even helping along, the annihilation of human speech, hence of the human? And then I think: Heidegger cannot hear the difference between the useful non-speak or moon-talk of acronyms (UNESCO, NATO, MIRV, AIDS) and the intimacy (call it nearness) of passing colloquialisms and cult abbreviations (Kino, flick, shrink, Poli Sci). But then I think: No, it must be just that the force of Heidegger's thought here is not manifest in his choice of examples any more than it is in his poor efforts to describe the present state of industrial society (as if our awareness of

159

the surface of these matters is to be taken for granted, as either sophisticated or as irredeemably naive). In descriptions of the present state of
Western society, the passion and accuracy of, say, John Stuart Mill's
prose quite eclipses Heidegger's. And as to his invoking of popular language and culture, Heidegger simply hasn't the touch for it, the ear for
it. These matters are more deeply perceived in, say, a movie of Alfred
Hitchcock's.

To dispel for myself Heidegger's condescension in this region I
glance at a line from Hitchcock's *North by Northwest* (the one in which
Cary Grant is attacked by a crop-dusting plane in a Midwestern corn-
field and in which he rescues a woman from the Mount Rushmore
monument of the heads of four American presidents). The line is said
by a man in response to Grant's asking him whether he is from the
F.B.I.: "F.B.I., C.I.A., we're all in the same alphabet soup"; after which
the conversation is drowned out by the roar of an airplane, toward
which they are walking. At first glance, that line says that it doesn't
matter what you say; but at second glance, or listening to the growl of
the invisible motor, the line suggests that it matters that this does not
matter. That line invokes (1) the name of a child's food, something to
begin from; and (2) a colloquialism meaning that we are in a common
peril; and (3) is a sentence whose six opening letters (initials) signal
that we have forgotten, to our peril, the ABC's of communication,
namely the ability to speak together out of common interest. But have
we forgotten it because we lack long or ancient words? It seems more
worthwhile to ask why "F.B.I." abbreviates a name that has in it the
same word as Wittgenstein's *Philosophical Investigations,* and to ask what
the concept of intelligence is that the military have agencies and com-
munities of it whereas universities do not. But if I am willing to excuse
Heidegger provisionally for his lack of ear in such regions, then I must
wait for my approach to them until later in this chapter when I invoke
the writing of Ralph Waldo Emerson and of his disciple Henry David
Thoreau, for both of whom the idea of nearness, or as Thoreau puts it,
of nextness (by which he explicitly says he means *the nearest*), is also
decisive, and whose concepts I feel I can follow on.

For the moment, I turn to the other material I mentioned that is
apparently antagonistic to ordinary language and its philosophy, that
represented in my seminar on recent psychoanalytically shaped literary
criticism, which began—in my effort to begin studying recent French
thought in some systematic way—by reading moments in Jacques Lacan's controversial and perhaps too famous study of Edgar Allan Poe's
tale "The Purloined Letter." Lacan's professed reason for taking up the
Poe story is its serviceability as an illustration of Freud's speculations

concerning the repetition compulsion in *Beyond the Pleasure Principle,* an illustration suggested by the narrative feature of Poe's tale that a compromising letter, stolen by one person who leaves a substitute in its place, is restolen and returned to its original position by another person who leaves another substitute (or construction), in turn, in its place. Fastening on the shifts of identification established by this repeated structure of thefts or displacements of a letter, Lacan in effect treats Poe's tale as an allegory of what he understands psychoanalytic understanding to require—the tracing and return of displaced signifiers. This understanding, together with the special art by which the letter is concealed, also constitutes the tale as an allegory of writing. I ask those for whom this, and the aftermath it has inspired, has all become too familiar to bear with me while I go over the tale again just far enough to indicate (something that has surprised me, even alarmed me) that it also forms at least as exact and developed an allegory of ordinary language philosophy. The sense of this application is given in Poe's tale's all but identifying itself as a study—and hence perhaps as an act—of mind-reading.

I believe that a certain offense taken toward ordinary language philosophy (from its inception in Austin and Wittgenstein until the present) is a function of some feeling that it claims mind-reading powers for itself: what else in fact could be the source of the ferocious knowledge the ordinary language philosophers will claim to divine by going over stupidly familiar words that we are every bit as much the master of as they? For example, Austin claims in "Other Minds" that when I say "I know" I am not claiming to penetrate more deeply or certainly into reality than when I say "I believe"; I am, rather, taking a different stance toward what I communicate: I give my word, stake my mind, differently—the greater penetration is perhaps into my trustworthiness (p. 78). And it seems to me that an immediate philosophical yield Austin wants from this observation (and perhaps similar yields from a thousand similar observations) is its questioning, perhaps repudiation, of Plato's ancient image of one set of ascending degrees of knowledge, an image Plato specifies in his allegory of the "divided line" of knowledge, an idea, if not an image, philosophers are still likely to hold without being able to question. From Austin's questioning or repudiation here a further consequence would be to question whether there is, or ought to be, or what the fantasy is that there is, a special class of persons to be called philosophers, who possess and are elevated by a special class or degree of knowledge. Austin's idea would seem to be that the decisive philosophical difference between minds lies not in their possession of facts and their agility of manipulation—these differences are reasonably obvious—but in, let us say, their intellectual scrupulousness, their sense of what one is or could be in a position to say, to claim authority for imparting, in our common finitude, to a fellow human being.

Does my elaboration of Austin's implication from the difference he has discovered between saying "I believe" and "I know" (that is, the difference between belief and knowledge) convey the kind of offense he may give, may indeed cultivate? I guess I was just now cultivating, or inviting, offense in my parenthetical, casual use of "that is" to move from our use of the words "belief" and "knowledge" to, perhaps I can say, the nature of belief and of knowledge. This casual move (or, as Emerson would put it, this casualty) is worded in Wittgenstein's motto "Grammar says what kind of object something is" (§373). This is, I think, not just one more offense. Without this sense of discovery (of the nature of things) the examples of ordinary language philosophy would altogether, to my mind, fail in their imagination. If this is right, its persistent obscurity is a reason that the production of such examples is so hard, perhaps impossible, to teach. When in the opening essays of *Must We Mean What We Say?* I sought to characterize and defend this move (from what there is to say, to what there is to word) by aligning the motivation of the *Investigations* with that of the *Critique of Pure Reason* as the exploration of transcendental logic, not only was I not given credit but my work was accused of being a discredit to empirically sound philosophy. (See especially my "Availability," p. 65.) While as an initial reaction this is understandable enough, and while I am not now attempting to add to the defenses I presented in that book, but rather to take up what I called at the beginning of this essay "fresh antagonisms" to the ordinary, I yet wish to derive a practical consequence from the move I described roughly as from language to nature (a move that cries out for further description, in particular descriptions that account for the sense of there being a "move" in question)—the practical consequence, namely, that one cannot know in advance when or whether an example from the appeal to ordinary language will *strike* the philosophical imagination, motivate conversation philosophically. As if ordinary language procedure *at each point* requires the experience of conversion, of being turned around. Talk about offense.

Take one further example, this time from Wittgenstein: "Other people cannot be said to learn of my sensations *only* from my behavior—for I cannot be said to *learn* of them. I *have* them" (*Investigations,* §246). But first of all, virtually every philosopher who has been gripped by the skeptical question whether and how we can know of the existence of so-called other minds has found himself or herself saying something of this sort, that others know of me at best from my behavior (as

if facing themselves with the queries: How else? Through mind-reading, or some other telepathy?). And one might imagine the fun an advanced Parisian sensibility might wish to make out of such a prim
appeal to what "cannot" be said, as though Wittgenstein were appealing
to our sense of propriety or of, say, linguistic cleanliness. Should we,
especially we serious philosophers, stoop to such considerations, or
propriety, mere manners? Is it even a fresh criticism? It seems to resemble the criticism Bertrand Russell and others in the English-
speaking world of philosophy initially leveled against the *Investigations*
upon its first appearance ("Some Replies to Criticism," p. 161) and to
Austin's work published in the preceding years ("The Cult of Common
Usage"), that such work amounted to exhortations about how we
ought to speak, that it sought to correct our, as it were, rough deport-
ment. This is surely not entirely, or on every understanding, wrong. It
is a piece of what Wittgenstein would mean in comparing the present
philosophically advanced human race with "primitives." Yet it may at
any time come over us, the truth of the matter, that we cannot, so to
speak, speak of someone learning of our sensations only from our behavior, without *insisting* that the words speak the obvious truth; and
on no apparent ground for this insistence than philosophical need: and
should this need be satisfied? But why should philosophy insist on the
significance of "only" here? "Only" here suggests some disappointment
with my behavior as a route to the knowledge of what is going on in
me, our route *faute de mieux*—not a disappointment with this or that
piece of my behavior, but with behavior as such, as if my body stands
in the way of your knowledge of my mind.

This now begins to show its madness, as though philosophy is
insisting on, driven to, some form of emptiness. And some such diagnosis is indeed Wittgenstein's philosophical conclusion, or his conviction about philosophy. His idea, I might say, is that this philosophical
use of "only"—that all but unnoticeable word in his apparently trivial
claim about what cannot be said (one triviality among a thousand
others)—is not merely a sign that we, say, underestimate the role of the
body and its behavior, but that we falsify it, I might even say, falsify the
body: in philosophizing we turn the body into as it were an impene-
trable integument. It is as though I, in philosophizing, *want* this metamorphosis, want to place the mind beyond reach, want to get the body
inexpressive, and at the same time find that I cannot quite want to, want
to without reserve. Wittgenstein is interested in this peculiar strain of
philosophy (it may be philosophy's peculiar crime) to want exactly the
impossible, thought torturing itself, language repudiating itself. In
Wittgenstein's philosophizing he seeks the source of this torture and
repudiation in language—what it is in language that makes this seem

163

necessary, and what about language makes it possible. He speaks of our being bewitched by language; hence his therapeutic procedures are to disenchant us. Lacan in a comparable way, I believe, speaks of his therapy as reading the unreadable. (Or Shoshana Felman speaks of it for him, in "On Reading Poetry," to which I am indebted in this and in further matters.)

Let this serve to indicate the kind of offense the claims of ordinary language philosophy can, and should, give. It is, at any rate, the attitude or level at which I find Poe's "The Purloined Letter" to serve as their allegory.

The tale opens, I remind you, as the Prefect of the Parisian police calls upon the detective Dupin to ask his opinion about some troublesome official business. The first words of dialogue are these (I use the Mabbott edition):

> "If it is any point requiring reflection," observed Dupin, as he forebore to enkindle the wick, "we shall examine it to better purpose in the dark."
>
> "That is another of your odd notions," said the Prefect, who had a fashion of calling everying "odd" that was beyond his comprehension, and thus lived amid an absolute legion of "oddities." . . . "The fact is, the business is *very* simple indeed, . . . but then I thought Dupin would like to hear the details of it, because it is so excessively *odd*."
>
> "Simple and odd," said Dupin. . . . "perhaps it is the very simplicity of the thing which puts you at fault."
>
> "What nonsense you *do* talk!" replied the Prefect, laughing heartily.
>
> "Perhaps the mystery is a little *too* plain," said Dupin.
>
> "Oh, good heavens! who ever heard of such an idea?"
>
> "A little *too* self-evident."
>
> "Ha! ha! ha!—-ha! ha! ha!—ho! ho! ho!" roared [the Prefect], profoundly amused, "Oh, Dupin, you will be the death of me yet!"

The narrative comes to turn on the fact that a purloined letter was hidden by being kept in plain view, as if a little too self-evident, a little too plain to notice, as it were beneath notice, say under the nose, and then moves to an examination of competing theories of the way to find the truth of hidden things. Now, of course, a reader of Wittgenstein's *Investigations* may well prick up his or her ears at the very announcement of a tale in which something is missed just because obvious. One remembers such characteristic remarks from the *Investigations* as these:

> The aspects of things that are most important for us are hidden because of their simplicity and [ordinariness, everydayness]. (One is unable to notice something—because it is always before one's eyes.) [§129]

Philosophy simply puts everything before us, and neither explains nor deduces anything.—Since everything lies open to view there is nothing to explain. For what is hidden, for example, is of no interest to us. [§126]

But a philosopher other than one of ordinary language may make comparable claims, for example the Heidegger of *Being and Time,* whose method can be said to be meant to unconceal the obvious, the always present. The allegorical pivot from Poe's tale specifically to ordinary language philosophy is the tale's repetition of the idea of the *odd,* and specifically its associating this idea of the odd with the consequence of laughter. For the producing of examples whose oddness rouses laughter (no doubt mostly muted) is a feature of Austin's and Wittgenstein's methods at once philosophically indispensable and (so far as I know) philosophically unique to them. Austin is the more hilarious perhaps, but here I remind you of this sound in the *Investigations:*

> Imagine someone saying: "But I know how tall I am!" and then laying his hand on top of his head to prove it. [§279]

> The chair is thinking to itself: . . . WHERE? In one of its parts? Or outside its body; in the air around it? Or not *anywhere* at all? But then what is the difference between this chair's saying something to itself and another one's doing so, next to it?—But then how is it with man: where does *he* say things to himself? [§361]

> It would be possible to imagine someone groaning out: "Someone is in pain—I don't know who!"—and our then hurrying to help him, the one who groaned. [§407]

But such examples only scratch the surface of the dimension of oddness in the *Investigations.* There is, beyond them, Wittgenstein's frequent use of the word *seltsam,* characteristically translated in the English as "queer," which also translates Wittgenstein's frequent use of *merkwürdig,* as does the English "strange." *Of course* they are frequent, since both exactly contrast with what is *alltäglich,* ordinary, everyday, the appeal to which is Wittgenstein's constant method and goal. Wittgenstein sometimes explicitly undertakes to instruct us when to find something odd ("Don't take it as a matter of course, but as a remarkable fact, that pictures and fictitious narratives give us pleasure, occupy our minds" [§524]); as well as sometimes to give directions for overcoming a self-imposed sense of strangeness ("Sometimes a sentence only seems queer when one imagines a different language-game for it from the one in which we actually use it." [§195]). He speaks to us quite as if we have become unfamiliar with the world, as if our mechanism of anxiety, which should signal danger, has gone out of order, working too much and too little.

The return of what we accept as the world will then present itself as a return of the familiar, which is to say, exactly under the concept of what Freud names the uncanny. That the familiar is a product of a sense of the unfamiliar and of the sense of a return means that what returns after skepticism is never (just) the same. (A tempting picture here could be expressed by the feeling that "there is no way back." Does this imply that there is a way ahead? Perhaps there are some "back's" or "once's" or pasts the presence to which requires no "way." Then that might mean that we have not found the way away, have never departed, have not entered history. What has to be developed here is the idea of difference so perfect that there is no way or feature in which the difference consists [I describe this by saying that in such a case there is no difference in criteria]—as in the difference between the waking world and the world of dreams, or between natural things and mechanical things, or between the masculine and the feminine, or between the past and the present. A difference in which everything and nothing differs is uncanny.)

But the angel of the odd hovers over the *Investigations* yet more persistently. The whole of the book can be seen to be contained in the book's opening of itself with a quotation from the *Confessions* of St. Augustine in which its subject describes his learning of language. This possibility depends upon seeing that the quotation contains the roots of the entire flowering of concepts in the rest of the *Investigations*. But it equally depends on seeing that the most remarkable fact about the quotation from Augustine is that anyone should find it remarkable, strange, odd, worth quoting, at all: "When they (my elders) named some object, and accordingly moved towards something, I saw this and I grasped that the thing was called by the sound they uttered when they meant to point it out. Their intention was shown by their bodily movements . . . and after I had trained my mouth to form these signs, I used them to express my own desires." (To glimpse the oddness, imagine the final sentence as from Samuel Beckett.) It presents the opening segment of countless moments in the book in which we are made uncertain whether an expression is remarkable or casual, where this turns out to be a function of whether we leave the expression ordinary or elevate it into philosophy, an elevation that depends on escaping our sense, let us say, of the ridiculous, one sense Wittgenstein undertakes to awaken. Philosophy in Wittgenstein turns out to require an understanding of how the seriousness of philosophy's preoccupations (with meaning, reference, intention, pointing, understanding, thinking, explaining, with the existence of the world, with whether my behavior consists of movements), its demand for satisfaction, its refusal of satisfaction—how this seriousness is dependent on disarming our sense of oddness and non-oddness, and therewith seeing why it is with the trivial, or superficial, that this philosophy finds itself in oscillation, as in an unearthly dance. (It was my sense of this unearthly oscillation that led me, early in my interest in Wittgenstein, to compare his writing with the writing of Beckett [for whom the extraordinary is ordinary] and with that of Chekhov [for whom the ordinary is extraordinary], who thus inescapably court the uncanny.)

I would love now to go on to a detailed working out of Poe's tale's allegory of ordinary language philosophy, but the most I can do here is flatly to assert a few claims about the issue. The second half of the tale is constituted by a narration of Dupin's narration and explanation of his powers of unconcealment. He begins by describing a childhood game of "even and odd" in which one player holds in his closed hand a number of marbles and demands of another whether that number is even or odd. An eight-year-old champion at the game explained his success to Dupin as one of determining whether his opponent was wise or stupid; and the method the boy used for this Dupin cites as the basis of the success of, among others, Tommaso Companella (whose system of mind-reading the boy had described) and of Machiavelli, no less. Lacan to my mind undervalues the relation of Dupin's story of the contest to the Prefect's opening vision of universal oddness. This relation depends on taking to heart Poe's pun, or pressure, on the English word *odd*. Baudelaire does not try in his translation to preserve, or bother to note, this recurrence; he uses *bizarre* for the Prefect's "odd," and for Dupin's "even or odd" he uses *pair ou impair*—what else? Lacan of course knows this, but he seems to me over-casual in deciding (certainly correctly) that a "better" translation of "odd" in this story is a word for "singular." Singular is, elsewhere, a sensitive word for Poe, but in the text of "The Purloined Letter" the separated uses of "odd" to name what is at once funnily obvious and at the same time constitutes a possibility in a mind-reading contest with concealed counts—the untranslatable coincidence in Poe's words—should not be smoothed but kept in friction. Smoothing them would help Lacan's apparent neglect of the mind-reading contest of odd and even (masterable by a child of eight) as some kind of figure for communication, say for writing and reading, in particular for reading this text of Poe's that recounts this contest. The funny obviousness of this figure, its banality, its depth concealed in plain view, ought not to cause us not to see what it is.

Lacan's fruitful perception that Poe's tale is built on a repetition of triangular structures in the theft of the letter is the basis of the ensuing controversies about the tale, and it is only in the way he reads the repetition, or stops reading it, that gives rise to my present reservation.

167

Here is the sort of thing I get out of stopping over the thematization of odd and even mind-reading. When in the second triangle Dupin takes the position of the Minister in the first (the position of thief, the one who sees what the others see, namely that the King does not see the letter and that the Queen sees that the King does not see, hence falsely feels secure), and the Minister in the second triangle takes the position of the Queen in the first (the position of the one stolen from, under her very eyes, or nose), then the position of the King in the first (the one who is blind) Lacan finds to be occupied in the second by the Police (who were blind to the thing hidden in plainness). Without denying this, we should also note that in the second interview (in which Dupin robs the robber) the third party of the triangle (the Police) is present only by implication (Dupin and the Minister are fictionally alone); and then note further that another party is equally present there, specifically present (only) by implication, namely the reader, myself, to whom the fictional letter is also invisible. So I am to that extent both the King and the Police of Poe's letter(s). But since I am (whoever I am) after all shown the contents of the literal thing called "The Purloined Letter" (that is, Poe's tale), since they are indeed, or in art, meant for me, even as it were privately, I am the Queen from whom it is stolen, as well as the pair of thieves who remove it and return it, therapeutically, to me (for who else but myself could have stolen *this* from myself?). And if I am to read the mind of the one whose hand it is in (that is, mine, so my mind) but also the mind going with the hand it is written in (that is, the author's—but which one, that of the literal "Letter" or that of the fictional letter?), it is also to be read as the work of one who opposes me, challenges me to guess whether each of its events is odd or even, everyday or remarkable, ordinary or out of the ordinary. (I am here invoking not what I understand as a reader-response theory, but something I would like to understand as a reader-identification theory.)

So this text of Poe's "tale" presents the following representation of textuality, or constitution of a text. It is an artifact, in a contested play of mind-reading, that is openly concealed in and by the hand. I steal it from myself and return it to myself—steal when I am wise or stupid (agree to play as a game of concealment) and return when I can relate concealment and revelation, or say repression and power (when I can know from whom the hand conceals by closing). Yet I am to know that no matching of minds can be open-handed either, that the artifact of the text is the scene of a crime, because it is an expression of guilt, because it is of knowledge that must be confessed, exacted, interpreted. Is this a representation? And what crime does the hand as such reveal? No doubt, along with other notorious matters (still typically consigned to psychoanalytic closets), it will have to do with the circumstance that only humans have hands (with those thumbs), and the consequent fascination of the hand for philosophers. The writer of *Walden* confesses at the opening of the book that the pages to follow are the work of his hands only; and later in his opening chapter, as he enumerates the debts he has encountered in setting out on his own life—saying that he "thus unblushingly publishes [his] guilt"—the arithmetic is of food, betraying the necessity of his having to eat, to preserve himself. As if his debt is for his existence as such, for asking acknowledgment (payable how? to whom? or is it forgivable? by whom?).

An urgent methodological issue of ordinary language philosophy—and the issue about which this cast of thought is philosophically at its weakest—is that of accounting for the fact that we are the victims of the very words of which we are at the same time the masters; victims and masters of the fact of words. I have mentioned that one of Wittgenstein's favorite terms of criticism, or accounts of this recurrent failure in our possession by or of language (if failure is what it is), speaks of our being bewitched by language. But that hardly accounts for such a crossroads as the emptiness of the word "only" in "knowing only from behavior." Perhaps my suggestion of "emptiness" and of a "will to emptiness" will prove to be an advance as a term of criticism (if, say, its invocation of Nietzsche's perception of nihilism can be made out usefully). And so perhaps will the idea of the unreadable, in the suggestion it would seem to carry, that ordinary language philosophy has not accounted for why the odd is laughable, for what it is we are laughing at philosophically, anxiously. Poe's "The Purloined Letter" imports a concrete and elaborate web of ways for conceptualizing these facts. What it may betoken that it at the same time allegorizes Lacanian psychoanalysis, together with the acts of writing and of reading, I am glad to leave open.

To complete the little topography I project for this occasion and bring Heidegger back explicitly into a bearing on the ordinary and the odd, I would, as I indicated in putting him aside earlier, have to undertake certain tasks pertaining to American transcendentalism, two in particular. First, to give an account of Thoreau's *Walden,* the major philosophical text in my life—other than the *Philosophical Investigations*—that deals in endless repetition, that begins with a vision of the extreme oddness of the everyday world, and that portrays its goal as the discovery of the day, his day, as one among others. Thoreau's guiding vision of the oddness of our everyday (its nextness, flushness, with another way) produces a response, that is, a texture of prose, lining the border between comedy and tragedy. Second, I would have to say what I have meant in expressing my intuition that Thoreau, together with Emerson (having insisted upon their relation to Heidegger), underwrite the procedures of ordinary language philosophy, an intuition I have expressed by speaking of them as inheritors of Kant's transcendentalism and as writing out of a sense of the intimacy of words with the world, or of intimacy lost. Again there is time here only for mere assertion.

The background of the intuition is the work of mine I cited earlier that I count on to show that both the *Investigations* and *Walden* share an aspiration of the *Critique of Pure Reason,* namely to demonstrate the necessity in the world's satisfaction of the human conditions of knowledge. *Walden*'s way of summarizing the first *Critique* may be heard in its announcement that "the universe constantly and obediently answers to our conceptions." And when in the *Investigations* Wittgenstein calls his investigation "a grammatical one," and says, "Our investigation is directed not toward phenomena but, as one might say, toward the '*possibilities*' of phenomena" (§907), this may be taken as saying that what he means by grammar, or a grammatical investigation, plays the role of a transcendental deduction of human concepts. The difference relevant for me is that in Wittgenstein's practice every word in our ordinary language requires deduction, where this means that each is to be tracked, in its application to the world, in terms of what he calls criteria that govern it; and our grammar is in some sense to be understood as a priori.[3] (It is the sense in which human beings are "in agreement" in their judgments.)

The mutual relation to Kant I called the background of the intuition of American transcendentalism as underwriting ordinary language philosophy. The foreground is the recognition that the *Investigations,* like the work of Emerson and Thoreau, is written in continuous response to the threat of skepticism. It seems to me that the originality of the *Investigations* is a function of the originality of its response to skepticism, one that undertakes not to deny skepticism's power (on the contrary) but to diagnose the source (or say the possibility) of that power—to ask, as I put it a while ago, what it is about human language that allows us, even invites us, in its own name, to repudiate its everyday functioning, to find it wanting. ("In its own name": we finite beings as it were share the sense of language's self-dissatisfaction, finding itself wanting.) I might epitomize Wittgenstein's originality in this regard by saying that he takes the drift toward skepticism as the *discovery* of the everyday, a discovery of exactly *what* it is that skepticism would deny. It turns out to be something that the very impulse to philosophy, the

3. This is a way of putting the burden of chapters 1 and 4 of my *The Claim of Reason: Wittgenstein, Skepticism, Morality, and Tragedy.* This generalization, as it were, of Kant is something I claim for Emerson in chapter 2 of the present volume.

impulse to take thought about our lives, inherently seeks to deny, as if what philosophy is dissatisfied by is inherently the everyday.

So the everyday is not merely one topic among others that philosophers might take an interest in, but one that a philosopher is fated to an interest in so long as he or she seeks a certain kind of response to the threat of skepticism. (It is a response that would regard science not as constituting an answer to skepticism but rather, taken as an answer, as a continuation of skepticism—as if the mad scientist in us is the double of the mad skeptic.) The everyday is what we cannot but aspire to, since it appears to us as lost to us. This is what Thoreau means when he says, after describing several of what he calls his adventures (a number of which take place while he describes himself as sitting down), "The present was my next experiment of this kind, which I purpose to describe at more length." By "the present experiment" he means of course the book in our hands, but he simultaneously means that the experiment is the present, that is, that the book sets itself to test ways of arriving at the present, not merely at what people call "current events," which for him are not current, but old news, and are not events, but fancies. He is repeating the thought when he says, "The phenomena of the year take place every day in a pond on a small scale." That is, there is nothing beyond the succession of each and every day; and grasping a day, accepting the everyday, the ordinary, is not a given but a task. This is also why Emerson says, "Give me insight into today, and you may have the antique and future worlds." His words have the rhetoric of a bargain, or a prayer, as in "Give us this day our daily bread"; it is not something to take for granted.

The implication of this view of skepticism as the measure of the everyday is worked out in torturous detail in *The Claim of Reason* and I will not try to characterize it further here. Instead I will head for a conclusion by asking where Emerson and Thoreau see the answer to skepticism to lie.

I still concentrate on *Walden* and cite two foci of its conceptual elaboration. The first focus is the theme of mourning (or grieving) which, in conjuction with morning (as dawning) forms a dominating pun of *Walden* as a whole; it proposes human existence as the finding of ecstasy in the knowledge of loss. I call *Walden* a book of losses, saying of the book's creation of the region of Walden Pond, the world as an image of Paradise (Walled In), that it is everything there is to lose, and the book opens with it gone, forgone. Hume had said in the *Treatise of Human Nature* that skepticism is a malady than can never be cured (bk. 1, pt. 4, §2). But the scene Hume thereupon portrays for us is one in which he returns from the isolation of his philosophical study into the company of his friends, where he finds welcome distraction from

171

the sickening news his philosophical powers have uncovered. Incurable malady, as a metaphor for some grievous human condition, suggests an imaginable alternative, yet one not open to us. It would seem to have to be an alternative to the grievousness of the condition of being human. (Philosophers do sometimes suggest that the human possession of, say, the five senses is an unfortunate fact about us. It is within and against such a suggestion of the contingency of human existence that Beckett's character Hamm in *Endgame* protests when he cries, "You're on earth, you're on earth, there's no cure for that!")

Distraction (as in Hume's *Treatise,* bk. 1, pt. 4, §§2 and 7) is one reaction to these tidings. But, depending on how you take the alternative to the malady of skepticism, a more direct response, perhaps in a more acute stage, is that, as in *Walden,* of mourning—the path of accepting the loss of the world (you might say, accepting its loss of presence), accepting it as something which exists for us only in its loss (you might say its absence), or what presents itself as loss. *The Claim of Reason* suggests the moral of skepticism to be that the existence of the world and others in it is not a matter to be known, but one to be acknowledged. And now what emerges is that what is to be acknowledged is this existence as separate from me, as if gone from me. Since I lose the world in every impulse to philosophy, say in each of the countless ways the ordinary language philosophers find that I make my expressions unreadable, the world must be regained every day, in repetition, regained as gone. Here is a way of seeing what it means that Freud too thinks of mourning as an essentially repetitive exercise. It can also be made out, in his little essay "Transience," that Freud regards mourning as the condition of the possibility of accepting the world's beauty, the condition, that is to say, of allowing its independence from me, its objectivity. Learning mourning may be the achievement of a lifetime. ("I am in mourning for my life." Chekhov's second line in *The Sea Gull* is, as it were, given its comic face in the preceding citations of Thoreau and of Freud.)

In addition to distraction and to mourning, Heidegger's perception of the violence of philosophical thinking, its imperative to dominance of the earth, I see as something like a competing response to, or consequence of, skepticism. One might take this violence as the response that supervenes when neither distraction nor mourning are any longer available human options. Twenty years ago, in an essay on *King Lear* ("The Avoidance of Love"), I put the matter, or left an open suggestion for putting the matter, somewhat differently, in a way that I must interpolate here. (My early suggestion originally occurs within an interpolation in the *Lear* essay [pp. 322–26]. Its recurrence here suggests, more or less impossibly, that the entire present paper could or should have been that earlier interpolation.)

> In the unbroken tradition of epistemology since Descartes and Locke (radically questioned from within itself only in our period), the concept of knowledge (of the world) disengages from its connections with matters of information and skill and learning, and becomes fixed to the concept of certainty alone, and in particular to a certainty provided by the (by my) senses. At some early point in epistemological investigations, the world normally present to us (the world in whose existence, as it is typically put, we "believe") is brought into question and vanishes, whereupon all connection with a world is found to hang upon what can be said to be "present to the senses"; and that turns out, shockingly, not to be the world. It is at this point that the doubter finds himself cast into skepticism, turning the existence of the external world into a problem. Kant called it a scandal to philosophy and committed his genius to putting a stop to it, but it remains active in the conflicts between traditional philosophers and their ordinary language critics, and it inhabits the void of comprehension between Continental ontology and Anglo-American analysis as a whole. Its relevance to us at the moment is only this: The skeptic does not gleefully and mindlessly forgo the world we share, or thought we shared; he is neither the knave Austin took him to be, nor the fool the pragmatists took him for, nor the simpleton he seems to men of culture and of the world. He forgoes the world for just the reason that the world is important, that it is the scene and stage of connection with the present: he finds that it vanishes exactly with the effort to *make* it present. If this makes him unsuccessful, that is because the presentness achieved by certainty of the senses cannot compensate for the presentness which had been elaborated through our old absorption in the world. But the wish for genuine connection is there, and there was a time when the effort, however hysterical, to assure epistemological presentness was the best expression of seriousness about our relation to the world, the expression of an awareness that presentness was threatened, gone. If epistemology wished to make knowing a substitute for that fact, that is scarcely foolish or knavish, and scarcely some simple mistake. It is, in fact, one way to describe the tragedy *King Lear* records.

It took a good lapse of time for me to come to see how to unfold the implications in this juxtaposition, to see how tragedy is a projection or an enactment of a skeptical problematic and at the same time how skepticism traces in advance, or prophesies, a tragic structure, say a structure of revenge. What the passage I just quoted accordingly says to me now is that the loss of presentness (to and of the world) is something that the violence of skepticism deepens exactly in its desperation to correct it, a violence assured in philosophy's desperation to answer or refute skepticism, to deny skepticism's disovery of the absence or withdrawal of the world, that is, the withdrawal of my presentness to it; which for me means the withdrawal of my presentness to (the denial of our inheritance of) language.

Here again (as in my first postscript to chapter 5, on deconstruction) I find myself called upon to assess the affinities of my work with that of Derrida. I have most often responded to this demand by in effect suggesting that it was, for me, always too late or too early for such an assessment. But sometimes there are specific steps of perspective it might be worth my pointing to. So let me say here that differences between what I do and what deconstruction does seem to me registered in my speaking of presentness (which is about me and my world) instead of (meaning what?) presence (which is about Being, not something I will ever be in a position, so far as I can judge, to judge); and in my criticism of "philosophy" (by which I take myself to mean a way human beings have of being led to think about themselves, instead of something I can spell "Western metaphysics") which is not, anyway not at first, that it originates in a domineering construction of (false) presence, but that it institutes an (a false) absence for which it falsely offers compensations. Even if it could be shown, and were worth someone's while to show, that these institutions are not so different, my claims do not arise from a study of the period of classical philosophy but are limited to strands within the period of philosophy since the emergence of modern skepticism. While I take it that this radical skeptical suspicion of the "external" world as a whole, and of others in it, is not a speculation known to the classical philosophers, I also take modern skepticism to be philosophy's expression or interpretation of the thing known to literature (among other places) in melodrama and in tragedy. (By the thing known in melodrama and in tragedy I mean, roughly, the dependence of the human self on society for its definition, but at the same time its transcendence of that definition, its infinite insecurity in maintaining its existence. Which seems to mean, on this description, in determining and maintaining what "belongs" to it. "It.") Something like what we mean by melodrama and tragedy helped form the classical philosophers, hence would always have been implicated in the "Western" impulse to epistemology and metaphysics. It is perhaps this relation to tragedy that allows me the patience to put aside the metaphysical mode, in which *all* false presence is to be brought to an end before its own impossible beginning, and instead to speak within the sense that *each* impulse to metaphysical presence is to be brought to its own end by diagnosing its own beginning. In Derrida's heritage we "cannot" truly escape from the tradition of philosophy; in mine we cannot truly escape *to* philosophy. For him philosophy is apparently as primordial as language, or anyway as prose; for me it is skepticism that is thus primordial (or its possibility).

The other focus in *Walden,* in conjunction with mourning, around which skepticism tracks its answer, is constituted by the overarching narrative of the book, the building of a house, that is, the finding of one's habitation, of where it is one is at home; you can call it one's edification. The guiding thought of Heidegger's essay "Building Dwelling Thinking," a companion essay to his "The Thing," is that dwelling comes before building, not the other way around; and one can take this as the moral of *Walden.* But in *Walden* the proof that what you have found you have made your own, your home, is that you are free to leave it. *Walden* begins and ends with statements of departure from Walden. Emerson's complex structuring concept for this departure is *abandonment,* abandonment of and to language and the world. The significance Heidegger finds in his words, and Emerson and Thoreau find in theirs, is remarkable enough; but in the face of this significance, to discover that their thoughts are intimately, endlessly related, has become for me unforgettably interesting. The direct historical connection (of Emerson with Heidegger) is through Nietzsche, but the intellectual conjunction has been a touchstone for me in the past few years in exploring the idea that romanticism generally is to be understood as in struggle with skepticism, and at the same time in struggle with philosophy's responses to skepticism. (How generally this applies is not yet important. It is indicated by the figures of Coleridge and Wordsworth behind Emerson and Thoreau, and by Hölderlin's shadow in Heidegger.)

With one further corner in the topography of the everyday that I am outlining I will be ready to take up a moment of unfinished business with Heidegger's "The Thing" and then tell you a parting story. (I first sketched this corner in the concluding two paragraphs of the preceding chapter, "Being Odd, Getting Even." What follows in the present paragraph is the same and different. Reformulation seems forever an essential piece of my intellectual business.) If you take Edgar Allan Poe (together with Nathaniel Hawthorne), on some opposite side of the American mind from Emerson and Thoreau, also to be writing in response to skepticism, then it becomes significant that they too write repetitively about dwelling, settling, houses; about, call it, domestication. Since their tales, unlike the scenes of Emerson and Thoreau, typically have other people in them, they think of domestication habitually in terms of marriage or betrothal. And habitually they think not about its ecstasies but about its horrors, about houses that fall or enclose, ones which are unleavable and hence unlivable. I said that the new philosophical step in the criticism of skepticism developed in ordinary language philosophy is its discovery of skepticism's discovery, by displacement, of the everyday; hence its discovery that the answer to skepticism must take the form not of philosophical construction but of the reconstruction or resettlement of the everyday. This shows in its treatment of skepticism's threat of world-consuming doubt by means of its own uncanny homeliness, stubbornly resting within its relentless superficiality; and not, as other philosophies have felt compelled to proceed, by way of isolated, specialized, highly refined examples (Descartes's piece of wax [end of Second Meditation], Kant's house [*Critique of Pure Reason,* A190, B235], Heidegger's automobile turn signal [*Being and Time,* pp. 108–9], G. E. Moore's envelope [*Some Main Problems,* p. 30]). This is the level at which I hear Poe's declaration, at the beginning of one of his most famous tales of horror, "The Black Cat," that he "[is placing] before the world, plainly, sincerely, and without comment, a series of mere household events." It stands to reason that if some image of human intimacy, call it marriage, or domestication, is the fictional equivalent of what the philosophers of ordinary language understand as the ordinary, call this the image of the everyday as the domestic, then the threat to the ordinary that philosophy names skepticism should show up in fiction's favorite threats to forms of marriage, namely, in forms of melodrama and tragedy.

This takes me back to Heidegger's "The Thing," in which the overcoming of our distancelessness, of our loss of connection, or rather our unconnectedness, with things, with the thing, *das Ding,* our being unbethinged, *unbedingt,* which is German for *unconditioned* (hence inhuman, monstrous, figures of a horror story), is expressed by Heidegger in terms of "the marriage of sky and earth," of the "betrothal" of "the earth's nourishment and the sky's sun." One might have imagined that this image is only accidental in Heidegger's essay, but it is essentially what goes into his extraordinary account of the thinging of the world as requiring the joining of earth, sky, gods, and mortals in what he calls "the round dance of appropriating" (*der Reigen des Ereignens*); and when he goes on to say "the round dance is the ring" that grapples and plays, he can hardly not have in mind the wedding band (an image in this connection that he would have taken from Nietzsche's Zarathustra ["The Seven Seals," §7, p. 231]), something confirmed by Heidegger's speaking of "the ringing of the ring" (*das Gering des Ringes*), where what he seems to want from the word *Gering* is both the intensification of the idea of being hooped together and at the same time the idea of this activity as slight, trivial, humble: it is the idea of diurnal devotedness. Thus does the idea of the everyday, which Heidegger has apparently disdained, recur, repeat itself, transformed, as the metaphysical answer to that empirical disdain.

Heidegger's idea of the humble, with its implication of cosmic radiance, may not seem very close to what Wittgenstein means in his insistence on looking for the humble use of famously philosophical words (like "language," "experience," and "world"). But the connection serves to register our sense that neither of these writers is as clear as their admirers would like them to be in philosophically accounting for their philosophical practice. Both wrestle against the human will to explain, but when Wittgenstein says "explanations come to an end somewhere," what he means is that philosophy must show, of *each* effort at philosophical explanation, the plain place at which it ends. Whereas Heidegger means to portray the shining place before which *all* explanations end. Still, we are reminded that both Wittgenstein and Heidegger were readers of Kierkegaard and that Kierkegaard's Knight of Faith exhibited what in English translates as "the sublime in the pedestrian" (*Fear and Trembling,* p. 52).

For the parting story I wish to tell you, I gesture toward that favorite region of mine that came up earlier for a glancing blow in Heidegger's allusion to it as symptomatic of our common, annihilating one-track thinking—the region of movies. I turn in conclusion here to a passage from a movie as also symptomatic of everyday thinking, but this time as symptomatic of the everyday recognition that our habitual modes of thought are destructive, and as an everyday effort to step back from them. The passage is from the concluding sequence of a film called *Woman of the Year* (directed by George Stevens in 1942, with Katharine Hepburn and Spencer Tracy), a worthy if somewhat flawed member of a genre of movie I have called (in *Pursuits of Happiness*) "the comedy of remarriage" and that I define through certain movies from the Hollywood 1930s and 1940s. The woman in *Woman of the Year* is a world-famous, syndicated political journalist, the man a lower-class sports reporter on her house newspaper. After satisfying a number of features required by the genre (their separation and threatened divorce; the woman's particular understanding with her father and the absence of her mother; a solemn discussion of what constitutes marriage and a scene of instruction of the woman by the man which is later undermined [in this case it is instruction in the rules of baseball]; an explicit renunciation of children and the establishing of a sense that while these two may not manage to live together they are certainly not prepared to share their lives with anyone else; and a move to a smaller, more modest dwelling than they begin in), there is a final sequence in which the woman appears about dawn at her estranged husband's apartment and while he is asleep attempts, with hopeless incompetence, to cook breakfast for him. He is awakened by the noise of her incompetence, interrupts her pitiful efforts, and is treated to a humble declaration from her which begins, significantly for the genre of remarriage, "I love you, Sam. Will you marry me?" He treats this outburst from his wife with a mocking tirade of disbelief, to which she replies: "You don't think I can do the ordinary things that any idiot can do, do you?" He says no; she asks why not; upon which he delivers a long remarkable lecture which begins, "Because you're incapable of doing them," and ends by saying that she is trained to do things incompatible with the training that doing those ordinary things demands. All I call attention to here is that this proves to be all right with him, with both of them; that for example in this genre of movie if anyone is seen to cook it is the man, never the woman (or never without him); that, uniquely in this genre of comedy, so far as I know, the happiness of marriage is dissociated from any a priori concept of what constitutes domesticity (you might also call marriage in these films the taking of mutual pleasure without a concept—whether two people are married does not necessarily depend on what age they are, or what gender, or whether legally). Marriage here is being presented as an estate meant not as a distraction from the pain of constructing happiness from a helpless, absent world, but as the scene in which the chance for happiness is shown as the mutual acknowledgment of separateness, in which the prospect is not for the passing of years (until death parts us) but for the willing repetition of days, willingness for the everyday (until our true minds become unreadable to one another).

At Vienna

CELEBRATION
LECTURE (1986)

7

The Fantastic of Philosophy

It IS WONDERFUL TO BE HERE—here in this house that Witt-genstein designed, and in this city that fashioned Wittgenstein.

It is almost seven years since I began visiting the Philosophical Institute at the University of Vienna and first met the young philoso-phers whose conception and publication we are celebrating today. Our intellectual companionship over the years has been an inspiration to me. It cheers me to think that our exchanges have played some part in the story that leads to today's event, and I take the event as a promise of continued and growing exchanges between Austrian and American philosophers.

This companionship has, of course, allowed me a perspective on my own temperament and tendencies in philosophizing; but beyond this, it has encouraged my sense that the task of cultural perspective is not only privately useful but philosophically creative. The interests among philosophers here in the richness of specifically Austrian thought has helped my own preoccupation with the richness, and the poverty, of specifically American thought, above all with the extraordi-nary fact that those I regard as the founders of American think-ing—Ralph Waldo Emerson and Henry David Thoreau—are philosophically repressed in the culture they founded. My efforts to release this repression are not interested, perhaps I should say explicitly, any more than I understand the attention to Austrian thought here to be interested, in ridding itself of foreign influence and participation. On the contrary, my wish to inherit Emerson and Thoreau as philosophers, my claim for them as founding American thinking, is a claim both that America contains an unacknowledged current of thinking, *and* that this thinking accomplishes itself by teaching the inheritance of European philosophy—an inheritance that should make me not the master of this European philosophy, but also not its slave.

Something apparently common to philosophy among the cultures of the West is, in recent centuries, philosophy's attention to the claims of science as the highest, or sole, access to knowledge. A way to attend to the distinctness of a culture's thinking is to meditate on the relation between its institutions of philosophy and literature. It is imaginable that a philosopher inspired by the German-speaking tradition of philosophy would not be content with results that failed to encompass, or say release, the knowledge embodied in his or her history of literature; whereas for a philosopher inspired by the English-speaking tradition, the invocation of Shakespeare or Milton or Wordsworth or Dickens was always apt at best to be a matter of occasional personal taste or embellishment, of essentially no professional interest. American thought, in my view, runs between these inspirations. To claim Emerson and Thoreau as of the origin in America, not alone of what is called literature but of what may be called philosophy, is to claim that literature is neither the arbitrary embellishment nor the necessary other of philosophy. You can either say that in the New World, distinctive philosophy and literature do not exist in separation, or you can say that the American task is to create them from one another, as if the New World is still to remember, if not exactly to recapitulate, the cultural labors of the Old World.

As an emblem of such issues of exchange within cultures, and between cultures, and between generations, I have chosen, for this day of celebration, to report my intervention upon being invited twelve months ago by the graduate student association of a literary-philosophical culture as foreign to American as to Austrian culture—namely by the Ph.D. students of the Japan Institute of Harvard University—invited to participate in one of the panels in a day-long symposium they were organizing on the topic of the fantastic in Japanese literature, and specifically to comment on two scholarly papers by members of their association.[1] The fact that the association was of the young, at the beginning of their scholarly careers, helped to reassure me that the invitation was meant not to verify my ignorance of Japanese literature but extended in hopes that I might like to learn something about

---

1. "Some Contours of the Fantastic in Modern Japanese Fiction," by Joel Cohn; "Fantastic Voyage: Refractions of the Real, Re-Visions of the Imagined," by Regine Johnson.

it and to respond, if I had a response, from my corner of the American world—even perhaps to learn something more about how I got into that corner.

Our panel of the symposium was entitled We Are Not Alone, and reading over the papers I was to comment on created in me something like the haunted experience of the fantastic, call it the uncanny, since the literature they describe is completely unfamiliar to me but the descriptions they give of that literature seem so familiar that I feel I have known what they speak of forever. The papers invoked such ideas as that of the imaginary journey, especially in quest of the self; and such ideas as that of being on some boundary or threshold, as between the impossible and the possible; and ideas of the confrontation of otherness; and of some adverse relation to the modern scientific sensibility.

My sense of the familiar here is not, I think, sufficiently accounted for by noting that our Western literature contains its own vein of the fantastic in literature, a vein represented, say, in the works that Tzvetan Todorov adduces as evidence for his theory of the fantastic, exemplified by the tales of E. T. A. Hoffmann. My feeling seems more particularly to do with the sense that American literature as such is eccentric in relation to the European, a deviation familiarly expressed by saying (almost inevitably with a certain prejudice) that where Europeans have written novels the Americans have composed something else, call them romances. If we consider that Nathaniel Hawthorne himself uses this distinction to permit himself an appeal to "the Marvelous" and remember that Anthony Trollope, in reviewing Hawthorne's *The Marble Faun*, speaks of Hawthorne's "weird imagination" and compares him with Monk Lewis; and further consider the imagination of Poe, and then the uncanniness of a white whale, it suggests itself that in contrast to Europe's definite but marginal interest in the fantastic, America has been centrally preoccupied with it. Accepting accordingly a point insisted upon by both the papers I was commenting on, that the literature of the fantastic has generally either in fact or in principle found it hard to be accepted and lifted out of the realm of the unserious or twilight zone into the central day of literature, I was led to pose the following supplementary question for consideration: What might it betoken about a culture's literature that its *founding* works are works of the fantastic?

Let me begin to specify this question by placing within our circle of concern a founding text of American writing that I do not imagine has been proposed before as an instance of the fantastic, Thoreau's *Walden*. That work obviously exhibits two of the principal characteristics of the fantastic I just listed, since *Walden* may accurately and well be characterized as an imaginary journey, and along lines that present themselves as boundaries or thresholds. That it situates itself in terms of a range of dualities has I believe struck many of its readers—between civilization and wilderness, between the future and the past, between human and animal, between heaven and earth, between dream and waking life, and, I would like to say, between philosophy and literature. That it is a book of imaginary travel is perhaps less remarked, but the fact is declared in the book's third paragraph:

> I have traveled a good deal in Concord; and everywhere, in ships, and offices, and fields, the inhabitants have appeared to me to be doing penance in a thousand remarkable ways. What I have heard of Bramins sitting exposed to four fires and looking in the face of the sun; or hanging suspended, with their heads downward, over flames; ... or dwelling, chained for life, at the foot of a tree; or measuring with their bodies, like caterpillars, the breadth of vast empires; or standing on one leg on the tops of pillars—even these forms of conscious penance are hardly more incredible and astonishing than the scenes which I daily witness.

People may call such a description literary as a way of dismissing it, but it is no more or less literary than, say Rousseau's vision of the human with which he opens his *Social Contract,* as born free and everywhere in chains. That is a vision, as Thoreau's is, essential to the theorizing that follows it, one that identifies the audience of the writing (as well as its author) and that defines the harm it means to undo. Thoreau's sense of what he sees as "incredible and astonishing" more openly identifies his work as partaking of the fantastic, the implication being that what is fantastic is our ordinary lives and that nothing more persistently, you may say uncannily, proves this than his readers' finding *him*—who is the soul of practicality—to be fantastic. Of all the writers who have suggested something like this idea, that the reader of the book, not the exceptional figures within it, is (the other that inhabits the realm of) the fantastic, none can go beyond Thoreau's systematic notation of the idea, nor (what is most pertinent for me) beyond his seriousness in claiming the uncanny vision as essential to philosophy—to the extent that philosophy is what attacks false necessities and false ideas of the necessary, as in Rousseau, but no less in Plato and Descartes and Hume and Kant and Marx and Nietzsche and Heidegger and Wittgenstein. But this claim of philosophy to the uncanny (and vice versa) requires a further inflection of what it means to see the reader as fantastic, a matter we will come to.

To prepare for it, let us ask if *Walden*'s vision really fits a further essential characteristic of the fantastic, the confrontation of otherness (hence of selfhood), emphasized by Todorov. Surely the point of Thoreau's depicted journey is to depart from others, not to confront them;

he knows from the beginning that others are the curse of human existence. This is humanly, surely, his greatest limitation. And surely no supernatural creature or enchanted habitat suddenly comes upon him in his woods. Or is this true?

Now we have to guard against taking the encounter with otherness or strangeness too narrowly. If this encounter is a wish both to find and to escape solitude, to escape the unnecessary isolations of selfhood, call this narcissism; and if the fantastic (as again Todorov suggests) is in some adverse relation to the modern scientific sensibility; then look what happens to Freud's famous observation (in "A Difficulty in the Path of Psycho-Analysis") that "the univeral narcissism of men, their self-love, has up to the present suffered three severe blows from the researches of science." Freud lists Copernicus's cosmological blow, recognizing that mankind is not the center and lord of the world; Darwin's biological blow, putting an end to the presumption that man is different from and superior to animals; and that blow of psychoanalysis, which discovered that "the ego is not master in its own house," its own mind. These blows are each understandable as discoveries of otherness or estrangement: cosmologically, estrangement from the universe as our home; biologically, from the idea of ourselves as superior to our origins; psychologically, estrangement from our own soul. But exactly these sad estrangements are for Thoreau ecstatic or fantastic opportunities: the sun is but a *morning* star (there is room for hope); we are indeed animals, and moreover we are still in a larval state, awaiting metamorphosis; we are each of us double and each must learn "to be beside oneself in a sane sense" (as opposed to our present madness). (In another context we would have to cite a fourth dimension of otherness in *Walden,* one more in focus these days, concerning the so-called discovery of America and *its* others. Thoreau's book is dominated by his sense of America's accursed, fantastic failure to recognize that native otherness; it amounts for him to the failure yet to discover America.)

Now Freud would have had his reasons for not mentioning the blow delivered by *philosophy,* within the scientific era, to human narcissism—philosophy's discovery of the limitation of human knowledge, as it were *despite* the advent of modern science and its own narcissism; limitation especially in its radical form as the threat of skepticism, the threat that the world, and the others in it, may, for all I can know, not exist. This is the traumatic thought that Descartes's *Meditations* undertakes to recover from, and it is pertinent for us that at one point Descartes declares his philosophical purpose to be to check the possibility that he is alone in the world, thus anticipating the title of the symposium panel my participation in which I am reporting on here. The proof that he is not alone demands for Descartes no less than the ontological proof for God's existence, a proof that God's existence is necessary. It follows that if that proof is not, or is no longer, credible to us—as it has not been credible in respectable philosophy since its apparent annihilation in Hume's *Dialogues on Natural Religion* and in Kant's *Critique of Pure Reason*—then the question of metaphysical isolation is in principle again torn open, and the literature of the fantastic appears as a philosophical underworld of attempted answers to skepticism. (Here I have to say that I cannot imagine for myself having come upon this perception of the material of this literature apart from my understanding of Wittgenstein's *Philosophical Investigations* as a project to allow skepticism its permanent role in the human mind, one not to be denied but to be placed (within different historical guises and economies). What this requires, as I read Wittgenstein, is learning to bear up under, and to take back home, the inevitable cracks or leaps of madness that haunt the act of philosophizing and haunt the construction of the world—to take the madness back to our shared home of language, and take it back not once for all [for there is no once for all within life] but each day, in each specific, everyday site of its eruption.)

This points to a good place for me to begin, hence a proper place for me to stop in a moment, in thinking about the experience of the fantastic: namely, to Freud's study of a major instance of the literature of the fantastic in his essay "The Uncanny." A good place for me because (as I go into at more length in the preceding chapter, "The Uncanniness of the Ordinary") in taking up E. T. A. Hoffmann's romantic tale "The Sandman," Freud begins by denying that the uncanniness of the tale is traceable to the point in the story of "uncertainty whether an object is living or inanimate," which is to say, to a point precisely recognizable as an issue of philosophical skepticism—skepticism with respect to the experience of others like myself, things philosophy in its English-speaking manifestation calls other minds. Freud insists that instead the uncanny in Hoffmann's tale is directly attached to the idea of being robbed of one's eyes, and hence, given his earlier finding, to the castration complex. But since no denial is called for (the castration complex may precisely constitute a new explanation or interpretation of the particular uncertainty in question), Freud's denial that the acknowledgment of the existence of others is at stake reads to me suspiciously like a Freudian confession that philosophy and its constition of otherness (in its existence and as its topic) is as fearful to him as castration is. It should give us to think.

This issue of skepticism toward and acknowledgment of the existence of others, the question whether we see their humanity, turns out to be the guiding issue of *Walden*'s fantastic language, hence of its own existence. In its thirteenth paragraph we find:

> What distant and different beings in the various mansions of the universe are contemplating the same one at the same moment! . . . Who shall say what prospect life offers to another? Could a greater miracle take place than for us to look through each other's eyes for an instant?

Looking through each other's eyes would be a way of putting a solution to the skeptical problem of others, a way past looking at others through our unkind eyes, alone, before which their existence cannot be proven, whether in Descartes's world, or in Hoffmann's, or in Freud's, or in Wittgenstein's. But the miracle of looking through each other's eyes is also a Thoreauvian description of what the writer of *Walden* means writing to be—his anticipating his reader's eyes, and his offering them his. So that the fact of writing, of the possibility of language as such, is the miracle, the fantastic. Accordingly the brunt of proving that others exist falls upon writing and reading (whatever these are), or say on the literary, on the fact of its existence between us, constituting us—so long, that is to say, as the genuinely literary, the conversation, exchange, of genuine words, lasts.

The inflection of the idea of the reader as fantastic, required in Thoreau's claim of the uncanny for philosophy, is thus an idea of the reader's willingness to subject himself or herself to taking the eyes of the writer, which is in effect yielding his or her own, an exchange interpretable as a sacrifice of one another, of what we think we know of one another, which may present itself as mutual castration, in service either of our mutual victimization or else our liberation. That to imagine the forgoing of a primary narcissism requires so primary an image of violence as the threat of castration—or: that to take one another's eyes is an image whose terror has to be faced in seizing its beauty; call this the sublimity of otherness—warns us not to sentimentalize our interventions. (One sentimentality is to say that writing, art generally, is meant for entertainment—as though entertainment were itself less violent and greedy than, say, instruction.) Taking one another's eyes is the chance outside science to learn something new; which is to say, outside science, to learn something. This seems to me a decent answer to my opening question concerning the task betokened by a culture's literature (and philosophy) that takes the fantastic as not less than central. It is perhaps what you would expect of a literature attempting to invent itself, to convince itself that it exists; as it is surely something you would expect of a literature attempting to preserve the literary as such from perishing, which is a way of defining romanticism's uncanny task.

It would not become a philosopher with my interests to quit my contribution to this symposium without mentioning a realm of the fantastic in which the distinction and issue of low versus high art, or marginal versus central art, precisely disappear, I mean the realm of cinema. What I have in mind here is not especially films of explicit magic or fantasy, the sort of thing special effects are perfectly suited to. I have in mind rather film's unaided perfect power to juxtapose fantasy and reality, to show their lacing as precisely not special. I once had occasion to put together a number of films constructed on the fantastic principle that the world of unyielding fact and the world of satisfied wish look the same, become juxtaposed without cinematic marking to set one world off from the other, creating in their viewers moments, I think one may say, of uncanny disorientation. (This is in my "What Becomes of Things on Film?") The principal films I began with were Bergman's *Persona*, Buñuel's *Belle de Jour*, Godard's *Two or Three Things I Know about Her*, and Hitchcock's *Vertigo*. To these I added Mizoguchi's *Ugetsui*, whose closing image is of a husband returned from a marvelous journey of the erotic to find his poor old house as he had left it, but empty. He lies down on the floor, curled like a child, and in the grey light his wife circles the room. We ache with the man for her to be real, for the beautifully familiar to succeed, or resucceed, the beautiful unfamiliar; but the stern, intermittent tap of a wood block wedges itself between time and eternity, and she vanishes. It is as great an image of the uncanny as I know on film. The experience of it scatters our always regrouping doubts whether we are any longer capable of that hesitation between the empirical and the supernatural on which the experience of the fantastic depends (or, having invoked Thoreau, let me say, instead of the supernatural, the transcendental). And we are reminded that the capacity to let fact and fantasy interpret one another is the basis at once of the soul's sickness and of its health.

Bibliography

Abrams, M. H. "English Romanticism: The Spirit of the Age." In *English Romanticism*, ed. Northrop Frye. New York: Columbia University Press, 1971.

————. *The Mirror and the Lamp*. New York: Oxford University Press, 1971.

Adams, James Trustlow. "Emerson Re-read." *Atlantic Monthly* (October 1930). Collected in *The Recognition of Ralph Waldo Emerson*, ed. Milton Konvitz, pp. 182–93 (Ann Arbor: University of Michigan Press, 1972).

Austin, John. "A Plea for Excuses." In *Philosophical Papers*.

————. "Other Minds." In *Philosophical Papers*.

————. *Philosophical Papers*. 3d ed., ed J. O. Urmson and G. J. Warnock. New York: Oxford University Press, 1979.

————. *Sense and Sensibilia*. Ed. G. J. Warnock. New York: Oxford University Press, 1962.

————. "Three Ways of Spilling Ink." In the 2d ed. of *Philosophical Papers* (1970), pp. 272–87. Also in *Philosophy Today No. 1*, ed. Jerry H. Gill (New York: The Macmillan Company, 1968).

Babbitt, Irving. *Rousseau and Romanticism*. Boston: Houghton Mifflin Company, 1919.

Beckett, Samuel. *Endgame*. New York: Grove Press, 1958.

Bloom, Harold. "The Central Man." Chapter 16 of *The Ringers in the Towers: Studies in Romantic Tradition*. Chicago: University of Chicago Press, 1971.

————. "Emerson and Influence." Chapter 9 of *A Map of Misreading*. New York: Oxford University Press, 1975.

————. "Emerson and Whitman: The American Sublime." In *Poetry and Repression*. New Haven: Yale University Press, 1976.

189

———. "Emerson: The American Religion." Chapter 6 of *Agon*. New York: Oxford University Press, 1982.

———. "Emerson: The Glory and the Sorrows of American Romanticism." In *Romanticism: Vistas, Instances, Continuities,* ed. David Thorburn and Geoffrey Hartman, pp. 155–76. Ithaca, N.Y.: Cornell University Press, 1973.

———. "The Internalization of Quest Romance." In *Romanticism and Consciousness,* pp. 3–23. New York: W. W. Norton and Company, 1970.

Burke, Kenneth. *The Philosophy of Literary Form.* Baton Rouge: Louisiana State University Press, 1941.

Carnap, Rudolph. "Empiricism, Semantics, and Ontology." In *Semantics and the Philosophy of Language,* ed. L. Linsky, pp. 208–30. Urbana: University of Illinois Press, 1952.

Cavell, Stanley. "Aesthetic Problems of Modern Philosophy." In *Must We Mean What We Say?* pp. 73–96.

———. "The Availability of Wittgenstein's Later Philosophy." In *Must We Mean What We Say?* pp. 44–72.

———. "The Avoidance of Love: A Reading of *King Lear.* In *Must We Mean What We Say?* pp. 267–356; also in *Disowning Knowledge,* pp. 39–124.

———. *The Claim of Reason: Wittgenstein, Skepticism, Morality, and Tragedy.* New York: Oxford University Press, 1979.

———. *Disowning Knowledge: In Six Plays of Shakespeare.* Cambridge: At the University Press, 1987.

———. "Declining Decline: Wittgenstein as a Philosopher of Culture." In *This New Yet Unapproachable America.*

———. "Ending the Waiting Game: A Reading of Beckett's *Endgame.*" In *Must We Mean What We Say?* pp. 115–62.

———. "Finding as Founding: A Reading of Emerson's 'Experience.'" In *This New Yet Unapproachable America.*

———. *Must We Mean What We Say?* Cambridge: At the University Press, 1976.

———. "On Makavejev On Bergman." In *Themes Out of School,* pp. 106–41.

———. "Othello and the Stake of the Other." In *Disowning Knowledge,* pp. 125–42.

———. "The Politics of Interpretation (Politics As Opposed to What?)." In *Themes Out of School,* pp. 27–59.

———. "Psychoanalysis and Cinema: The Melodrama of the Unknown Woman." In *Images in Our Souls: Cavell, Psychoanalysis, Cinema,* ed. Joseph Smith and William Kerrigan, pp. 11–43. Baltimore: Johns Hopkins University Press, 1987.

———. *Pursuits of Happiness: The Hollywood Comedy of Remarriage.* Cambridge, Mass.: Harvard University Press, 1981.

———. *Senses of Walden.* San Francisco: North Point Press, 1980.

———. *Themes Out of School: Effects and Causes.* San Francisco: North Point Press, 1984.

———. *This New Yet Unapproachable America.* Albuquerque: Living Batch Press, 1988.

Chekhov, Anton. *The Seagull.* In *Chekhov: The Major Plays,* trans. Ann Dunnigan. New York: New American Library, 1964.

Coleridge, Samuel Taylor. *Biographia Literaria.* Ed. J. Shawcross. New York: Oxford University Press, 1949.

———. "Othello." In *Coleridge: Shakespeare Criticism,* vol. 1, ed. Thomas Middleton Raysor. London: Everyman's Library, 1960.

———. *The Rime of the Ancient Mariner.* In *The Portable Coleridge,* ed. I. A. Richards, pp. 80–104. New York: Penguin Books, 1978.

Derrida, Jacques. "Coming into One's Own" (which is an abridged version of "Freud's Legacy"). In *Psychoanalysis and the Question of the Text,* ed. Geoffrey Hartman, pp. 114–48. Baltimore: Johns Hopkins University Press, 1978.

———. "Freud's Legacy." In *The Post Card,* trans. Alan Bass, pp. 229–337. Chicago: University of Chicago Press, 1987.

Descartes, René. *Meditations.* Ed. Laurence J. Lafleur. Indianapolis: Bobbs Merrill, 1951.

Emerson, Ralph Waldo. *Essays and Lectures.* Ed. Joel Porte. New York: The Library of America, 1983.

Empson, William. *The Structure of Complex Words.* Ann Arbor: University of Michigan Press, 1967.

Felman, Shoshanna. "On Reading Poetry: Reflections on the Limits and Possibilities of Psychoanalytical Approaches." In *The Literary Freud: Mechanisms of Defense and the Poetic Will,* ed. Joseph Smith, pp. 119–48. New Haven: Yale University Press, 1980.

Ferguson, Frances. *Wordsworth: Language as Counter-Spirit.* New Haven: Yale University Press, 1977.

Freud, Sigmund. "Analysis of a Phobia in a Five-Year-Old Boy." In the *Standard Edition,* vol. 10, pp. 3–149.

———. *Beyond the Pleasure Principle.* In the *Standard Edition,* vol. 17, pp. 3–64.

———. "A Difficulty in the Path of Psycho-Analysis." In the *Standard Edition,* vol. 17, pp. 137–44.

———. "Remembering, Repeating, and Working-Through." In the *Standard Edition,* vol. 12, pp. 145–56.

———. *The Standard Edition of the Complete Psychological Works of Sigmund Freud.* 24 vols. London: Hogarth Press, 1966.

———. "Three Essays on the Theory of Sexuality." In the *Standard Edition,* vol. 7, pp. 125–243.

———. "Transience." In the *Standard Edition,* vol. 14, pp. 305–7.

———. "The Uncanny." In the *Standard Edition,* vol. 17, pp. 219–52.

Goedel, Kurt. "On Formally Undecidable Propositions of *Principia Mathematica* and Related Systems. I." In *From Frege to Goedel: A Source Book in Mathematical Logic, 1879–1931,* ed. Jean van Heijenoort, pp. 596–616. Cambridge, Mass.: Harvard University Press, 1967.

Greene, Robert. *Pandosto. The Triumph of Time.* In *Narrative and Dramatic Sources of Shakespeare,* vol. 8, ed. Geoffrey Bullough, pp. 156–98. London and New York: Routledge and Kegan Paul and Columbia University Press, 1975.

Hacking, Ian. "Making Up People." In *Reconstructing Individualism,* ed. Thomas Heller, Morton Sosna, and David Wellbery, pp. 222–36. Stanford: Stanford University Press, 1986.

———. "Prussian Numbers 1860–1882." In *The Probabilistic Revolution*, vol. 1, *Ideas in History,* ed. Lorenz Krueger, Lorraine J. Daston, and Michael Heidelberger, pp. 377–94. Cambridge, Mass.: M.I.T. Press, 1988.

Hartman, Geoffrey. *Wordsworth's Poetry, 1787–1814.* New Haven: Yale University Press, 1965.

Hawthorne, Nathaniel. "Wakefield." In *The Celestial Railroad and Other Stories,* pp. 67–76. New York: New American Library, 1963.

Hearne, Vicki. "Talking with Dogs, Chimps, and Others." *Raritan* 2, no. 1 (Summer 1982): 71–91. Reprinted in her book *Adam's Talk* as "A Walk with Washoe: How Far Can We Go? pp. 18–41. (New York: Alfred A. Knopf, 1986.

Heidegger, Martin. *Being and Time.* Trans. J. Macquarrie and E. Robinson. New York: Harper and Brothers, 1962.

———. "Building, Dwelling, Thinking." In *Poetry, Language, Thought,* pp. 143–62.

———. "The Origin of the Work of Art." In *Poetry, Language, Thought,* pp. 143–62.

———. *Poetry, Language, Thought.* Trans. Albert Hofstadter. New York: Harper and Row, 1971.

———. "The Thing." In *Poetry, Language, Thought,* pp. 163–86.

———. *What is Called Thinking?* New York: Harper and Row, 1968.

Hintikka, Jaakko. "Cogito, Ergo Sum: Inference or Performance?" In *Descartes: A Collection of Critical Essays,* ed. Willis Doney, pp. 108–40. South Bend, Ind.: University of Notre Dame Press, 1967.

Hoffmann, E. T. A. "The Sandman." In *Selected Writings of E. T. A. Hoffmann,* vol. 1, ed. and trans. Elizabeth C. Knight and Leonard J. Kent, pp. 137–67. Chicago: University of Chicago Press, 1969.

Hume, David. *Dialogues Concerning Natural Religion.* Ed. N. K. Smith. Oxford: Clarendon Press, 1935.

———. *A Treatise of Human Nature.* Ed. L. A. Selby-Bigge. Oxford: Clarendon Press, 1951.

Kant, Immanuel. "Conjectural Beginning of Human History." Trans. Emil Fackenheim. In *Kant: On History,* ed. Lewis White Beck, pp. 53–68. Indianapolis: Bobbs Merrill, 1950.

———. *Critique of Pure Reason.* Trans. Norman Kemp Smith. New York: St. Martin's Press, 1965.

———. *Prolegomena to Any Future Metaphysics.* Revised translation by Lewis White Beck. Indianapolis: Bobbs Merrill, 1950.

Kierkegaard, Søren. *Fear and Trembling* and *Sickness Unto Death.* Trans. Walter Lowrie. Garden City, N.Y.: Doubleday Anchor, 1954.

————. *On Authority and Revelation: The Book on Adler, or A Cycle of Ethico-Religious Essays*. Trans. Walter Lowrie. Princeton, N.J.: Princeton University Press, 1955.

Kuklick, Bruce. *The Rise of American Philosophy: Cambridge, Massachusetts, 1860–1930*. New Haven: Yale University Press, 1977.

Lacan, Jacques. "Seminar on the Purloined Letter." Trans. Jeffrey Mehlman. In *French Freud: Structural Studies in Psychoanalysis, Yale French Studies* 48 (1972). Reprinted in *The Purloined Poe: Lacan, Derrida, and Psychoanalytic Reading,* ed. John P. Muller and William J. Richardson, pp. 55–76. (Baltimore: Johns Hopkins University Press, 1988.

Laplanche, Jean. *Life and Death in Psychoanalysis*. Trans. Jeffrey Mehlman. Baltimore: Johns Hopkins University Press, 1985.

Laplanche, J., and Pontalis, J. B. *The Language of Psychoanalysis*. Trans. D. Nicholson-Smith. New York: W. W. Norton and Company, 1973.

McFarland, Thomas. "A Complex Dialogue: Coleridge's Doctrine of Polarity and Its European Contexts." In *Reading Coleridge: Approaches and Applications,* ed. Walter B. Crawford. Ithaca, N.Y.: Cornell University Press, 1979.

Mankin, Robert. "An Introduction to *The Claim of Reason.*" *Salmagundi* 67 (Summer 1985): 66–89.

Marx, Karl. "Towards a Critique of Hegel's *Philosophy of Right:* Introduction." In *Karl Marx: Selected Writings,* ed. David McLellan, pp. 63–74. New York: Oxford University Press, 1977.

Mencken, H. L. *The Philosophy of Nietzsche*. New York, 1913.

Mill, John Stuart. *On Liberty*. Ed. Elizabeth Rapaport. Indianapolis: Hackett Publishing Company, 1978.

Milton, John. *Complete Poems and Major Prose*. Ed. Merrit Y. Hughes. New York: The Odyssey Press, 1957.

Moore, G. E. "A Defense of Common Sense." In *Philosophical Papers,* pp. 32–59. London: The Muirhead Library of Philosophy, George Allen Unwin, 1959.

————. *Some Main Problems of Philosophy*. London: The Muirhead Library of Philosophy, George Allen Unwin, 1953.

Nietzsche, Friedrich. *The Gay Science*. Trans. Walter Kaufmann. New York: Vintage Press, 1974.

————. *On the Genealogy of Morals* and *Ecce Homo*. Trans. Walter Kaufmann and R. J. Hollingdale. New York: Vintage Press, 1969.

————. *Thus Spoke Zarathustra*. Trans. Walter Kaufmann. New York: Penguin Books, 1978.

Poe, Edgar Allen. "The Black Cat." In *Collected Works,* vol. 3, pp. 847–59.

————. *Collected Works*. 3 vols. Ed. Thomas Ollive Mabbot. Cambridge, Mass.: Harvard University Press, 1978.

————. "The Imp of the Perverse." In *Collected Works,* vol. 3, pp. 1217–27.

————. "The Purloined Letter." In *Collected Works,* vol. 3, pp. 972–96.

Ransom, John Crowe. *The World's Body*. Baton Rouge: Louisiana State University Press, 1968.

Rousseau, Jean-Jacques. *On the Social Contract*. Trans. Judith R. Masters. New York: St. Martin's Press, 1978.

Ruskin, John. "Of the Pathetic Fallacy." In *The Genius of John Ruskin: Selections from His Writings*, ed. John D. Rosenberg, pp. 61–71. London: Routledge and Kegan Paul, 1979.

Russell, Bertrand. "The Cult of Common Usage." In *Portraits from Memory and Other Essays*, pp. 154–59. London: George Allen Unwin, 1956.

———. "My Mental Development." In *The Philosophy of Bertrand Russell*, ed. P. A. Schilpp, pp. 1–20. New York: Tudor Publishing Company, 1951.

———. "Some Replies to Criticism." In *My Philosophical Development*, pp. 159–87. London: George Allen Unwin, 1985.

Ryle, Gilbert. *The Concept of Mind*. New York: Barnes and Noble, 1949.

Santayana, George. "The Absence of Religion in Shakespeare." In *Interpretations of Poetry and Religion*, pp. 147–65.

———. "Emerson." In *Interpretations of Poetry and Religion*, pp. 217–33.

———. "The Genteel Tradition in American Philosophy." In *The Genteel Tradition: Nine Essays by George Santayana*, ed. Douglas L. Wilson, pp. 37–64. Cambridge, Mass.: Harvard University Press, 1967.

———. *Interpretations of Poetry and Religion*. New York: Harper Torchbooks, 1957.

———. *Skepticism and Animal Faith*. New York: Dover Publications, 1955.

Shakespeare, William. *A Winter's Tale*. Ed. J. H. P. Pafford. London: Methuen, 1963.

Shelley, Mary. *Frankenstein* (Text of 1818). Ed. James Rieger. Indianapolis: Bobbs Merrill, 1974.

Thompson, G. R. "Introduction" to *Great Short Works of Edgar Allen Poe*, pp. 1–45. New York: Harper and Row, 1970.

Thoreau, Henry David. *Walden*. Annotated by Walter Harding. New York: Washington Square Press, 1963.

Todorov, Tzvetan. *The Fantastic*. Trans. Richard Howard. Ithaca, N.Y.: Cornell University Press, 1975.

Trollope, Anthony. "On Hawthorne." *North American Review* (1879). Reprinted in Richard Ruland, *The Native Muse* (New York: E. P. Dutton, 1976).

Warren, Robert Penn. "A Poem of Pure Imagination: An Experiment in Reading." In *Selected Essays*, pp. 198–305. New York: Random House, 1951.

Weber, Max. "Science as a Vocation." In *From Max Weber: Essays in Sociology*, ed. H. H. Gerth and C. Wright Mills, pp. 129–58. New York: Oxford University Press, 1980.

Weber, Samuel. "The Sideshow, or: Remarks on a Canny Moment." *Modern Language Notes* 88 (1973).

Whicher, Stephen. "Introductory Note to 'Experience." In *Selections from Ralph Waldo Emerson*, ed. Stephen Whicher, pp. 253–54. Boston: Houghton Mifflin Co., 1957.

Williams, Bernard. "The Certainty of the *Cogito*." In *Descartes: A Collection of Critical Essays*, ed. Willis Doney, pp. 88–107. South Bend, Ind.: University of Notre Dame Press, 1967. An expanded version of this article can be found in "*Cogito* and *Sum*," chapter 3 of *Descartes: The Project of Pure Enquiry*, pp. 72–102 (Atlantic Highlands, N.J.: Humanities Press, 1978).

Wisdom, John. "Gods." In *Philosophy and Psychoanalysis*, pp. 149–68. New York: Barnes and Noble, 1969.

Wittgenstein, Ludwig. *Philosophical Investigations*. Trans. G. E. M. Anscombe. New York: Macmillan Company, 1953.

Wordsworth, William. "Ode: Intimations of Immortality from Recollections of Early Childhood." In *Selected Poems and Prefaces*, pp. 186–90.

———. "Preface to the Second Edition of *Lyrical Ballads*." In *Selected Poems and Prefaces*, pp. 445–64.

———. *The Prelude* (Text of 1805). Ed. E. de Selincourt. London: Oxford University Press, 1964.

———. *Selected Poems and Prefaces*. Ed. Jack Stillinger. Boston: Houghton Mifflin Company, 1965.

Index of Names and Titles